T0354894

The Difference Makers

John P. Sutton

Order this book online at www.trafford.com
or email orders@trafford.com

Most Trafford titles are also available at major online book retailers.

Print information available on the last page.

ISBN: 978-1-4251-4149-3 (sc)
ISBN: 978-1-4269-2241-1 (hc)

Trafford rev.

 www.trafford.com
North America & international
toll-free: 1 888 232 4444 (USA & Canada)
fax: 812 355 4082

FOREWARD

AS A BLACK American, based on many of my life's experiences, I can easily relate to a Black person asserting disparate treatment based on race, which in most cases is valid. Racial disparity in America continues to be a reality. It is very difficult, if not impossible, for a non-Black to sense or imagine with any degree of accuracy what has happened and continues to happen to many Blacks in America.

Often uninformed and insensitive people assert that one is "playing the race card" for some special dispensation or compensation. Hearing "race card" statements has subconsciously made many victimized Blacks passive in accepting disparate treatment.

Almost every Black American experiences racially disparate treatment on many occasions. I have observed many Blacks experiencing disparate treatment primarily because they were Black. I have been the victim of disparate treatment. The story that follows is my story: a firsthand accounting of what I, John Sutton, have experienced, in addition to what I saw others experience. Albeit fait accompli, my love for America hasn't waned nor has it caused me to hate others; conversely, I am more loving, caring and understanding.

I believe everything in this story is true, most certainly that which I have personally experienced. Despite it all, I love America and feel a need to recount certain chapters of my life to provide a perspective of the Black experience to the Black, White, Red, Brown and Yellow communities. Perhaps more importantly, despite all the shortcomings I have experienced, there are those who have been— Profound Difference Makers—in my life; I call them the "Difference Makers."

The word Black will be used in lieu of African-American or Negro. Profanity is used, as I experienced it, to provide a realistic accounting of how the events actually transpired. This is my experience, even from historical points of view; this is my accounting.

During the settlement of America, Blacks were imported from Africa and sold into slavery. Slavery was justified in the colonies because it existed in biblical times and the Bible instructs slaves to obey their master. Blacks have always been profoundly loyal to America. It is believed that there were Blacks with Columbus on his second voyage to America. Black men fought on the side of the colonists in the Revolutionary War against Great Britain. Black U.S. Calvary Soldiers assisted the U.S. Government, during slavery, in the forced relocation of over 17,000 Cherokee Indians from north Georgia, North Carolina, Tennessee and Alabama to Oklahoma in 1838, known as the "Trail of Tears". They also assisted in forcibly taking 2,000 slaves from rich Cherokee Indians. The Civil War started in 1861 in an effort to keep the Union intact. Over 200,000 Black soldiers fought on the side of the Union. During this period, there were a lot of pros and cons regarding slavery. In 1862, President Abraham Lincoln issued the Emancipation Proclamation (EP), effective January 1, 1863. After the EP, the Civil War intensified and continued until April 1865: ending slavery and supposedly the Southern Aristocracy. The Ku Klux Klan (KKK), an organization made up of White Anglo-Saxon Protestants (WASP), was formed to completely suppress the rights of Blacks as a kind of revenge against both The Union and its Black allies. The KKK, in the form of mobs, killed Blacks all over the South without restraint. It is postulated, with a sense of accuracy, that as many as 500,000 Blacks have been murdered by the KKK, affiliated and non-affiliated "mob crowds" from its inception well into the late 1970's. Almost contemporaneous with Blacks moving from the South to the Industrial Belt in the Midwest, the KKK also expanded its operations and organizations to the Industrial Belt.

In the South after the Civil War the further enslavement of Blacks took another form called "sharecropping", where freed Blacks having no money, things of value, poor knowledge and little to no skills, had to enter into verbal contractual agreements with farmers and large landowners. In this arrangement, Blacks were provided meager quarters, allowed to charge food, clothing and other provisions at the owner's country store. In turn, the freed Black would farm large acres. After reaping the crops, the freed Black's charge account would be settled and he would supposedly be paid half of the profits from sell of the crops. Poorly or uneducated freed Blacks had to rely on the honesty of their landowners. Many were cheated after harvest and some purportedly incurred debts that were carried over to the next crop harvest season, which caused a compilation of purported debts that could never be paid. As a result, they were in essence enslaved to the landowners. Because they seldom earned a significant amount of money, they were therefore restricted to the plantation and its owner like their enslaved ancestors. This practice was passed on to future generations. After a few decades, the Black population in many areas of the South exceeded the White population, in some areas by two-fold. Blacks, left out of the mainstream to fend for themselves, started building their own churches and schools. For a long time, churches also served as schools. Blacks started their own communities, elected officials and held various offices. They ventured to isolated areas and built Black towns. Mound Bayou, Mississippi was one, established by a Black family in 1887. It later grew to become a prosperous incorporated town. The Supreme Court case Plessy v. Ferguson in 1896 allowed states to separate Blacks from Whites, giving rise to the purported policy of "separate but equal."

Older Black Mississippians believed that "Jim Crow" started immediately after the end of the Civil War. During slavery, there was race mixing (miscegenation) in epidemic proportions, perpetrated by White males involving only Black females. Most of the nonconsensual sexual encounters—rapes—resulted in the siring of mixed offspring, "mulattoes", referred to in some circles derisively as "mud children, zebras, blue veins, red bones and high yellows." There has long been a large mulatto population throughout the South.

The southern states passed laws prohibiting consorting or marriages between the White and Black races, which did not really apply to the White male. Blacks were considered inferior to Whites. Separate facilities were erected to limit social or incidental contacts. Black males were prohibited from looking at White women or staring at them for any significant time. A broad definition of rape involves "having sexual intercourse with a person without his/her consent." Some Blacks were lynched for verbal or visual rape or mere accusations. Although Blacks were segregated when smuggled to America, it proliferated after the Civil war. In Black folklore, the term "Jim Crow" was derived from several sources; the main source was from a purported White male who traveled throughout the South performing skits with black painted face and white lips mocking Blacks in various acts of ignorant buffoonery. Southern newspapers joined the trend with regular cartoons and caricatures denigrating Blacks. Under Jim Crow laws and for no other reason than the color of a Black person's skin, many Blacks were slain by the KKK, white mobs and small angry groups.

During this period, Blacks, whether rich or poor, lived a humbling life of profound angst in having to deal with Whites. The word white was seldom spoken out of fear. White bread was called "light bread" and regular milk was called "light milk." In conversations with one another around Whites, to avoid confrontations, Blacks called a White person an "ofay" or "fay" or "gray man or gray woman." To avoid further conflicts, Blacks developed a kind of language called "Pig Latin."

As a Black living part of my teenage life in Greenwood, Mississippi, the heart of the Jim Crow South, and attending segregated schools, were the most unpleasant experiences of my life. This story, containing chapters of my life, is intended to be an inspiration to all and to emphasize my great love for America despite its shortcomings and my bad experiences.

DEDICATION

THIS BOOK IS dedicated to my daughters Ila Sutton-De Abreu, Ivonia Tinessa Sutton-Bryant and Heather Sutton; my grandchildren Caila, Caleb "Baby Brother" and Hubert E. Bryant III "Tre."

This book is further dedicated to Ray Griffin, Eddie Hill, Richard Smith, Regina Bledsoe, Lisa McBride, Tim Jones, Morris "Cookie" Walters, Walter Brown, Monica Harvey, Charlie Boyce, Craig Johnson, Matthew Fog, Ann Vernado and other Blacks, whose names escape me at the moment, who were shown a different level of justice by the U. S. Department of Justice; some who were prosecuted and others persecuted based mostly on an accusation; to those Black victims who were never made whole from the wrongs perpetrated against them despite favorable court rulings; to those Black victims who now know the difference between perjury, subornation of perjury and "not candid"; to those Blacks whose EEO complaints were shelved and never really acted on according to established policy, procedures and guidelines; to those Blacks who knew they were discriminated against, but never filed an action to redress the issue because they did not want to be labeled as "playing the race card."

This book is also dedicated to those Blacks and non-Blacks in fiduciary and administrative positions who have been fair in making rulings and decisions based on facts, devoid of political, racial or employment influences.

I

IN BLACK SEGREGATED schools in the South, certainly in Greenwood, Mississippi, we were not taught that: Black soldiers fought along
with White soldiers during America's fight for independence from Eng-
land. During that same period, Blacks were enslaved in various parts
of the colonies and other parts of the British Empire, which obviously
influenced other countries to go into the slave business.

We were not taught that there were Black U. S. Calvary Soldiers who
assisted the U.S. Government in the infamous "Trail of Tears" march;
where approximately 17,000 Cherokee Indians were uprooted from rich
arable land in the east and relocated to poor farming land in Oklahoma.
We were not taught that there were approximately 2,000 Black slaves
taken from wealthy Cherokee Indians during this ordeal. During this trek,
approximately 6,000 Cherokees died from various diseases, sickness and
fatigue. During this same period, there were approximately 4,000,000
Blacks enslaved in the South.

Segregated schools in Greenwood did not teach Blacks that approximately 200,000 Blacks soldiers fought in the Civil War.

There was no such thing as Black History and the history we were
taught was skewed and incorrect. In your lifetime, you experience a sea of
things that influence your life, the way you think, walk, talk, treat others,

1

and desire to be treated and perhaps most importantly, where you will go or what you will do within the years of your existence. All persons have experiences that are of interest to others. Many are wasted and never benefit others because they are seldom recorded. They die when you die, leaving very little to almost no evidence of your existence. People live forever when they publish stories, especially autobiographies or even fictional stories. They provide readers, after they have died some insight into their life experiences and in some way provide a guide or reference of how to deal with life's everlasting challenges. Many readers today prefer reading books involving fantasy, intrigue, power, money, drugs, crime, espionage, violence, science fiction and sex.

There are approximately 300 million people in the United States, each with many interesting stories to tell. I believe many Americans live and die with the only recording of their life printed in obituaries. Even then, their lives are often exaggerated out of respect for surviving family members and friends.

The "rich and famous" are often immortalized with buildings, edifices, stars, photographs, music, or works of art that seemingly last forever. It provides opportunities for future generations to know them vicariously long after they have been deceased. Perhaps equally important is that it provides future generation family members some insight into their existence: how they coped with certain issues and more importantly how they survived.

By existing, one is confronted with oceans of experiences that shape his personality: some good, bad, pretty, ugly and unforgettable.

This is my autobiography, which describes many of my experiences, including trials, tribulations, prejudices, and disappointments that I experienced as a Black American. I love America, despite my numerous bad experiences. I would be remiss not mentioning that my good experiences far outnumbered the bad ones. It was unthinkable that a little Black boy, born in the Jim Crow South, would one day have the opportunity to shake the hands of two U.S. presidents and a U.S. attorney general.

There were many people I encountered that were major Difference Makers in my life. The most important were my mother and father, who were married and together until death. I was one of the 40 percent of Black Americans fortunate to be raised in a two-parent home. The only time I ever recall being hungry as a child was at my own doing. I was also fortunate to have parents that did not have to eke out a living at a time when there was less wealth in America and a large percentage of the population was less educated than they are today.

On August 31, 1994, I retired from the U. S. Department of Justice, Drug Enforcement Administration (DEA) after 25 years of credible service. When I retired I had been the Special Agent in Charge of the DEA St. Louis Field Division (SLFD) for four years. The SLFD covered the states of Missouri, Kansas, South Dakota, Nebraska, Iowa and the Southern U. S. District of Illinois. Before joining the DEA's predecessor agency, the Bureau of Narcotics and Dangerous Drugs, I was a Compton, California police officer for four years.

In all of my years of law enforcement, I arrested, caused the arrest or participated in the arrest of many individuals for offenses ranging from misdemeanors to major felonies such as murder and drug trafficking. In encountering the arrestees, I often wondered what made or caused them to pursue such a life. It was equally as easy for me to have gone into a life of crime as it was for some of my classmates and friends who eventually did.

For some, I had similar experiences, born Black during a time when seemingly everything associated with Black humans was inferior and viewed with suspicion. I could have easily chosen the criminal subculture as a way of life.

Like many criminals, I have had numerous storms in my life and have experienced being left out of mainstream America; have experienced some of the most profound depths of disparity, ridicule, scorn and disappointments, however, I did not resort to the criminal way of life. I love America to the maximum degree and will forever be loyal and true to her. I am not bitter and believe that my path in life was heavily influenced by the Difference Makers, those persons I encountered along the way that made a profound Aesopian difference in my life. Like many people, I have experienced storms that at times seemed unbearable and unending.

I was born in the small Mississippi delta town of Cruger in the late 30's when Jim Crow was as prevalent as the rising sun. There were eight children in my family and two other siblings that died shortly after birth. My mother was a teacher and my father was a skilled Baptist preacher. He was also a skilled carpenter and barber. They both had college degrees. We were not as poor as the late Jerry Clower because we had an indoor toilet and electricity in our house. I had a further edge on him because I had two parents at home.

Like Jerry Clower, I love America and am very patriotic. My mother emulated his mother, that is, she always gave her children the best parts of the chicken and was the last in the family to sit down to eat.

While living in Cruger, World War II started. I recall the blackouts when the town electricity was turned off and we were not allowed to even burn candles, lamps or to illuminate anything at night until the "all clear" was shouted. The sky around our house in those days always seemed to be filled with the roar of airplanes going and coming.

During the war my oldest brother Dave, very large for his age, enlisted in the Army at the age of 15. I recall the talk around town of the Japanese bombing Pearl Harbor.

My second oldest sister told me that: several years before I was born, that a White man named Joseph Alford, President of the Bank of Cruger, came down with tuberculosis (TB). The local doctors treated him at a distance that is, allowed him to reside at home. In those days everybody stepped wide of TB patients. Mr. Alford summoned my father to his house with instructions to wear a red bandana over his face and to come in via the front door instead of the customary rear door for Blacks.

My father, a Black man, obviously then as he would have been today, was leery of entering the residence of a White family's home or any home wearing a bandana masking his face. Mr. Alford reassured him it would be okay for him to wear the bandana and instructed him not to enter the customary rear door but to enter his residence via the front door. My father was further assured that the "High Sheriff" would be aware of his coming to Mr. Alford's house.

My father reluctantly went as instructed to Mr. Alford's house. It was widely known that he had TB. As a consequence, even close friends and relatives avoided him. All of his neighbors avoided him, making him almost a prisoner in his own home.

Mr. Alford told my father that before he became sick, he had seen him on many occasions downtown and he (my dad) always seemed peaceful, at ease, wore a smile and was very friendly and respectful. When he asked what made my Dad like that, he replied "God, Mr. Alford. I have God in my life. I am a servant of God. He protects me and keeps me." Mr. Alford asked, "Preacher do you really believe in a God?" He responded, "Yes sir I do. I believe in him unconditionally through his son Jesus Christ."

According to my dad, he spoke about God, the Bible, various stories in the Bible and heaven with Mr. Alford carefully listening to his every word. He asked numerous questions that my dad had no problem answering.

Mr. Alford asked, "Preacher do you think you can cut my hair and shave me without cutting me?" "Yes sir Mr. Alford, If I had the proper tools", my father advised. Mr. Alford gave him $20.00 to travel to Greenwood to purchase clippers, scissors, razor, soap cup, brush, talcum powder and after-shave lotion. After my father initially cut Mr. Alford's hair and shaved him, he asked my father to pray for him. About the third occasion of this arrangement, Mr. Alford asked my dad if he could save him. Could he provide him a passage to heaven? My father advised he could, and had Mr. Alford accept Jesus Christ as his savior. He gave him a Bible to read and study from one of his four churches. He shaved Mr. Alford twice a week and cut his hair every 10 days. They prayed and had Bible study on each occasion. With this additional income, my father moved our family 15 miles north to Greenwood. He continued this arrangement with Mr. Alford, always praying and discussing the Bible with him.

About 10 years later, my father, while returning home from one of his churches one Sunday night, was carjacked by five young White males, in two cars on Highway 49 between Tchula and Cruger. The leader of the group handed one of the White males a tire iron and instructed him to, "Kill that nigger, niggers don't have a soul; kill this nigger!" The young White male nervously approached my father waving the tire iron in his hand. After he came within a few feet, he stopped abruptly and yelled, "Hell I can't kill this man. He is my granddaddy's friend."

The White young males entered their cars and hurriedly drove away. My mother for years described how scared my dad was when he returned home that night. My father acknowledged that the incident did occur but denied that he was at anytime scared, relating that he had Jesus or an angel at his side.

Several years later Mr. Alford died. About six months after his death, a lawyer, the executor of Mr. Alford's estate called my father to his office in Cruger. The executor gave my father $3,300 that Mr. Alford left him in his will. With this inheritance, my father paid cash for our home at 413

Nichols Street in Greenwood, Mississippi in 1943 and had a few dollars left. We were one of the few families, and certainly fewest of Black families, in America at that time to own a home that was mortgage free.

Shortly after we moved on Nichols, Reverend Pleas and his family moved into the adjacent house to our right. Almost contemporaneously, Reverend Jackson and his family moved into the house to our left, three preachers' families all living in the first three houses on the corner of Nichols and McLaurin streets.

My Aunt Rosa Mae worked on the assembly line in a defense plant. She was a very beautiful, dark complexion, buxom lady with dimples in each cheek and one in her chin. She was very shapely with curves and had the most beautiful legs I had ever seen. Other women on the assembly line were jealous of her. One in particular suspected that she was having an affair with her husband and reportedly put a "hex" on her that caused her to faint and her left eye to turn in a manner resulting in a fixated stare to the left side of her face. I went with my father to the plant to take my aunt to Dr. Layne. I overheard Dr. Layne advise that he had no idea what was wrong with my aunt. Unable to see out of her left eye, my aunt lost her job at the defense plant. She then went into the beer making business. Leflore County was a dry county. My aunt bottled the beer in Mason jars and sold it to juke joints in the area. She was the first person that I knew that could make beer.

There was an U.S. Naval Armory behind our house that housed German prisoners in numerous little black huts on the Armory Compound immediately rear of our house. It was surrounded with barbed wires and reinforced with electrical shocking wires. As children we would go to the fence and talk to the prisoners, those that spoke English. The expressions on many of their faces indicated that they had never seen a Black person up close.

I saw a lot of young Black men in our neighborhood and in the city go off to war. Some came home with amputated arms, legs, scarred and mutilated bodies. Others never returned and were reported as missing in action (MIA).

I remember a naval official driving up to a neighbor's house delivering a flag and leaving. The lady of the house immediately came over to our house and asked my mother the meaning of "missing in action." I recall how gentle and soothing my mother's words were to her and two

6

other ladies who later consulted with her. On each occasion my mother related that it meant that they were lost somewhere on the battlefield or had possibly been taken as a prisoner of war (POW). She further consoled them by relating that if they were prisoners they were being treated nicely like the German prisoners behind our house were being treated.

When the grieving mother departed, my mother explained that "missing in action" meant that the soldier had most likely been hit by a bomb and obliterated to smithereens. She would then lead us in a prayer for God to bring our brother Dave home safely, to be his protector, and to ward off all evil that is being thrown or shot at him.

The Commanding Officer of the Armory, a White male dressed in white uniform, was walking along the perimeter one day and spoke to my friend Norman and me. He told us his name was Jack and invited us to visit him sometime. Later my friends Norman, Matthew and I went to the front of the Armory on Carrollton Avenue and visited our new White friend Jack. He was approximately 35 years old, stoutly built with a thin mustache. Jack showed us the first pair of leather boxing gloves I had ever seen and invited us to a "Smokum", an in-service boxing program. He gave us snacks and invited us back anytime. We paid Jack numerous visits, especially since he always had snacks. On a few occasions, we even ate lunch with Jack, which to our astonishment was served to us, at a table, by White sailors. On one occasion, while visiting Jack, a car pulled up front that seemed to catch him by surprise. An older White superior officer entered Jack's office where we were and shouted, "What the hell are these niggers doing in here Jack?" Jack responded, "These are my little friends from the neighborhood." The White superior officer said, "Get these little Black nigger motherfuckers outta here. They don't belong in here. We are running a war not a local bird tavern." The expression on Jack's face indicated that not only was he embarrassed, but that we should leave.

We left hurriedly, not really knowing what the word "nigger" really meant but knowing the profanity was bad. We rarely visited Jack again unless he asked us from inside of the prison fence. My mother later explained to me, "in this world, there are evil people; people will hate you because of the color of your skin." My mother further explained that within our own race there were Blacks that hate other Blacks because of the darkness of their skin. Dark complexion Blacks would hate light complexion Blacks and vice versa. She assured me that I was equally as important as the next person, that we were all created by God; all God's children.

During each visit with Jack, he offered us the best of food. I saw a roast in the kitchen that was as big we were. Jack's demeanor never faltered from being nice. Conversely, he seemed to treat us better as though to make up for the hurt his commanding officer had subjected us to.

In my mind today, sixty years later, Jack remains forever one of the kindest and friendliest White men I have ever met. He was an anomaly. From Jack, I learned to be kind to people in general, to have ugly, cute, maimed, disfigured, obese, thin, popular, and unpopular friends. As I matured, I learned that providing a meal or sharing a meal with a person is kind of a spiritual thing that enhances friendship and love for one another. It often reminds me of when God asked: how can you say you love me who you cannot see when you do not love your brethren who you can see.

In history I learned that approximately 3,000,000 Blacks, mostly males, served in the armed forces during World War II. Most of them were from the South where Jim Crow was prevalent, subjecting them to discrimination and prejudice; however, they served our country well devoid of any reservation or hesitation. They served with great pride. The first servicewoman I ever saw was my second cousin Lee, a Black female, strutting proudly in her WAC uniform.

Shortly after Blacks were allowed to serve in the U.S. Marine Corps, Odis Gresham, from Greenwood, Mississippi, volunteered for the Marine Corps after graduating from Stone Street High School where he had been a good football player. He was one of the first Blacks from our area to join the Marines.

In 1944, while walking barefoot on our back porch, I stuck a splinter in my left foot that caused me to be stricken with "lockjaw" (tetanus). In those days, everybody was dying from lockjaw. I recall the spasms I suffered when my body temperature reached 104 degrees or higher. I remember being hospitalized in a Black hospital in Greenwood at the brink of death. I had a vocational nurse (VN) in my room 24-7. One day a young new VN was at my bedside as I was sipping orange juice through a glass quill (paper and plastic straws had not been invented). I had a spasm and my jaws locked on the glass quill shattering it in my mouth.

8

The young VN pried my mouth open and commenced raking the glass shards out of my mouth. The spasm came again and my jaws locked on her fingers. She screamed and hollered until a doctor and nurse came in and unlocked my jaws. The young VN voided all over the place.

One day my mother was visiting me when a group of church ladies came in, gave me a bunch of quarters, a card, some flowers and prayed for me. One of the ladies came over and chatted with me about God, then using one of her fingers and thumb, she pried my left eye open and stated, "Lord, I can look into this boy's eyes and tell that he's gonna die." My mother, sitting next to my bed immediately stood up, fainted and fell flat on the floor. After she was revived, I heard her tell my father that when she stood up she was preparing to strike the "remarking" woman, but instead God struck her down.

I was in a private room with the drapes drawn across the door, which was a sign that there was no hope for recovery, that I had reached the end of life. I was fortunate in two ways. First, a self-assured White doctor came into my room and asked my mother what time of day was I born? When she related that I was born during the early morning hours, he advised that he would not let me die even if he had to amputate my leg at the knee. Second, penicillin had just hit the treatment circuit and was being touted as the panacea for all bacterial infections. The sulfur drugs were no cure for lockjaw. I learned that lockjaw is a deadly bacterial infection that causes the body temperature to rise even after death.

The doctor immediately cut the wound open, removed dead tissue from my left foot and put me on penicillin every hour. When my father visited and I was given a penicillin shot, I saw him flinch and grimace. Later in my life I suspected his reaction was not from seeing the pain inflicted on me but because of the high cost of the hourly penicillin shots. About 10 days later I was released from the hospital. After this close call with death, my mother wanted me to be a minister, not a preacher. She made me read the Bible nightly and taught me how to pronounce certain words. I had to read the Bible for two hours a day. If my mother thought I was not reading, she made me read aloud.

I recall when the war in Europe (V-E Day) was over. It was a Sunday. We saw the prison guards drinking and jubilating. At nightfall the German prisoners escaped from the camp behind our house. Eight German prisoners stormed our house while my father was away at church. My brother Walter pulled a Daisy air rifle out, cocked it and attempted to scare the prisoners. They were very kind and advised my brother that he only had a BB-gun and that it was ineffective, that they meant no harm. They begged for food and clothing, referred to my mother as Mrs. and answered her "yes mam." They convinced her that the war was over and of their desire to stay in America. Despite my mother telling them to go north to the White neighborhood for help, they insisted on staying in the Black neighborhood and asked for directions to the railroad track. They asked for shoe polish and mixed brown paste and brown liquid separately with lard, and covered their hands and faces with the mixture.

Perhaps it was the politeness they showed and the begging that softened my mother's heart. I knew she was aware that many American soldiers had been killed or were "missing in action" in Germany, some from our immediate neighborhood. She relented and fixed eight care packages, some included pieces of fried chicken that were left over from our dinner. My mother gave them some of my father's clothing and even threw in some of my brother Walter's clothing. They left our home resembling Black men and walked to McLaurin Street toward the railroad tracks.

Later that night when my father returned and learned what had happened, he was initially angry, but told my mother that she had done the Christian thing. He later commented that she was brave for doing what she did.

A large number of Black soldiers returned home to Greenwood from various parts of the world where they had experienced life much different than Jim Crow life in Mississippi; some had even experienced miscegenation, which was taboo and the root for Blacks being lynched. Some Black soldiers that served in Germany where the National Anthem was "Deutschland, Deutschland Over All" during the period when Hitler had espoused a "Master Aryan Race", returned home leaving a significant number of German/Black babies behind. Black and White soldiers, returned home, unbeknownst to many including themselves, with morphine addictions, called "soldiers disease."

They masked it in alcohol abuse, paregoric (an over the counter opiate used to treat babies with colic and teething) abuse, strong cigarettes smoking habits, often exhibiting erratic and bizarre behavior patterns.

My uncle, Nick, the first Black sailor I ever saw, returned to Greenwood an unheralded hero. He had sustained almost total hearing lost but did not want to go through all the red tape of trying to qualify for a partial disability. In those days it was difficult for a Black man to qualify for anything that benefited him, despite having served in the armed forces during a world war. He had served aboard a gun ship in the capacity of some sort of wait staff. During the war, all U.S. military branches were mostly segregated, with the U.S. Navy being the most segregated.

Uncle Nick was a tall Black man, jet-black, with dimples in his cheeks and chin. He was apparently considered handsome because, despite being married, women threw themselves at him. Somewhere in his upbringing my mother was his teacher; my father was his brother. Despite my mother being his sister-in law, he always called her by her teaching name "Ms A.B." This was strange because my mother's name was Arbunyan--one word. It was even stranger that my father also called her "A. B." and she called him by his initial "W.H."

Uncle Nick had difficulty turning down gifts, especially from attractive women. He got involved in a tryst and sired two children by his minor wife. In order to provide for the minor family, he went to trade school on the G.I. Bill and became a certified mechanic. After saving a little money, Uncle Nick deserted his first wife and moved his minor wife and children to Los Angeles, California.

My oldest brother Dave was honorably discharged from the service and returned to Greenwood. He told of numerous foreign countries where he had been and showed photographs of himself hugging attractive European women. Dave had photographs of men with bones stuck in their noses. I listened to him for hours recalling some of his exploits in the service. Dave advised that he was a tail gunner on a B-29 bomber.

On one occasion, he related how his plane had been shot down over Germany and he was taken prisoner for three weeks. According to Dave, he and others escaped the German prison camp. He reportedly ran 22 miles to the American front line. Dave showed me a quarter-size black scar on the right side of his right lower leg and a large black scar on the opposite side.

I admired my brother Dave and would listen to him recall his experiences in Europe and Africa for hours. He was dispirited that not much had changed when he returned home. Jobs were scarce for Blacks and most Black families were merely eking out a living doing petty jobs that had no future, offered no pride and had no benefits.

A few veterans utilized the G.I. Bill to learn certain skills, not many of which proved useable in this Jim Crow South area. There was no college for Blacks to attend in the immediate area. To accommodate Black veterans, marginal technical skills were taught at the Black high school. My brother Dave took a job driving a taxi that paid peanuts. Shortly after his return home, he had a run-in with a White policeman named Teddy Shanks wherein a scuffle ensued. Dave was the victor of the scuffle and fled from the area to avoid being arrested.

The police came by our house several times looking for him. My father, fearing that Dave would succumb to a lynching, put him in the trunk of his Hudson car and drove him to Grenada. Dave was put on the City of Chicago train to Memphis where he boarded a train to Los Angeles, California.

Around the time my brother Dave left for California, my uncle Jodie Smith, my mother's brother was honorably discharged from the Army. He had served his country well and was home seeking to enjoy the type of life he had experienced overseas. Like the wives of many returning soldiers, his wife had forgotten that she was married. She was having an affair and continued it after he returned. Jodie unable to find postwar work, decided to go into the moonshine whiskey making business. He did well for a long time, especially paying the "High Sheriff" his toll fees. The sheriff became angry at the large amount of money that Jodie was making in the liquor business. He arrested Jodie and confiscated his stills and hired his own people—his relatives—to run the business.

One day I was playing on our front porch as a county prison crew was working across the street from our house. A shotgun carrying guard watched over them as they worked and counseled them about certain movements that were indicative of one contemplating escaping. The prisoners were clad in black and white striped uniforms.

I casually looked across the street and noticed that one of the prisoners was staring at me almost continuously. He had stopped working completely and was leaning on a shovel staring at me. I walked up the street on the opposite side and noted that he continued to stare at me. As I came closer, I recognized that he was my Uncle Jodie. He had a dejected and sad look on his face, one that I imagined slaves had. It was then that

I noticed that all of the prisoners had a ball and chain attached to their ankle. I ran back into the house and told my mother that Uncle Jodie was one of the prisoners in the work crew. She came outside, looked in his direction and immediately started crying as she re-entered the house. She wept for what seemed like hours.

When my mother regained her composure, she apologized for crying in front of me, advising that she could not help it. She then called me into the living room and gave me a big lecture about crime. My mother advised me that if I ever went to jail that she would just die. She further advised that if I ever became a drug addict that it would kill her. She then asked me what I wanted to be when I grew up. I gave her a canned answer of a teacher, preacher, musician, or a professional athlete. She had a strong aversion to any of her children being a professional athlete or musician. She gave a big talk about our two national heroes, Joe Louis and Jessie Owens. She explained how both had been exploited and would eventually end up poor. She was most convincing when she showed me a picture of World Heavyweight Champion Joe Louis advertising for Camel cigarettes. Even in those days, my mother had the insight that there was something addictive about cigarettes. She had a strong belief that most Black musicians were drug users, some actually addicted to heroin.

My mother was so emphatic about her desires that none of her sons went to jail that she then encouraged that I become a minister or a preacher just like my father. She convinced my father to assist me in becoming a preacher by taking me to one of his four churches on Sundays. My mother was a member of New Zion Baptist Church in Greenwood and on occasions she would accompany my father to one of his churches.

II

A SUNDAY CAME around when my father decided to take me to one of his churches. We drove to a little town, outside of the town of Sidon, called Rising Sun. We drove through the town into the rural area until we came upon a gravel road. We rode down the gravel road several miles and pulled onto a meandering red clay road, about 500 yards off the gravel road until we came upon a beautiful white frame church, St. Peter's Rock Missionary Baptist Church. There were approximately 220 people, including children and adults, present. I attended the Sunday School with children my age. Everybody in the church knew that I was Reverend Sutton's son and likewise treated me as some sort of celebrity. My father preached a sermon titled, "The Eagle Stirred its' Nest." He started off in a slow monotone, increasing the pitch of his voice to a baritone and started preaching loudly, rhythmically as he hollered and screamed to stress a point. Several women got the Holy Ghost and danced about the church as in some kind of catatonic trance. One, a rather robust big chest woman started pulling her blouse apart at the chest as though trying to become comfortable. She fell from the pew heavily upon the floor with her legs agape and screamed something indecipherable. A deaconess ran over and comforted her by raising her legs above the level of her head; she then placed her purse under her head and fanned her. When the woman appeared to be unconscious, the deaconess removed her shoe and held it to the woman's nose like an ammonia ampoule. Another woman ran up and down the center aisle screaming and jerking her body from side to side in a kind of locomotive ataxia way. A very light complexion woman stood up in the middle of a pew and threw her hat first, followed by her purse across the aisle. She then screamed in a loud soprano voice, a voice so beautiful it belonged in the choir.

My father preached harder and with the completion of one and sometimes two screaming sentences, he grunted, wiped his face, paused momentarily and belted out loud gospel stories. He hummed and increased the sound of his voice in a kind of rhythmic motion. About 15 women got the Holy Ghost and danced uncontrollably around the outer and center aisles; deacons and deaconesses assisted some. My father preached on with deacons yelling intermittently, "well, well, well, amen, hallelujah" and screams of "preach Reverend, preach", followed by a barrage of hallelujahs. Despite the windows being opened, it was very hot inside the church. The droning of the ceiling fans was a hypnotic device for those unable to experience the Holy Ghost. They slept, some snored and others woke momentarily and dozed back into a kind of hypnotic sleepy state. The whirling fans had a strong hypnotic effect on me, but being the preacher's son; it would have embarrassed my father of all people, if I slept during his sermon or even slept in church. My father preached for about 45 minutes until the front of his shirt, from the collar down to almost his waist, was drenched with perspiration. He said something about Paul and Silas and ended the sermon singing a solo of "Amazing Grace".

After my father finished singing, the choir stood and sang "Swing Low Sweet Chariot." Seeing my father preach and the effect it had on the congregation was awe-inspiring. After service, we went to one of the deacon's houses and ate country fried chicken, collard greens with okra, potato salad, corn bread, candied yams and peach cobbler with home made ice cream.

About 6:00pm, we went back to church for the evening service. My father preached again but with less alacrity. The evening service ended around 9:00pm. Shortly thereafter my father and I headed home. En route home I learned a great deal from my father and today I still remember the quality time he and I spent on those trips to and from his churches.

All four of his churches were rural churches. Each would have a full service once a month, which included Sunday School, morning service and an evening service.

On one of our trips home, my father explained why my mother had such great fear of her children going to jail or something untoward happening to us. He related that before they got married, my mother was a rural schoolteacher in Gages Spring, a community near Lexington. In those days Black rural teachers taught all classes from primer (kindergarten) through grade 12.

My mother was rooming with a family close to her school. One night while grading tests, she heard the noise from a "mob crowd" between her rooming house and the school. Numerous shots were fired and the sound of angry White men rang in the air for over an hour.

The next morning when she walked toward her school, about half way there, she saw two bullet-riddled bodies of Black males hanging in a tree. One was the body of one of her students and the other was an older brother of another one of her students. Their tongues were protruding from their mouths. She gathered all of the students together and they prayed, some cried, all that day.

Later that day before school was let out, several Black men from the community removed the bodies from the tree. All of the Blacks in the community went about their business as though nothing had transpired. According to my father, my mother harbored a great fear that something tragic like that would one day happen to one of her children. He was dramatic in his expression of the horror of the incident and related how God would deal with them in the afterlife.

My father was a very intelligent man and had tremendous insight about many facets of life. Over the years, I watched him provide sage advice to members and non-members of his churches and the community. In the Jim Crow South, it was common for Whites to talk to and treat Blacks in a condescending manner. For some reason, my father was highly respected.

He once related that even KKK members were strong believers in God, reputed to be strong God-fearing people. They made biblical references that they were superior to Blacks by reading various scriptures. According to my father, their beliefs were strengthened by the bible stating that slaves should obey their masters.

My father often terminated his sermons singing either "Amazing Grace" or "Swing Low Sweet Chariot." He related that most "Negro Spirituals" were written by Black American slaves depicting suffering, sadness, despair, anger, dejection, pain, and a promise of a better life after death. He further related that the church was the only institution that slaves had and that the church served in many capacities. My father also added that the song, "Amazing Grace" was written by a White slave trader who became a born again Christian; after accepting Jesus as his savior he continued in slave trading, but started treating slaves more humanely.

I witnessed one of the most prejudiced of Whites, instead of calling my father "boy, bubba, slick, hey you or uncle" called him preacher— never reverend— but preacher.

I believe some of my father's strongest God-given gifts were: helping others and giving to others. Although he had a set salary from each of his four churches, the members gave him additional pay in kind. On several occasions, I accompanied him on visits to ailing and less financially able members and saw him, in addition to giving them the collection the church raised for them; reach into his pocket and give them some of his money. I saw him also share many of his gifts in kind. Perhaps his most impressive sermons centered on, not giving but sharing, how he encouraged church members to share with those in need and one another. A profound lesson I will never forget is that a Christian does not give but shares with others and that all things are given to us by our Creator; we share some of the things that are given to us by God.

Several farmers in his congregations owned their own land; some owned hundreds of acres and a few owned a thousand acres or more. The three Malone brothers from Pickens were some of the larger Black landowners. The two older brothers were big deacons and leaders of my father's church in Pickens. According to my father, many of the Blacks in his congregations acquired land from their parents who had acquired it from either their parents or grandparents. While others either purchased it or it was given to them by dying former slave owners. According to my father, most Agnostics and Atheists tried to atone for their sins on their deathbed. I find this to be a truism even today.

From fall to winter when the crops were gathered and livestock butchered, his churches paid him a monthly salary and gifts in kind such as: large bags of flour, corn meal, canned fruits, vegetables, prime cuts of beef and pork, peanuts, pecans, chicken, fish, ducks, geese, rabbits, squirrels, venison from their hunts and molasses that some made on their land.

One Sunday I observed my father preach to the point of almost fainting. About 20 women got the "Holy Ghost" and screamed, gyrated, danced, ranted, frothed at the mouth, while some fainted as though they were having a nervous breakdown. Women and children cried and the whole church seemed to rock as if being struck intermittently by spurts of lightning bolts. One lady got so engrossed that she gave the appearance of being in a coma for a long time with most of the whites of her eyes showing and saliva drooling from her mouth as though having a grand mal epileptic seizure. Children cried and ushers and deacons rushed to and fro toweling women and trying to comfort them. After that sermon, I decided that preaching was not for me. At the end of the service, I heard two men commenting about my father. One remarked," he's quite a whooper. He lit 'em up in there today." Since he was such a prolific preacher, he was offered numerous rural churches, some of which he referred to other ministers.

Greenwood, the cotton capital of the world, was one of those cities where the White residents refused to cede that the Union had won the war. There was little to no other industry in the city or surrounding area and there were perhaps more needy non-Blacks in the county than needy Blacks. The cotton industry was the chief source of income. Most Black residents lived in Black belts of the city: Gritney, GP, The Buckeye and Baptist Town. Most of the families on Nichols Street were large families with six or more children.

The Gardners lived in the second house to our right. Mr. Willie Gardner, a mulatto, had six children. It was rumored that he had a good relationship with his White father and White brothers who were all in the logging business. Mr. Gardner was a logger. He showed me the first $500 and $1000 U.S. notes that I had ever seen. Although he was not a God-fearing man, he always carried himself in a regal and dignified manner. He was not flashy, often wore khaki and regular work pants. Mr. Gardner was a very good provider and his children wanted for nothing.

Mr. Robert Woods, a one-armed veteran, lived in a shotgun house (a small house with a direct line of sight through the front door and out the rear door) next door to the Gardners. He had a small truck that he used to collect scrap iron and to eke out a living. Mr. Woods wore his army jacket and pants often as though they were his only clothing.

Mr. Frank Hemphill, one of the oldest men on our street, lived next to Mr. Woods. He ran a neighborhood store and was the first animal trapper I ever met. He trapped, trapped, dressed and sold minks and foxes to furriers; his wife had apparently died long ago.

My best friend Norman Smith lived next door to Mr. Hemphill. Norman had six brothers and one sister. His mother died during the birth of his youngest brother. Norman's father, Mr. Richard Smith, represented some of the firsts I would encounter in my life: he was the first Black master plumber and the first single parent I ever met. Mr. Smith was tall and muscular with broad shoulders topped by his muscular neck that was wider than his head. His complexion was very dark. He was one of the first "saggers" I ever met; he never wore a belt and his pants always sagged.

The Evans family lived next door to the Smith family. Mr. Evans had approximately 12 children. Most of them had asthma, always wheezed with labored breathing. To make matters worse, they smoked some kind of powder called Asthmaderm that was supposed to alleviate the suffering, all the while they wheezed and coughed violently when smoking it.

Next door to the Evans's lived the Matlock family. Mr. Matlock was very fair, almost White. Mrs. Matlock was mulatto. They had two children, John and Jean. Standing directly in front of Jean one could not discern if she was Black or White. Although she attended an all Black school, it was very difficult for her to date Black males because the police thinking they had crossed the color line, would always stop them.

Across the street from the Gardners was the Lenoir family. Mr. Lenoir, often called Reverend Lenoir, was a very tall robust Black man weighing approximately 300 pounds. He had the type of eyes often depicted in movies as evil eyes. Mr. Lenoir always wore black and smoked a cigar. One day while talking to him, he showed me a large safe in his house and related that he was an insurance agent. Mr. Lenoir further related that he was a voodoo doctor, that he had learned the art from an older man. I apprised my mother what he had said. I took her advice and stepped wide of Mr. Lenoir and only spoke to his wife when passing.

Across the street from the Pleas family lived Mother Beck. She was a mulatto and owned her house and the duplex next door. Mother Beck was a spinster. Like the Pleas and Jackson families, she was a member of the Church of God in Christ (COGIC), often referred to as "Holy Rollers".

A Black man named Jimmy whose wife was also named Jimmie lived in one of Mother Beck's duplexes, the one closest to her house. I thought she had a funny shape because her stomach stuck out all the time. She had eight boys and always seemed to be pregnant. One day I sat on the porch when Jimmie was visiting my mother. I overheard them talking about her having a baby in a few months and my mother telling her she should have her husband castrated. After she went home, I asked my mother how do people have babies and what was the meaning of castration. I learned from my mother that you pray to God to have a baby and that castration was asking God not to bless you with more children.

The COGIC Christians were different from the Baptist Christians. They used drums, saxophones, guitars and tambourines during their services. Reverends Pleas and Jackson were COGIC preachers. My father was a Baptist preacher. We lived in the middle of the two COGIC preachers.

All three preachers would have had a cardiac infarction if they'd been aware that their 12 and 13 year old sons were crap shooters, gamblers and additionally two were smokers and occasional wine drinkers.

I attended a COGIC church once and was amazed how they reacted to the "Holy Ghost." The music led them into a kind of singing and dancing trance-like state. Their cajoling and dancing seemed more confined than in the Baptist churches. There was less hollering and less shouting. They beat tambourines on their hips and hands and stomped.

III

AFTER THE END of the war, the German prison huts at the U.S. Naval Armory behind our house were razed, leaving a large vacant lot. Having no city park we used the now vacant armory lot as a park. We played football, baseball and on occasions had crapshoots there. There were several small shotgun houses on the street, on the east end of the lot, occupied by not so prosperous White families. In the first house to the north lived a large White boy about our age. He watched us play with great interest. We noticed over a period of time he would come closer to the yard and shyly speak. One day we learned from his mother calling him that his name was Billy.

One day after not having enough players to play baseball, we asked Billy if he wanted to play. He ran into his house, returned and started playing baseball with us. When the summer came close to an end, we started playing football. Billy joined us. We were especially cautious not to hurt Billy in any way.

After a year of playing with Billy, Norman asked him to have dinner at my house, which he promptly accepted and followed us to my house. Billy, Norman and I ate on our back porch. Billy thanked my mother and left. He ate at our house on many subsequent occasions and sometimes he would walk across the lot to my house just to play.

About two years later, Billy surprised us. He invited Norman and me over to his house for lunch. We had never been in Billy's house before but had seen his mother, a wiry blonde lady that smoked frequently, walked around barefoot and had a habit often seen in southern women, when not smoking, she would stand back in her legs, suck her right thumb and hold the hem of her dress with her left hand. We were impressed when Billy led us into his house through the front door. In Jim Crow Mississippi it was customary for Blacks to enter a White family's residence through the rear door and to limit your presence to only the kitchen. When we entered Billy's house there was a muscular White male sitting at the table. He remarked, "So Billy these 're your little nigga friends your momma wrote and told me about." Billy responded, "Naw daddy, these ain't niggers daddy. These 're my best friends." His daddy said, "I'm sorry son, I didn't mean no harm. Y'all come sit down and eat with us!" Norman and I sat at the table with Billy and his father. Billy's mother served us a triple-decker sandwich, a sandwich that I had never eaten before. It had jelly and mayonnaise between two pieces of "light bread" and peanut butter between the second and third slice of bread. We drank grape flavored Kool-Aid made in a gallon pickle jar, with squeezed lemon halves and lots of sugar at the bottom.

When I went home I apprised my mother what had happened. She advised that we had just met Billy's father who had just been released from state prison. My mother further advised me that I had had something that Billy did not have until now—a father. According to my mother, she could sense that Billy did not have a father at home the first time he had dinner with us. She remarked how he constantly watched my father and paid strict attention to almost everything he did.

There were three movie theaters in the city. The Dixie and Walt Hall were Black theaters located in Black neighborhoods. The Paramount was located downtown and was considered the White theater, where Blacks were relegated to sitting in the balcony and using the restrooms and water fountains marked "Colored".

There was an advantage to having two Black theaters. They featured many Black movies with Blacks in subhuman, starring, and decent roles. Blacks were also featured in atmospheric scenes and as minor characters in subplots. We were able to enjoy the entertainment of White cowboys like Gene Autry, Roy Rogers, Buster Crabbe, Sunset Carson, Lash La

Rue, Whip Wilson, Bob Steele, Eddie Dean, John Wayne, Rod Cameron, Tom Mix, Tim McCoy, Johnny Mack Brown and others.

Several of these cowboys played the guitar and sang, while some had accordions and harmonicas in their movies. The most famous were Gene Autry and Roy Rogers. Gene Autry had a few Blacks in some of his movies. They were featured as musicians instead of being engaged in ignorant racially debilitating buffoonery.

We had our own famous Black cowboy, Louis Jordan and his Tympani Five. Louis Jordan was a Black cowboy that played the piano and saxophone in his movies. He combined fighting bad guys with singing and comedy, mixed with a little romance. It was nice seeing Black heroes and role models in decent and respectful roles.

On the other hand, it was very disheartening and sad seeing Blacks reduced to below human level via frequent depictions in the media—newspapers, television, radio and movies—as buffoons. Perhaps more disheartening than the media portrayals was being subjected to separate eating, dining, drinking, living, transportation and comfort facilities. One of my deepest hurts occurred in the Paramount Theater where I had gone to see "Cease Fire," a movie purported to depict an American army unit that had not yet gotten the word that the war had ended. Some soldiers from Greenwood were in the movie. I saw a White lady let her poodle drink water from a fountain marked "Whites only." As Blacks we were supposed to know our place; supposed to realize that we were inferior to Whites.

Then there was McLaurin Street Elementary and Middle School for Blacks and Stone Street was the Black high school. Although the schools were supposed to be equal, the Black schools had the worst of all equipment. We would only get new books on rare occasions. Most of the books we were issued had been used in the White schools for two or three years. Even with the used books, at the end of the semester we were assessed a "damage" fee that had to be paid before receiving your grades. Even the furniture had been used in the White schools before it was handed down to the Black schools.

Our textbooks were redacted and amended to only depict Whites and everything that they did in a positive manner. We were never taught, nor did we have access to books relating that Haiti, a Black nation was the second republic in the Western Hemisphere. In the libraries we could read

Currier and Ives's "Illustration of America" with depictions of Blacks in derogatory situations as: braggarts, idiots, buffoons, and ignorant beings, with large eyes, white lips and very white teeth. They were depicted as inarticulate, speaking an ignorant form of English; always enunciating words incorrectly, misusing verbs and using non-existent words while constantly engaging in some kind of chicanery.

Norman and I were classmates from pre-primer through middle school. On one occasion, Norman copied so much from my test that he also mistakenly copied my name. The movie star Morgan Freeman was an upper classman. Five-time Olympian Willie B. White was an under classmate.

We ate dinner, always a home cooked meal, around 6:00pm daily. Norman had a habit of being at or around my house at that time. On each occasion my mother offered him dinner, which he always accepted by responding, "Yes mam, thank you Mrs. Sutton." One day at dinnertime my mother said, "Norman we are about to have dinner, won't you join us?' Before she could finish asking, Norman responded, "Yes mam, thank you Mrs. Sutton." I screamed, "Hey Norman you ought to go home and eat, you eat at our house every day!" Before I could finish speaking my mother told me to shut up and simultaneously mauled my head (took her bent index finger and pressed it hard against my head until it became painful). We had meatballs and spaghetti, string beans, corn on the cob and corn bread. Norman informed my mother that he did not eat meatballs and spaghetti. She then cooked him a large slab of ham and a portion of cabbage.

After dinner, Norman thanked my mother and as always told her that she was the best cook he had ever known. He offered to wash the dishes, which my mother always refused. Shortly after Norman left, my mother gave me the biggest lecture about giving and caring for others. She then told me that I had something that Norman did not have, a mother. She surprised me when she related that she was aware that Norman had a habit of hanging around doing dinnertime. She told me that Norman was welcome to eat at our house anytime. I started to think that she cared more for Norman than she did for me. She then told me that sometimes when I'm at Norman's house and asked to have dinner that I should accept, that it was the Christian thing to do—Share. One day while at Norman's house his father asked me to have dinner with them and I accepted. After we sat down to eat meatballs and spaghetti and after blessing the food, I told Norman that I thought he did not eat meatballs and spaghetti. His father blurted out in a deep bass voice, "That's not so Baby John, we eat whatever is cooked here, don't we Norman?" Norman responded, "Yes sir."

I learned from Norman's father that the foremost things in any real man's mind and energy were: caring for his family, teaching them good morals, ethics, values and how to get along with others. I also learned to be thankful for what you have; to sometimes eat those foods prepared for you, even if to your displeasure, be appreciative. As a plumber, Mr. Smith was required to work hard and in dirty, unsanitary conditions. Upon returning home from work, he cooked or purchased meals for six waiting sons. He was one of the best, if not the best, single parent I ever met. Mr. Smith never went to college and there was some talk that he never graduated from high school. Despite the foregoing, he accomplished something many men White and Black failed to do. He acquired a very good paying skill as a master plumber. Mr. Smith did what all real men should do, cared and provided for his family. He sent six children to college.

Shortly after Odis Gresham was honorably discharged from the Marines, he returned to Greenwood and like many Black veterans found that nothing had changed. Since the war was over, all of the Blacks, males and females that worked in the defense plants were laid off. There were no jobs for them. Odis utilized the G.I. Bill and attended Morris Brown College, a historically Black college in Atlanta, Georgia. He played football for a few years and when returning home during the summer recesses, he saw Greenwood remaining the same as it was before he left for the war. There were a few houses that were being built for veterans that were small and shaped like matchboxes. In Baptist Town most of the houses had not been painted in years and were in various stages of dry rotting.

Black farmers came to town from Browning, Black Hawk, Little Egypt, and Charles Whittington Plantation to frequent the shops, juke joints and cafes on Carrollton Avenue. Some of them were sharecroppers and some owned their own farm, some small and yielding funds slightly sufficient to sustain a living. Among them were snuff-dippers, smokers and tobacco chewers. They thumped cigarette butts everywhere and deposited their tobacco and snuff saliva on the floor of the Dixie Theater.

The Marine Corps had made a man out of Odis and had drilled him into a fine fighting machine. Odis, an articulate light complexion Black man, decided that he wanted to exercise his right to vote. Blacks had to past a test in order to qualify to vote. With almost three years of college under his belt and three years of military service, Odis thought that he was smart enough to pass a Voter's Qualification Test. Despite his education and training, he brushed up on local, state and federal government, learned the names of the governor, lieutenant governor, state attorney general and the mayor and other local officials before the test. From his days at Morris Brown College, he had learned the names of all of the presidents and the total number of senators and representatives.

Odis, ready as ever to take the Voter's Qualification Test, put on a coat and tie and went to the Leflore County Courthouse to register to vote. The registrant, an elderly White lady gave him a form to complete. After he turned in the completed form, she asked if he was ready to take the test. He replied that he was, thinking that she would give him a list of written questions. When he asked her where he had to go to take the test, she advised him that he could take it right there and asked again if he was ready, "Yes mam, I am as ready as ever."

The registrant looked Odis seriously in the face and asked, "How many bubbles are in a bar of soap?" Odis, so stunned by the question responded, "five million, two hundred fifty-five thousand, four hundred and twenty-two (5,255,422)." The registrant advised, "You have failed the Voter's Qualification Test." When Odis asked her how many bubbles are in a bar of soap, she told him that he was being smart and to move on.

She further advised him that she is the tester not the test taker and reiterated that he was being smart and to move on; before he got into trouble.

According to Odis, some of his friends were asked questions such as: the distance between Mars and Jupiter; the distance between the sun and the moon; how many rabbit hairs are in a mature rabbit's fur; how many birds are in a covey, or how fast does the lead goose fly when geese are flying south for the winter? Additionally, they would levy non-existent poll taxes. Votes from the handful of Blacks that were allowed to vote, were usually routed to favorable candidates, not counted or thrown away.

Almost all of the Black veterans with the wherewithal migrated from Greenwood to northern and western states, with the majority moving to Chicago. Some, while en route to Chicago, went to other cities and states in the Industrial Belt where industries were anxiously awaiting good, reliable and honest hard workers.

Odis departed Greenwood for Chicago and en route landed a good paying job at LaClede Steel in Belleville, Illinois. He moved to East St. Louis, Illinois. Odis married Susie Sutton, my second oldest sister, in 1950. They lived in East St Louis, Illinois. East St. Louis was then a predominantly Black city with a population of approximately 100,000. There were numerous meatpacking houses located in East St. Louis. Jobs were plentiful. From the mid '50s to the mid '80s East St. Louis had the largest Black home ownership per capita in the United States.

Odis worked for LaClede Steel for 39 years, never missing one day of work. He and other Black veterans established a Veterans of Foreign Wars (V.F.W.) organization in East St. Louis. About 15 years ago they burned the mortgage for the building.

Odis was one of the most honest, loyal, civic-oriented and law-abiding citizens I have ever met. He was a giver. He gave a lot to many people, some he knew and some he did not. The horrors he experienced in the war were too painful for him to explain. The pain he suffered upon returning to Greenwood was equally as horrible.

Greenwood is a city of approximately 20,000 inhabitants, located in the heart of the Mississippi Delta and about midway between the capitol Jackson, and Memphis, Tennessee. The Yazoo River borders the downtown section on the north. All of the purportedly rich Whites lived north of the Yazoo River, near the Tallahatchie River.

Greenwood was the county seat for Leflore County. There was no city park, swimming pool, recreation facility or boys or girls club for Blacks. Before the end of WW II, my parents purchased a television. A 30-foot antenna, which cost almost as much as the television, was attached to our house. We were one of the first families in Greenwood to own a television set. Neighbors, friends and others, including some strangers, came to our house to watch television.

There was a private country club (golf course) in the city open to Whites only. Bernie Beale, a well to do Jewish man and an avid golfer attempted to join the Greenwood Country Club and was denied. Angered by the refusal, Bernie built a 9-hole golf course 10 miles south of the Greenwood Country Club. I went to the Greenwood Country Club with friends on numerous occasions as a young teenager hoping to be a caddy. The Black Caddy Master never called me to caddy. I suspected it was because of my dark complexion. He was darker than I was. It was strange having other Blacks treat me differently because of the deep pigmentation of my skin. It was stranger seeing Whites treat light complexion Blacks better. I later thought that maybe the White golfers preferred lighter complexion caddies instead of darker ones. I decided that once I became an adult, that I would move from Greenwood, learn to play golf and that I would have someone caddy for me one day. There were no places for Blacks to swim or learn to swim in the city. We hitchhiked to a small lake about 10 miles outside of Greenwood called West Hughes where we swam and cajoled in the water. The small lake was like an oasis located off a gravel road complete with a sandy shore and almost clear water. Sometimes while swimming, water moccasins were seen swimming in various parts of the small lake. We learned early that they are territorial. There were wild plum trees around the lake. After swimming, we often feasted on wild plums. One day after swimming, we started gathering plums and found several snakes in the trees also eating plums.

One of our favorite movie stars was Johnny Weissmueller who portrayed the starring characters in "Tarzan" and "Jungle Jim." My little buddies and I always admired the scenes when he would dive into a river and fight a huge crocodile or boa constrictor with his knife, always being victorious and emerging out of the water without a scratch. We timed several of his underwater fight scenes and we learned that he was under water fighting for 8 to 10 minutes. We wanted to be famous swimmers like "Jungle Jim."

One day I was late joining my friends going swimming. When I got up to the corner of Highway 82 and the Greenwood Country Club, they had already hitched a ride. I started thumbing and in a short while was picked up by two White males in a pickup truck. They told me to get in the bed and to knock on the top of the cab when I wanted to get off. We rode down the gravel road and as we approached the swimming spot at West Hughes, I tapped hard on the top of the cab. The driver and passenger turned, looked at me and sped up. I knocked several times and on each occasion they looked back at me smiling and increasing the speed. When we came to a loose gravel trench in the road that slowed the truck down to about 50 miles per hour, I jumped out and flipped over and over several times on the gravel road into a ditch. I was unconscious for a while. At some point during the fall part of my body landed on my left arm causing a 6-inch long and wide scrape of flesh to be torn from my upper left arm and deltoid area. I told my parents several different lies regarding how I had gotten hurt. I had long been forewarned not to hitchhike.

After telling my buddies about the incident, we decided not to hitchhike again and to swim in a creek that abutted the Greenwood Country Club on the east. We swam there on numerous occasions. One Sunday morning I played hooky from church and went swimming in the creek with my buddies. After swimming for about and hour, Bo Dent told us to watch him dive into the creek. He was the best swimmer among us, as good as or better than his older brother Bucky. Bo dived into the creek several times and stayed underwater for a while. When he surfaced, he would come up about 20 yards up the creek.

Bo dove into the creek again and did not surface for a long time. We screamed for him to quit playing around. His older brother Bucky dived into the creek in the same area and swam around but there was no sign of Bo. All of us dived into the creek and searched the muddy part of the creek but failed to find Bo.

We stayed there for hours later watching the emergency team drag the creek for Bo. When they initially dropped the dragline with large gaff hooks into the water, Bucky screamed and hollered about the hooks hurting his brother. So young and naïve about life, all of us protested the use of the gaff hooks relating that they would hurt Bo. We were too naïve and too young to know that humans cannot live for hours without oxygen or that the dead cannot feel or sense pain.

The search team found Bo about three hours later. He was a light complexion Black teenager. His cyanotic face made it difficult to recognize him. It was frightening, for boys who had just reached puberty, to experience the death of a peer for the first time. There was eeriness about Bo's death that's hard to explain. All of us felt guilty, felt that we could have done something to save Bo.

I dreaded telling my parents that I was there when Bo drowned, especially when I had left home supposedly for church. I anticipated that I would be physically punished. I will always remember that my mother knew that I, at only 12 years old, was hurt by the death of a friend and did not warrant physical punishment. When my father suggested it, she told him that I had been hurt enough. "There is no need to pour salt on an open wound," she said. Perhaps the most important lessons I learned from Bo's death are: God calls us home when he wants to and by whatever mean he desires, that in reality God is the giver and the taker. Neither good, bad, pretty, fat, thin, ugly, rich, poor, atheist nor Christian has an inkling of when God will decide to take their life. Consequently, in essence even now we are all living on death row.

Shortly after this incident and after realizing that I was not the best swimmer in the gang, I accepted Jesus Christ as my Savior and joined Mt. Zion Baptist Church. For years I pondered that if Bo had been a Christian that he would have not drowned that very sad Sunday.

McLaurin Street School was a sad looking two-story brown/black brick building that resembled a prison. It was fenced in almost like a prison and located close to the railroad tracks that traversed the center of town. There was no cafeteria or eating facility on the premises like at the White schools.

The most exciting part of each school day commenced with the recitation of The Pledge of Allegiance. A couple of my classmates and I would end it by saying "with liberty and justice for y'all. After the pledge we would sing three songs. When all classes sang different songs: Ten Little Indians, The Farmer In The Dell, Go Tell Aunt Rhody, Shrimp Boats Are Coming, Heidi Rune, and The Mouse That Lived On The Hill, the whole school appeared to be a place of happiness, joy and peace despite being a government institution designed to provide its Black students poor, substandard education and second and third class citizenship all designed to make Black students forever feel inferior to Whites.

We had the potential to be even greater athletes but lacked the money or facilities necessary to participate in expensive sports like golf, fencing, water polo, gymnastics, ice skating, hockey, tennis, swimming, or soccer.

The Jews were at a stratum just above Blacks. Teachers had the authority to physically punish students for bad behavior. If the teachers were too fragile, timid or nervous to punish a student the student would be sent to the Principal's Office to be physically punished. There were no written guidelines and Black students were physically punished based on the discretion of the teacher.

We were provided educational material that, in itself, was demeaning and condescending, with a basic theme of teaching how unworthy we were as people. Most of the literature in our libraries depicted stories of Blacks at the lowest level of human existence. We had books like: Uncle Tom's Cabin, Gone with the Wind, Stories of Uncle Remus, Little Black Sambo, Tar Baby, Cabin in the Sky, A Raisin In The Sun. The only Black writer we knew was Richard Wright, the author of Native Son, a story about a Black man wanted for murder and running from the police in Chicago. In class, the teacher had us study newspaper articles and a book about the "Scottsboro Boys" that involved nine Black males, ranging in age from 13 to 19 years old who were accused of the alleged raping of two White women. The older Black males were sentenced to death and the 13-year-old Black male was sentenced to life in prison. These young Blacks were reportedly beaten almost daily and were subjected to the most inhumane punishment imaginable.

This was a manner by which Black teachers instilled in us that there are two, possibly three or more standards of justice, with Blacks receiving the most severe punishment; that a Black person could easily be convicted based mainly on an accusation, devoid of good evidence. Although most of the Scottsboro Boys were eventually acquitted after numerous appeals and after serving long prison terms, it was uncertain if the 13-year-old boy had reached puberty, nevertheless he was initially sentenced to life in prison. Another lesson we gleaned from this case was that the Scottsboro Boys, in one sense, were lucky that their fate did not end in a lynching by a mob crowd or the KKK.

Albeit, rape is a dastardly, cruel, barbaric crime, some Black teachers then discussed whether the act warranted the death penalty for Blacks. Even in those discussions, none of the teachers offered an opinion but asked the class for individual thoughts. The teachers, although formally educated mostly in southern Black colleges, had learned how to navigate safely in the Jim Crow South. Sometimes when asked what they thought about Mississippi's U. S. Senator Theodore Bilbo calling Blacks "niggers" in his radio broadcast and his talks about sending "all niggers back to Africa", they would skirt the issue. Some would merely say "well" and shrug their shoulders.

I remember many of my former Black teachers; the majority was female. There was Mrs. Threadgill, Mrs. Topps, Ms. Banks, Ms. Wilson, Ms. Bonds, and Mr. Leonard and lastly there was Ms. Martin, a graduate of the University of Iowa, she was the weirdest of them all. While all other classes sang popular songs, Ms. Martin had us sing a weird song as follows:

"Alley Vee Voe, Alley Vee Voe, Alley Vee Voe Vie Voe Voom
Alley Vee Voe, Alley Vee Voe, Alley Vee Voe Vie Voe Voom
A cat trap is bigger than a rattrap; a rattrap is bigger than a cat trap
Alley Vee Voe, Alley Vee Voe, Alley Vee Voe Vie Voe Voom"

We would repeat these verses three times and sing— The Mouse that Lived on a Hill. Part of the class would sing the lyrics and the other part would sing a kind of descant of "um huh, um huh, um huh" throughout the whole song. Some of the words Ms. Martin used, even after many years, continue to linger in my mind. One of her favorite declarations was "incline planes are sloping surfaces."

She often would call a misbehaving boy, "you little Pee George ex-sprout" and follow it up by telling him "you are smelling your little wet."

Ms. Martin was probably one of the best formally trained Black teachers at McLaurin Street School. She had several really weird quirks. When a student yawned and did not cover his mouth, she would dip her fingers in a water bowl she kept on her desk, then flick drops of water on her lower face area. She would then remove a dirty rag from her desk, wipe her mouth and call that person an uncouth devil and ask, "Where are your manners? Haven't you ever been told to cover your mouth when you yawn? Nobody wants to see your tonsils."

Even then, this little ritual led us to believe that she had some notion that when a person yawned, germs and bacteria would bombard from his mouth to the mouth of others far away or within his immediate sight.

Ms. Martin was a middle age, olive-colored Black woman with straight black hair; she lived alone, had no sisters or brothers and never spoke of any.

It was rumored that she had once been jilted by a Black philanderer name "Lightfoot." Often we would sneak into her classroom and print the name Lightfoot on the blackboard and leave before she arrived. We would then re-enter with her or shortly thereafter to see her become discombobulated. From this discomfiture, Ms. Martin would lecture all day on a potpourri of subjects, from manners, history, English, to getting a decent education and moving northward for a better life. She spoke of beautiful places where she had been that seemed magical to us.

Most of us had never left the state of Mississippi and were experiencing poverty in Greenwood and vicariously in other places, as depicted in newspapers, books, magazines and films. .

We could not imagine a place where Blacks were accepted as equal humans as non-blacks. Ms. Martin spoke often about an elegant mansion outside of Greenwood called Malmaison. She was a strong history buff. She taught us that the city of Greenwood and the county of Leflore were named after a rich Choctaw Indian who was chief of the Choctaw nation. He owned a lot of Black slaves and used them to build the mansion. Leflore became rich through a deal he made with the U.S. Government in assisting the relocation of approximately 20,000 of his Choctaw Indians from Mississippi to Oklahoma. According to Ms. Martin, almost half of the Choctaw Indians died from diseases during the transfer. He was given large parcels of land and slaves for his betrayal. Leflore was reportedly a friend of Jefferson Davis and other politicians.

To slow down or dissuade Blacks in Greenwood from migrating north, we were taught in certain classes about the slums in inner cities, especially Chicago where most southern Blacks were migrating in hordes. In Greenwood and other Mississippi cities, Blacks would suddenly disappear which was often reconciled by stating that he or she "up and left for Chicago." It was highly suspected that they had been snatched. They were never seen again. Since the Civil War, the Black population in Mississippi had grown by leaps and bounds. It was common for black families to consist of 8 to 12 siblings in a single household. It was evident that Blacks outnumbered Whites at least two-fold.

From its inception, the KKK operated as vigilante mobs with impunity. Their various enclaves consisted of policemen, preachers, politicians and even local judges. Although they formed mainly to suppress Blacks, after a short while they directed their hatred and violence toward Jews, Catholics, homosexuals, communists and other non-WASPs. They viewed every White person caught or thought to be sympathizing with Blacks as a communist, traitor or an insane person.

The KKK, if not by an agreement, had the tacit approval of all the U.S. presidents after Lincoln up to Truman. They were cognizant of the 14th Amendment to the Constitution, and in taking the oath of office they swore to "uphold the Constitution of the United States…" All of those presidents neglected the basic tenets of their office. This was a major influence that attracted a number of educated Blacks to the only party that recognized and appeared to treat Blacks as humans, the Communist Party. The KKK enclaves were sometimes correct with their assessment of some of the White sympathizers.

There is little information regarding how they treated the few Indians left in the area. They were apparently treated a level above the Jewish people. Some of the Cherokees and Choctaws left in the area were of a lighter complexion than their western counterparts. Some were mixed with European blood. They were allowed membership in the Greenwood Country Club.

The economy of Greenwood and surrounding areas were centered on the cotton industry. Cotton was harvested by hand by Blacks who were paid minimum wages; wages insufficient to sustain a living.

Black sharecroppers strove to have large families to enable them to farm large acres, supposedly to earn more. To the contrary, large families resulted in the charging of more at the country store, further increasing the debt. Devoid of money or a sponsor, sharecroppers were locked into a type of indentured servitude with their landowners, making it impossible for them to relocate to the Midwestern Industrial Belt.

In the Greenwood area, the KKK stepped up its violent activities against Blacks, and included Jews and non-WASPs as targets. The justification for the non-Wasps was that they were Communist or non-Christian. There were reports of Blacks being lynched in Mississippi and other southern states.

My mother developed a stronger fear of one of her sons being lynched by the KKK or an angry White "mob crowd." She tried to slyly monitor my movements and frequently gave a sigh of relief after I returned home. She had the same fear for my older brother Walter but in someway indicated that I was the one likely to get into trouble. She often told me that if I ever went to jail, it would kill her. My mother further mentioned that if I ever got on drugs that it would also kill her.

My mother frequently warned me about taking gifts from strangers or even people I knew. She often related that people did not give things without some underlying motive. She suspected that the four-pack cigarette samples frequently given out, by women clad in little skimpy outfits, had an ulterior motive. She suspected that they contained something to make the users develop a want and a need, which would later require that they be purchased. She further believed that the government cheese given to the public at certain times was possibly a kind of test instead of merely getting rid of excess stockpiled cheese.

I had a fear of drugs, especially after reading many articles about heroin addiction in the big cities in the north. For Greenwoodans, Chicago was the city we were most familiar with because of the people who had left and returned for short vacations. They always seemed to be prospering; always returned in new or newer cars and fancy clothing. I knew I would never become addicted or habituated to drugs. Getting arrested, I could not really control being Black. There were many Blacks arrested then on suspicion of uncommitted crimes.

In those days many police departments arrested people on charges of Vagrancy or Loitering, listed in The FBI National Crime Classification Index as "VAG-LOIT." The elements of that crime covered any person unemployed or without a permanent residence.

About this time Eddie Noel, a mulatto man, killed a White man and went on the lam. An all points bulletin (APB) was issued for his arrest. The APB described him as being armed and dangerous. He was further described as a sharpshooter who had frequently practiced shooting cigarettes out of his wife's mouth.

Blacks in Greenwood discussed their desire that the State Police arrest Eddie Noel, instead of a local police department. Various law enforcement agencies, organized posses, unofficial posses and the KKK sought him. The general consensus was that Eddie Noel would not be taken alive. This incident increased my mother's fears about the safety of her sons.

Eddie was later captured alive. It was reported that he was not killed or beaten like many Blacks had been because he was a "mud baby, a zebra" (the illegitimate son of a White politician).

My mother was big on lecturing us to not get into trouble. She was a big user of parables, similes, allegories and metaphors. She often emphasized her point by stressing how certain things we could do would hurt or kill her. Being the wife of a Baptist preacher and a rural school teacher, she believed it would be embarrassing if any of her children got arrested, involved in drugs or if one of her daughters got pregnant out of wedlock.

I remember once when my two older sisters, Daisy and Susie, were preparing to go to a high school dance, I heard my mother warn them repeatedly not to jump through fire, further advising that there are girls that jump through fire all the time and never get burned. She stressed that the first time either of them jumped through fire that they would certainly get burned.

This lecture went on for about twenty minutes as I sat close by listening. When my sisters departed for the dance, before they got to the corner I called for them to wait for me. I caught up with them and asked, "Daisy, why do girls like to jump through fire?" They screamed, "Boy, get the hell away from here."

I remember many stories my mother told me, most had some moral value or warnings about being a good child. So obsessed with my future behavior, on an occasion when the state was preparing to execute a Black male; my mother discussed taking me, a very young child, to see the execution but she was overruled by my father.

I can recall almost verbatim her many Aesopian tales like "The Turtle and The Hare", "The Fox and The Grapes" and phrases like " a monkey feels good until his peanuts run out", "if you run with dogs you will get fleas", and " little birds being thrown out of the nest". One of her favorites was, "a person is not known by the clothing he wears but by his belief in God, what he tries to teach and the company he keeps". I knew early in my life that I would not get involved in drugs or crime. I suspected even then there were Blacks that were jailed or convicted and merely on an accusation made by Whites.

During the fall carnivals, circuses, minstrel shows and Flim-Flam groups came to Greenwood and set up in a vacant field south of Highway 82 and west of Highway 49. On one occasion, I saw a purportedly headless woman in a tent, midgets, clowns, three card Monte and pea shell artists operate; awing the curious while separating them from their money. Flim-flam artists were separating others from their money by having them punch chads out of a board. Often when they left town, a Black person would come up missing. It would be reported that they had run away with the circus. One of the most memorable carnivals that came to town was called "Silas Greene from New Orleans". It was an all-Black carnival that consisted of rides, peep shows, cotton candy, candied apples, fried corn on the cob, and all kinds of delicious food items, tricks and games. There were dancers of all sorts. The most amusing were the tap dancers. There were tap dancers that made songs from the fast movements of their feet. In one of the peep shows, I saw an attractive medium complexion female smoke a cigarette with her vagina; in another a man ate razor blades and a magician pulled rabbits out of hats and long scarves out of the ears of onlookers. All of the employees, participants and tent-erecting people in Silas Greene's carnival were Black. Like the other circuses and carnivals I had seen, they were also rather weird people, who walked about like zombies indicating that they had no real purpose in life.

One day Ringling Bros. and Barnum & Bailey Circus came to town and marched elephants through downtown streets. Since there was no zoo, we had never seen wild animals like elephants, tigers, lions, zebras or camels. We were shocked by their sizes. As small children, we had imagined that they were slightly bigger than cats. The most popular of them all was Clyde Beatty, an animal trainer. He stepped into a cage of big tigers & lions with a whip and had them doing all kinds of antics as though they were human and understood him. They jumped through hoops and climbed steps all at Beatty's command. To me for years, Clyde Beatty was the toughest and bravest White man alive.

Some of the most colorful people were not the clowns or acrobats, or aerialist; they were the salesmen selling elixirs purported to cure everything from gout to runaway wives and girlfriends. Most of their concoctions were mixtures of liquor (potable alcohol), cocaine, opiates etc. They danced, gyrated, gave big testimonials about those who had been cured. They picked "any stranger" from the crowd and gave them a sample. Immediately, the "stranger" would relate that he or she felt better. They came with all kinds of gadgets, rides, performers, clowns, freaks and games designed mainly to separate customers from their money. The most enjoyable treats were the cotton candy and candied apples.

Some of the saddest days in Greenwood always occurred in the wintertime, when the sky was gray and there was no place for Blacks to go other than to the movies. There was the Elk's Club, a Black club for adults that had been acquired by a few enterprising WW II Black veterans. Most of the famous Black musicians played there.

One day I caught a glimpse of Fats Domino when he was entering to perform there. I was very impressed with the aura about him, especially a celebrity. Fats got out of a pink and light blue Cadillac after parking close to the front door. He wore a black suit and pink dress shirt with a black necktie. His shoes were as shiny as marble. I saw women coo and sigh at his presence. Like all of my buddies, I wanted to one day own a Cadillac like Fats. We visualized owning a Cadillac of various colors; the most favorite being fire engine red with white upholstery. As little boys, dreams were something that could not be taken away from us. Sometimes, even they seemingly were also taken away.

IV

IN GREENWOOD AND other parts of Mississippi from the end of WW II until 1950, jobs for Blacks continued to be scarce to none. The cotton industry had given in to automation. Corn, soybeans, hops, sorghum, sugar cane and even peas became automated; leaving would be farm workers and small Black farmers without work.

Education had long been thought to be the panacea for the high Black unemployment rate. There were only a few vocational schools in the area and the historically black colleges were geared toward training teachers, farmers and other vocational skills. Even with certain skills, there were no jobs for Blacks. Those with jobs were often fired to make a position for a non-Black.

Aunt Rosa Mae moved her family to California. Many Greenwoodans moved to Chicago, Gary, Detroit, St. Louis, Cleveland, Toledo, Columbus, Memphis, Philadelphia, Pittsburgh, Indianapolis and other cities near or north of the Mason-Dixon Line.

Uncle Walter, my mother's brother, was working for the railroad before I was born. He was from Durant, Mississippi but lived in Evansville, Indiana all the years I knew him, He was a tall, muscular very dark complexion man with strong teeth. Every time he came to visit he always brought each of us a large red and white stick of peppermint candy. Uncle

Walter worked 42 years for Union Pacific and 13 years for Burlington Northern. When he died, he had over $10,000 on his person and almost $100,000 in the bank. Although he was married, he never had children, he never owned a car or learned to drive.

I learned from Uncle Walter to be duty-oriented, to save part of my earnings, to be a good provider, to leave good memories of my existence with relatives and friends. I also learned what he had never really experienced during his life and that is to really live, not let a job or position be my all or the most important thing in life.

When The Korean War started, many Black males in Greenwood jubilated. Some were drafted and others, unable to find employment volunteered. Our neighbor Marion Pleas joined the Marines. My brother Walter was drafted and sent to Ft. Chaffee, Arkansas and then on to Korea. My mother beamed with a sigh of relief that he was in the army where she believed it was safer than being a young Black male in Greenwood.

Waddell Jackson nicknamed "Crying Child" volunteered for the Army and became a paratrooper. Before joining the Army, Crying Child was a big wimp who lived in Baptist Town. He was afraid to play even sandlot football. When he came home on leave wearing his uniform it was a sight to see. His pants were heavily starched and his creased uniform fit like a glove. The rigorous training had made him buff. Crying Child, who was about five years older than our group, kept us in awe describing the training he had received and the thrill of jumping out of airplanes. According to him, at the beginning he was a little scared, but after jumping so many times, when he was in the process of jumping and given the command to "Check your chutes", he would respond, "I'll check my chute in the wind" and then he would jump. Unbeknownst to himself, Crying Child encouraged five Black males from our neighborhood to join the Army and go airborne. I would have joined then, if I were of the age.

About the time the Korean War started, Uncle Nick came back to Greenwood on vacation driving an almost new car and wearing nice clothes. He even talked differently. Uncle Nick talked a lot about how beautiful it was in California and that it never snows in Southern California. I asked if I could go back to California to live with him. He was very agreeable. My mother told me she would consider it on my uncle's next trip. My brother Dave had been in California about four years but we seldom heard from him. He had always lived on the wild side.

Racial tension increased in Greenwood and other parts of Mississippi and Blacks were still denied the right to vote. My father at the time was heavily involved in helping members of his four churches prevent their land or portions of their land from being illegally confiscated by Whites through numerous contrivances. Some involved the all of a sudden alleged "back taxes" or "unpaid taxes." At the time he was the Moderator of the Rose Hill Baptist District, an area that covered 10 counties around Natchez, Yazoo City, Lexington, Durant and other areas.

About this time, a mob of angry whites hanged a Black male in Tupelo, Mississippi. Two days after the lynching, a tornado touched down in Tupelo, killed several people and destroyed buildings downtown. I heard my mother talking about it with a neighbor.

As always, she tried to talk above my head. She seemed perplexed as to how a Black male could commit a rape with his eyes or his voice. I knew then that she would likely relent and allow me to go live with my uncle in California. One of the positives in Mississippi was the ability to obtain a driver's license at the age of 15.

My brother Walter returned to Greenwood from Korea after being honorably discharged from the army. He survived a bullet wound in his lower leg. Like many Black veterans he moved to East St. Louis, Illinois with support from our parents.

My father had been kind enough to teach me how to drive. Sometimes on Sunday nights, he would let me drive on the country roads and on occasions on the highway. He taught me how to flash the headlights off and on as an alert for oncoming cars to dim their lights. I got my Mississippi Driver's License at the age of 15.

The next summer, Uncle Nick drove from California to Greenwood with his minor wife and two children. I asked him if I could come to California to live with him. He agreed; if my mother and father would agree to it. Because of the racial tension in Greenwood and Mississippi at the time, my parents agreed.

The day of our departure, my mother gave me a thousand do's and a thousand don'ts. As we entered Uncle Nick's 1950 black Ford sedan and were driving away, I watched my mother re-enter the house crying. It was a bittersweet moment for me.

We took U. S. Highway 82 west through Greenville, Mississippi and Arkansas, stopping for gasoline and using the bathrooms marked

"Colored" and drinking from water fountains equally marked. As we entered Texas, I drove for about 12 hours. Shortly after my uncle started driving a White Texas State Trooper (TST), wearing cowboy boots, a Stetson hat and Ray Ban sunglasses, stopped us. After he asked for and received my uncle's driver's license, he asked, "Boy, where're y'all going?" "Back to California sir", my uncle responded. When the TST asked for the registration, my uncle apparently did not hear him. Sitting in the front passenger side, I started to open the glove compartment to get the registration when the TST shouted, "Hold it nigger what the fuck are you doing fucking around in the glove box? You don't have a gun or weapon in there do ya?" He grabbed the handle of his revolver as though preparing to draw.

"No sir. I was getting the registration for my uncle, he's hard of hearing," I tried to explain. The TST stated, "You keep your Black ass still, now both of you get out of the car and step back to my vehicle." My aunt and two first cousins stayed in the car. When we were back at the patrol car, I again advised the TST that my uncle was "hard of hearing." The TST placed his hand on the handle of his service revolver again and remarked, "Huh, hard of hearing, with what I got here, this nigger will hear everything I say and will hear it loudly." My uncle smiling retorted, "Yes sir." The TST stated, "See this nigger can hear clearly. He's one of them niggers that hear what he wants to hear, when he wants to hear it. But he will hear what I got to say. He thinks he's some kind of hot shit 'cause he's got a California tag on his car. We don't give a shit about California tags around here." Uncle Nick, smiling, gave him another "yes sir." I again explained that he had a problem hearing and that he had gotten injured in the Navy.

The TST, after belittling us for several minutes and talking briefly about being in the service also, allowed us to leave with a verbal warning for an alleged traffic violation we had not committed. I'd always admired my Uncle Nick and admired him more after witnessing his demeanor with the TST. I knew that over a period of his life that he had learned to navigate safely in the troubled waters of Mississippi. In retrospect, I wonder how I would have responded to the TST demeaning me and treating me like dirt in the presence of my wife and family. I saw my uncle as a much stronger and spiritual man than the TST could ever be,

I surmised that demeaning humans different from him was perhaps his only means of entertainment.

We drove through the night and were still in Texas. We passed beautiful stucco homes, foothills, mountain ranges, and traversed mountains. We drove through dessert-like land, with cactuses, large Joshua trees that had the appearance of giant humans. Passing through cities and towns, we saw beautiful homes with various colored bougainvillea flowers climbing trellises and scaling verandas, beautiful green yards with colorful flowers, the prettiest of all were the Bird of Paradise plants and the giant Bird of Paradise trees. At sunset, the silhouette of mountains, foothills, valleys, gorges, and dry lakebeds were very picturesque; beyond anything I had seen or imagined. Many passing and oncoming cars had dripping water bags attached to the front bumper. During the early evenings and early mornings, huge jack rabbits jumped and ran about next to the highway, some ran across the highway in front of us.

When we drove into New Mexico, we saw numerous signs along the highway warning motorists to beware of Gila Monsters; some had a picture of an orange-reddish robust lizard with a black stripe and a thick tail. New Mexico, in most parts, was similarly dessert like parts of Texas. We passed stucco houses with flat roofs, more road signs warning not only of Gila Monsters, but rattlesnakes too. In small towns we saw Indians with medium complexions; Indian men with no facial hair. Their facial skin appeared bleached by the sun and resembled a type of tough skin or leather. They were the type of Indians I had seen in cowboy movies.

In Arizona, we saw scenes similar to the ones in New Mexico and Texas. In Arizona, my aunt asked me if I had noticed anything different lately. After admitting that I had not, my aunt related on the last few fuel stops and comfort breaks that we had used cleaner facilities that were not designated "for Blacks or Whites only." In New Mexico and Arizona, we were responding to Whites with yes or no and had dropped all of the sirs. We were now being treated with more respect and for what we are, human beings; members of the human race.

I was driving when we crossed the Colorado River and was awed at the sight. At the California border at Blythe, I stopped at the checkpoint. A White officer approached and asked if we were bringing any fruits or vegetables into the state. When I answered "No", he responded, "Thanks sir, you all have a nice trip home." I drove through the mountains to

Redlands and as we came to Indio, I noticed, like in Texas, New Mexico and Arizona heat waves dancing across the highway like a clear form of moving gas. We fueled up and took a comfort break in Indio. The temperature was 119 degrees in the shaded area of the service station but almost devoid of any moisture. It was cooler than some of the 90-plus degrees I had experienced in Mississippi.

I drove on until we descended from the West Covina foothills into the Los Angeles basin. While descending, for miles all I could see were large smoke stacks billowing skyward. The smog was so thick in the air you could almost cut it. The smell of burnt garlic, onions and newspapers filled the air and immediately caused irritation in my eyes. I began to cough and my eyes became watery. I was advised that California residents burn their newspapers in incinerators in their yard on Thursdays; normally it is not that smoggy.

We drove on to my uncle's house, at 848 E. 113th Street, in the heart of South Central Los Angeles. The neighborhood consisted of rows of pastel colored stucco houses with neatly trimmed lawns. It was made up of mostly Blacks, a few Mexicans, a few Whites and Orientals.

Los Angeles at the time was sprawling, had a population of less than one million people, but was growing daily population wise. The tallest building downtown was City Hall. After a heavy rain, it could be seen as far south as 120th Street. One of my disappointments, aside from the smog, was that the Los Angeles River, not like other rivers, in reality it's a large manmade concrete ditch that was cut throughout the city and eventually flows into the Pacific Ocean. Needless to say it is devoid of fish, snakes or the types of animals usually found in a river. During the summer it is completely dry with only occasional trickles of streams.

Aunt Rosa Mae also lived on 113th Street, up the street from us. She had married a man we called Walcott whose last name was Pendleton. His son Eugene was my age. There were lots of teenagers my age on our street. Most of them had cars, were very sexually active and a few smoked "weed." One day while visiting Eugene and my aunt, it was broadcasted on the radio that "the grunions are running tonight between 8:30 pm and midnight.

I rode with my cousin Eugene and several of his friends in a caravan of six cars south on Figueroa to Cabrillo Beach in San Pedro. I had two delightful experiences; the first time that I saw the Pacific Ocean was at night and I fished for the first time and caught fish without a fishing pole. When the tides came ashore, grunions were washed upon the beach when it receded. We picked them up, placed them in five-gallon plastic containers with ocean water. I was disappointed that the ocean water is not really blue as seen during the day and in the movies.

I developed a fondness for the ocean, the breeze coming inland, the freshness of the air and the beautiful buildings, trees, plants and the friendly people, including the vendors. I learned to fish on the ocean, catch cods, pylon perches, opal eyes, flounder, sharks and Bonita (tuna). The Bonita was the most challenging, would only bite live bait and appeared to swim at about 50 miles per hour. I learned to crab, to catch a five-gallon container of Dungeness crabs within a short period. In our neighborhood we improvised a lot. We built crab nets out of bicycle rims or pieces of chicken wire. We went to fish markets and got large fish heads out of their trashcans or asked for them from the owner or manager.

The Seven Seas Fish Market on Imperial Highway, west of Central Avenue provided us with large fish heads for years. They thought we were using them to make bouillabaisse. When they learned it was for crab bait, they started selling us fish heads as crab bait for 50 cents a pound.

My first job involved bailing recycled paper at a company in Vernon, California. My cousin Eugene and I worked there when we desired and were paid, not hourly, but by the bale. We were 17 years old and big for our age. We worked alone in the warehouse without supervision. There was a forklift that we quickly learned to operate and used it to load the paper bales on a large trailer.

When we learned of higher paying jobs at the piers, we wore long sleeve shirts, rolled them up to the middle of our upper arms to make us look more muscular. Eugene and I then went to the Unemployment Office in Compton just before it opened. Almost daily, they would ask all veterans if they wanted to work on a banana boat. They gave them first dibs, and then they would call large men out of the line and send us to contact a Pacific Maritime representative on a pier in Wilmington to work on a banana boat. We were paid $2.45 per hour for the first six hours and $4.90 per hour for all additional hours worked in that day. The work entailed lifting stalks of bananas onto several levels of the boat, walking to a conveyer and placing them into individual revolving chutes. Some of the stalks weighed as much as 180 to 200 pounds. On occasions, we saw large spiders that were lethargic from the cool temperature in the hatch. We only had to work 40 minutes per hour with a 20-minute break each hour.

I remember the rides with my uncle from our house on 113th Street to Central Avenue, north to 103rd Street (the Main street of Watts) and on to Alameda Avenue where he would purchase gasoline for 22.9 cents per gallon at a U-Pump Discount Service Station. Sometimes when northbound on Alameda Avenue, we were cutoff by trains. Uncle Nick always turned the engine off until the train passed. I learned to be frugal watching his habits.

One of Uncle Nick's most frugal habits was centered around making use of almost everything he encountered; from nails he'd pick up, to grocery bags. He used them as trash bags and trashcan liners and for storing. He was the most prolific improviser I ever met. I saw him take a large metal bean container and wrap it around a muffler as a muffler patch. Years later I saw Pep Boys selling similar patches. He would take a coat hanger and fashion it into a tailpipe hanger or for use as a radio or television antenna. Uncle Nick would change the oil in his car, save the old oil and later use it as a weed killer in the alley at the rear of his house.

We often poked fun at him, at one of his frugal habits. We had relatives living on Bonnie Brae, north of Temple. Bonnie Brae from Temple north had a rather large downhill slope. When we would turn off Temple on to Bonnie Brae, in order to save gasoline Uncle Nick would cut off his engine and coast downhill. He would restart it by popping the clutch, which he advised saved the battery and the wear on the starter.

Uncle Nick seldom purchased clothing for himself. He had two double-breasted black Navy dress-uniform suits from the war. He would wear one on "dress up" occasions.

One day after a heavy breakfast, Uncle Nick took a walk from his house west on 113th Street to Avalon. He walked to Imperial Highway then back to his house. Somewhere in that one-block area of Avalon, Uncle Nick found $65 on the sidewalk. Thereafter, he made a weekly ritual of taking these walks on Saturdays and Sundays. During these walks, he always looked somewhat searchingly down on the sidewalk. He continued these walks for almost 10 years and ended abruptly after he got robbed.

Uncle Nick lost most of his hearing during the war and like many

Black veterans was never awarded any disability. He was a strong man and always told me that he never wanted anything for free, never a hand out, that he preferred to work for everything he got. Often we questioned his hearing ability because he seemed to have perfect hearing whenever money was mentioned. Uncle Nick had an aversion to lending money to anybody and particularly relatives. He assured me that I was the only family member he would lend money. Even with this assurance, I never borrowed from him.

I saw one of the most spectacular events of my life, the 1956 Rose Parade in Pasadena and the Rose Bowl game featuring the mighty Michigan State University (MSU) Spartans and the UCLA Bruins. MSU had a Black running back named Sam Brown who did everything. He won the game for MSU, 17 to 14. It appeared that his name was the only one on the MSU team that the announcers knew. I had never seen so many people gathered in one place before and got somewhat a sense of how big California really was, especially seeing so many cars and heavy traffic jams.

When school started the next year I had earned enough money to purchase fashionable school clothing and had a little saved. I finally saw my oldest brother Dave. He was glad I had relocated to California and often picked me up on weekends for outings. He had a fancy Chevrolet Impala and kept it waxed and shiny. I learned that he was a construction superintendent and an official in the union. Dave felt a great sense of pride in his position and related how much concrete he had supervised in the construction of the Harbor Freeway. According to Dave, "Yeah boy, I am a big nigger in the construction business in this town. I even got White boys and Mexicans working for me. How's that for an ex-Crugeran?"

I was very proud of my brother, especially seeing him with a job that gave him a sense of pride and accomplishment, a real person, a man. He often joked like a southern White male and often called me "boy" with a coy smile. Dave got so carried away that he started mimicking White southern males; he called every male "boy" in his general conversations.

One day Dave called and asked me how much money had I saved. When I told him about $300, he agreed to pick me up in a short while.

I thought he wanted to borrow some money from me. He drove me over to a predominantly White neighborhood, where we met a man he knew. He asked the man, "Now how much do you want for that piece of junk?" The man smiled as we walked to a 1941 well-preserved black Chevrolet. The man advised he had wanted $150 for the car but since I was Dave's brother, he would sell it to me for $100. In a state of awe and shock, I paid the man $100 and I followed Dave back to Uncle Nick's house in my new car. At the age of 17: I had purchased a car with money I had earned during the summer. I also paid my aunt and uncle money, no specific amount, on a regular basis. One of the nice things that I found in California was that jobs were plentiful, so plentiful that you could select the type of job you desired. I was able to work the paper-recycling job at my own leisure and play high school football.

President Truman eliminated segregation in the armed forces. He was the first president to insist that Blacks deserved equal treatment under the law. Truman was the first U.S. president to speak before the National Association for the Advancement of Colored People (NAACP). Although he was a strong president, he had a Congress that fought him on racial parity issues.

In May 1954 when the Supreme Court in Brown v. Board of Education ruled that segregation of students in public schools violates the equal protection clause of the Fourteenth Amendment because separate schools are inherently unequal; it was called Black Monday. The Fourteenth Amendment, ratified in 1868 provided equal protection to all, but Blacks were up to this point left out, actually denied this constitutional right. It would take three additional years before the U.S. Government decided to ensure these rights.

The rights of Black U.S. citizens, especially to police protection, had been violated since ratification of the amendment, with the knowledge of U. S. legislative and executive officials, to include state and local elected white officials.

Southern law enforcement officials, whose duty required that they protect all citizens, had always been major participators and perpetrators of racial violence against Blacks. With the increase of racism escalating to unprecedented levels, most Blacks discussed relocating from Greenwood and other parts of Mississippi.

Racism in and around Greenwood peaked in the summer of 1955, when a 14 year-old Black male, Emmett Till, from Chicago visiting relatives in Money, Mississippi, a town ten miles north of Greenwood, reportedly told a White lady, "bye baby." Two White males later abducted him from his relative's house. A few days later his body was pulled from the Tallahatchie River. One of his eyes had been gouged, his head had been crushed and a bullet was lodged in his head.

Two men were arrested and subsequently acquitted by an all-white jury. This dastardly and murderous act became a wake up call for Black Americans all over the United States. It served as a stimulus encouraging Blacks to move from the South.

About a year later my father was helping two families, members of one of his churches, to keep from losing their property in a scheme of alleged unpaid back taxes. They prevailed with strong documentation. Two nights later a cross was burned on the lawn of our home at 413 Nichols Street in Greenwood. A week later, my father sold our home and furniture at a price way below the fair market value. My mother, father, two sisters and brother then packed enough clothing for a week and departed Greenwood during the early morning hour for California.

Shortly after their arrival, I then moved with my family to our home in the 1800 block of E. 124th Street in Compton, California where I also attended Centennial Senior High School. I was the co-captain of the football team for the 1956 season.

I found the California schools far superior to the Black segregated Mississippi schools. They offered advanced classes that were not available to even White students in Mississippi schools. They provided an atmosphere that indicated that what you learned would be useable in the future. The Pledge of Allegiance was more meaningful. It fostered a true belief in "Liberty and Justice for All."

We studied current events and were exposed to many subjects. The completion of the Senior Problems class prepared you with coping and survival skills beyond high school. This new educational system was like a renaissance to me and was highly conducive to learning. It made me hungry for knowledge.

In segregated schools, we were encouraged to learn merely enough to pass a test and not to view education as a lifelong benefit. It was refreshing having new books and secure well-educated teachers who spoke their minds and freely expressed their opinions about issues without fear of retribution. I was stimulated to learn more than merely what the school required; I developed a strong desire to know and to seek information and retain it for future use.

There were boy's counselors and vice principals who got to know you personally. They helped students to find part-time jobs during the regular school year and full-time jobs during summer vacation. We worked at the U.S. Post Office, Terminal Annex, in downtown Los Angeles during the Christmas holiday seasons.

V

MR. AARON C. Wade, my high school football coach, was a small man in stature with a giant aura about him and a heavy bass voice to match his motivating personality. I was about four inches taller than the coach and outweighed him by 40 pounds. In those days, I was very strong and as fit as could be, however, I had a reverent fear of the coach, despite knowing that his bark was more severe than his bite.

HE WAS VERY diplomatic at times and a screamer when he thought it was required to obtain a desired result. On one occasion, I told him that I wanted to play quarterback. He showed a lot of concern and assured me that I had the potential to be a good quarterback. The coach then assured me that I could be a "hellacious" defensive tackle or defensive end. He further assured me that I could also play both positions also on offense and defense. He patted me on the shoulder when I was leaving his office and remarked that in those positions I would have exposure to more playing time. When we practiced during the summer break, the coach would scream if he thought we were not putting forth our maximum efforts. One day in August it was very hot and we had started our seasonal training; we ran 100-yard wind sprints and performed the exercises according to then University of Oklahoma's Coach Bud Wilkinson's manual. We ran plays, did strengthening exercises and were told the types of foods we should include in our daily diets. About two weeks into training, I was put in an exercise called the bullpen, where you obtain a defensive position and attack line in the circle, and it is switched to when you are in the circle and are attacked by linemen in the ring. There was a big lineman named Riddell, who outweighed me by 50 pounds. I always got the best of him whether on offense or defense. Afterwards, we went one-on-one. I had fast forearm uplift and always wore a plastic shield across both. In the one-on-one, I snapped my right forearm up against the big lineman's helmet so hard it made a snap sound. Riddell jerked his head back, not in pain, but from the stun of my forearm. The linemen coach, Mr. Adams screamed, "That's it

John ring his bell." He then called other linemen over and told them that that was one way of getting the lineman's attention on defense.

We went into trap blocks, high-low blockings and two-on-one blocking tactics. Afterward we did 50-yard wind sprints at a fast run. After the wind sprints, we did a cool down exercise. We continued this type of training for three days when the big lineman, Riddell, all of a sudden pulled off his shoulder pads and jersey and started walking toward the gymnasium, which indicated he was quitting football. As he walked toward the gym, Coach Wade had us huddle up around him. He then pointed at the big lineman and stated, "There goes a quitter, the type of guy you never want to date your sister. Quitters develop a habit of quitting and many go through life never completing much before throwing in the towel and quitting. The mark of a man is one who when the going gets tough, he gets tougher and continues, does not quit." The coach continued talking about always giving all you can give and if necessary, reaching back somewhere and giving more in everything you do.

Coach Wade was a character builder, a role model, and a person you could confide in about anything from sex to sexually transmitted diseases. He made me realize, then, the important influences that a coach has in the life of his players, especially those fatherless players. I also realized that for some, a coach's voice is the only authoritative male voice they hear. A coach not only teaches the fundamentals of a particular sport, they teach sportsmanship. They teach endurance and perseverance and how to follow a task to the end; and how to work as a team.

One of Coach Wade's, pet peeves was for one of his football players to become engaged in a fight during a game or a fight per se.

On several occasions, I saw one of our players get into a fight and immediately Coach Wade would run onto the field, grab the player in his chest and escort him off the field. He always taught us that our main objective was to play football to the best of our ability and within the confines of rules and regulations. According to Coach Wade, usually when there is a fight on the field, the one who starts it realizes the opposing player is outplaying him.

One of the important things I learned from Coach Wade was to learn all you can learn in any field you desire to work, especially the policies, guidelines, procedures, change, and how others perform the same or similar duties. Initially, I was shocked when he advised that athletes should use the best equipment available when participating in any sport. This was contrary to the schools in Greenwood where we were accustomed to routinely receiving hand-me-downs from the White schools. All of our football equipment was new. The high school was new; built in 1954. Coach Wade taught us to learn all that we could about football, which is what he did. On one occasion, we had a New York Giants professional kicker conduct a kicking seminar at our school. Several years later, while watching a professional football game on television, I saw my old coach, Mr. Wade run onto the field being introduced as one of the referees. He was one of the first Black referees in professional football.

During my senior year, I had customized my car as a "low-rider' with baby moons chrome hubcaps, a flame drawn on both fenders, chrome lake plugs, chrome overhead valve cover, and new chrome front and rear bumpers. Additionally, I had a white fuzzy mirror warmer wrapped around my review mirror. My steering wheel was cut into a ¾ circle similar to those seen in small airplanes.

Almost all of the Black student car owners were "lowriders" and owned older cars except Errol Drew, a newly acquired friend and football teammate. Drew had a 1956 Ford with all of the chrome accessories and it hiked up in the back in a style White guys called a "rake" or on a "diego."

Drew was 5'8" and 255 pounds of solid muscle; he was an offensive guard. I liked to do the linemen exercise called "the bullpen." I, weighing 215 pounds, would beat Drew something fierce. One day after football practice he told me, "I think you enjoy whipping my ass out there on the football field, huh?"

I smiled and told him it was all just a game. We became friends after that. One night Drew and I had exited a café on Olympic Boulevard and Central Avenue, seeing no cars in either direction, we ran across Olympic to the north curb where Drew had parked. Before we entered the car, an LAPD unit seemingly came out of nowhere, turned on their emergency lights, flashed the spotlight in our faces and shouted on the Public Announcement system, "Freeze, both of you motherfuckers, put your goddamn hands in the air! If you move, we'll blow your goddamn brains out."

Two White officers got out of the police unit and placed us in a front leaning rest position with our legs spread wide apart and extended back. One officer stood watch as the other officer patted us down for weapons. He, while searching, called us every profane word he could think of prefacing it with boys and niggers. After running record checks, they cited us for "jaywalking." They told us how to appear in court or we could pay the fine and they left.

Drew's family had money. His dad and two of his brothers owned four famous Tulsa Barbeque restaurants in Los Angeles. Drew and his family lived in a new house at the west Compton city limit north of Alondra just east of Avalon. It was a very modern house with some of the latest fixtures and appliances. It was listed in "Better Homes and Gardens." I stopped associating with Drew after he and some thugs attempted to snatch a lady's purse in, what was then the all-White city of Inglewood. I found it very bizarre for Drew who was 5'8" and 255 pounds and wore thick bifocal glasses. Drew was driving his car during the offense. He abandoned his car and tried to hide between oleander bushes, which are poisonous, that lined the curb, while wearing a red bebop cap and a light blue shirt. Although a football player, he tried to introduce me to marijuana and Thunderbird wine.

My next newly acquired friend was classmate Leotis Sanders. He had a younger sister who had a tremendous crush one me. She was an underclass student and sent word of her interest one day. Leotis, very protective of his sisters, had a habit of befriending guys his sisters liked. He would threaten them or convince his sisters and his mother that they were unworthy.

Leotis was one of the most prolific thieves I've ever met. The word around campus was that he could steal Oldsmobile flipper or Dodge lancer hubcaps off of a car while it was being driven. He drove a low rider blue Chevrolet with fancy hubcaps. I came perilously close to getting arrested for curfew violation one night while hanging out with Leotis.

According to Leotis, my car was not equipped with up-to-date hubcaps. He came by my house with his little brother, Little Will, and Henry Powers one of our classmates. I joined them in his car and we went to Mona Park to meet some girls after they got out of a dance. We sat chatting for a long time noting that almost everybody had left the building, but we never saw the girls we were supposed to meet, after the dance, come out. Around 11:00 PM, then suddenly emergency lights of a Los Angeles Sheriff's patrol unit came on behind us and the spotlight was flashed before being steadied on the inside rear-view mirror. As a tall White sheriff's deputy approached the car, I learned several new words. Leotis shouted, "Ah fuck, goddamn Pigs, what the fuck." The deputy flashed the beam of his flashlight in our faces and said, "Leotis, Henry Powers and Little Will, son what's your name? Do you have any ID?" Before I could respond, Leotis blurted out, "You honky pig motherfuckers, all you cocksuckers know to do is come down here from Firestone Park and Bogart a nigger. You sack full of motherfuckers." Henry Powers followed with, "Yeah what's wrong with you honky whitey motherfuckers, why don't you go play Rango Billy on some whitey's fucking neighborhood. I bet when you drove up you told your white ass partner, let's go George Raft these niggers, they ain't nothing but niggers. You honky white-ass afterbirth eating sack full of motherfuckers."

While nervously trying to retrieve my driver's license, I felt my heart jump into my throat above my epiglottis as sweat broke out on my brow. As I caught a glimpse of the other deputy in our right rear, Little Will then blurted out, "Leotis why in the fuck these honky motherfuckers always ride down on us niggers, these no good honky motherfuckers. Look at this cocksucker, you honky son-of-a-bitch."

When handing the deputy my license, I felt my throat go dry and my tongue swell in my mouth. I thought of being jailed for curfew violation and although I feared being beaten to a pulp by the deputies, this fear paled in comparison to how I knew my parents would react.

While the deputy was reviewing my license, to my utter astonishment, Leotis, Henry and Little Will continued lambasting the deputy with tirades of profanity. I looked back at the deputy at our rear and saw him slapping his nightstick in his left hand and noted that he was wearing sap gloves. I heard him mumble something to his partner. Out of fear, I remained still, until the other deputy asked, "John what do you do for a living? Are you in school?" I replied, "Yes I am. I am a senior at Centennial High School." He looked at me and remarked that he had not seen me before. At this point, Henry shouted, "Man what the fuck, you just rolled down here and decided to Bogart us just because we are niggers huh? Don't you motherfuckers ever get tired of Bogarting and George Rafting niggers?" He then called him a lousy lowlife honky motherfucker. I, sitting in the left rear, was petrified of their demeanor. I knew we had flunked the "police attitude test" and would get arrested, spanked and booked into the county jail. I had never heard of any person, White or Black, demeaning the police and walking away without being arrested, beaten or both. Little Will continued to holler profanity at the officer and made a remark about the officer's mother performing fellatio on a well-endowed Black male. I felt my mouth become extremely dry, my heart beat increase and I started to sweat more profusely than before. When the other deputy approached and asked me if I attended Centennial High School, I responded, "Yes sir." Henry screamed, "Hey John you don't have to answer these motherfuckers no sir, yes sir. These cocksuckers already think they're better than we are. Motherfuck him and his mammy too." Leotis then added, "Hey don't cow-tow [sic] to this honky, this is California. They're just like niggers too. They ain't got shit but that badge. Motherfuck 'um."

The lead deputy surmised that Leotis had stolen hubcaps in the trunk. After Leotis, pressed the trunk button, the deputy came back with two Oldsmobile flipper hubcaps advising that they were likely stolen. The deputy advised, "John you are these guys savior. If you were not with them, they would be in jail by now. These guys are big-time crooks. You seem like a nice kid; find some other guys to pal around with. These guys will be in jail before they are 19 years old. All of you are lucky tonight because most of my colleagues are not as tolerant as I am." I thanked him. As we were leaving the parking lot, Henry gave them a parting remark, "I hope someone blows your goddamn brains out you honky motherfuckers." I knew then that I would heed the deputy's advice.

The first marijuana cigarette I'd ever seen, unbeknownst to me, was being smoked in my car while I was driving. Joe Liggins Jr., the son of the famous musician who wrote the song "The Honey Dripper" that sold

4,000,000 copies in 1953, had a deformed arm. I can clearly recall how his arm got injured. One night we were at a party in Willowbrook. Joe Jr. and several guys had started using drugs. While dancing, we heard the sound of someone getting struck by a car. We ran out and saw Joe Jr. sprawled on the street in front of a car. He appeared to be bleeding from his mouth, nose and elsewhere. The girl throwing the party screamed for her mother to call the police. She then remarked, "Oh my God, it's Joe Jr. He's going to die." An older lady said, "Let me through, and let me see what's going on here." She walked up to Joe Jr., moved his face from side to side and asked him to raise his foot. After he moved his leg, the old lady said, "naw this niggah ain't gonna die, he's full of those red devils (seconals), wine, weed (marijuana) and plus his hair is processed, it'll take a goddamn train to kill this niggah." Miraculously he recovered. His left arm, although not amputated, it was deformed leaving him partial use of his left fingers.

On occasions Joe Jr. would walk to my house and ride to school with me. One day I was driving westbound on 124th Street while Joe Jr., a passenger in the front, smoked what appeared to be a hand-rolled cigarette. I saw a California Highway Patrol (CHP) car behind me with the emergency lights activated a clear indicator for me to pull over. I remarked, "Aw shit there is a Chippy behind, pulling us over." Joe Jr. looked back and immediately started eating the cigarette, fire and all, while wincing from the pain.

After I presented my driver's license, registration and proof of insurance, the CHP officer advised me that my car was too low that I had scraped the street when backing out of my driveway. He gave me a verbal warning and let us go. It was when Joe Jr. complained that the Chippy made him eat his weed that I got angry. Possession of marijuana, regardless of the amount, was a felony. The police had authority to seize a car based on one marijuana cigarette. Thereafter I avoided Joe Jr. like a plague.

About two weeks later, Leotis called me and said he had a present for me and was coming by. He lived in Palm Lane, a housing area on 120th Street and Wilmington Avenue. When Leotis arrived with Henry, I was standing in our driveway talking to my father. Leotis got out of his car, walked up to me in the presence of my father and handed me a small cigar type cigarette wrapped in yellow paper. I immediately placed it in my pocket and walked with him back to his car. Leotis stated, "That's Panama red weed, the best there is. It will make you high off two good puffs and will keep your dick hard for three hours." I chatted with Leotis and Henry in the driveway for several minutes. When they left, I ran into the house and flushed the marijuana down the toilet.

One day while jogging at Centennial High School I started to slide from side-to-side and loose my balance. I stopped, steadied myself and began to think that I had exhausted myself to the point of near fainting. I felt better after I stopped but felt what I thought was the ground shaking underneath. After a few moments, I heard a loud snapping akin to that of a huge bone breaking and cracking. The ground swayed quickly, almost knocking me off my feet. Shortly after the first jolt, several more jolts occurred in waves. Nobody had to tell me what I was experiencing. My immediate thoughts were that the ground would eventually break open and I would be engulfed into an abyss. I ran to my car and turned on the radio. It was announced that there'd been an earthquake, followed by some number registered on a Richter scale. At this point I did not know if I wanted to really be a Californian; after learning that Southern California is located on the San Andreas Fault. It was an unforgettable experience.

James Garrett, an underclassman, lived around the corner from me. I kind of avoided associating with him because most of his conversations centered around how to steal cars, smoke dope and steal hubcaps. On a few occasions when visiting a neighbor, he would stop and we would chat about football, track and what school had the best team. On occasions when in his neighborhood, I would stop and visit with him. James a penchant for stealing cars and seemed to have a perversion to steal them under the watch of the owner.

He had been stopped by the police several times for driving stolen cars. Being a teenager, he would be detained and charged with "joyriding." The last time he went to Juvenile Court, the hearing judge advised James and his parents that this had to cease and told James that he was "skating on thin ice." He warned James that on the next occasion he would be confined for a period of time.

To prevent James from stealing cars, his dad decided to buy James a car. They bought him a 1950 black and white Buick. James picked up one of my habits, shuttling cute girls to and from school. About six months later Los Angeles Sheriff's Department deputies arrested him driving a stolen 1954 Chevrolet.

I went over to his house when I saw his dad coming home from work. I was nosy and wanted to hear his explanation of why he stole the car. A friend and I were sitting in the living room with James and his mother when his father entered. After exchanging pleasantries with us, his father started off by telling him that he was disappointed with his behavior and perplexed as to why he would stoop to steal a car when he had a car of his own. James slowly started saying, "Daddy, it's kinda hard to explain it." His father said, "Well son do the best you can, we are listening." James said, "Well er, er, er Daddy those other cars just ride better." My friend and I immediately left his house suspecting that he was about to be the recipient of some physical corrective action.

There were many unique students at Centennial High School and there was an informal dress code. It was taboo to wear jeans or khaki pants in high school. In our high school we had a number of students that became famous: the Olympian Charles Dumas, the first person to high jump seven feet; Marlene Brown, an Olympic decathlete; Walter Ward and the Imperials, a rock group; the Sweet Sixteens, a singing group with a number one hit, "A Casual Look"; Peter Bryant, a singer and brother of famed chanteuse Joyce Bryant; a number of athletes that became professional football, baseball and basketball players.

One of the weirdest was underclassman Clyde Scruggs. Clyde had an unusually large head with saliva always dripping from his mouth. We thought he was retarded. Clyde, although his brother was one of the few known young heroin addicts in town, never used drugs and never mentioned his brother's addiction in our presence. He had a penchant for consorting with prostitutes and playing the horses at illegal off-track betting locations.

He often won and many people consulted with him on various horses as though he was some kind of tout or handicapper. Clyde was one of the few Black Cross Country runners and pole-vaulters around. The last time I saw him, he was Dr. Clyde Scruggs, PhD, a professor at Stanford University. He had been in Mexico with another Stanford professor charting the eclipse of the sun. That professor, whose name escapes me, won a Nobel Prize.

Although California was integrated, there were no Blacks playing football at Stanford University. One of my Black teammates and a Black player a class above me, both honor students, were denied admission based on a purported failure to pass the entrance exam. There were no Blacks playing on any of the Southeast Conference (SEC) teams or any major college team in the South. Black athletes in the South were heavily recruited by major colleges (Divisions I & II) in the North, West, East and parts of the Midwest. Arizona, Arizona State, Idaho, Idaho State, Oregon, Oregon State, Washington, Washington State and Iowa recruited Blacks heavily from all over America.

UCLA, with Kenny Washington, was one of the first major universities to allow a Black to play the quarterback position. I saw athleticism playing a major role in causing integration in the American college system.

When graduating from high school, I was being offered a football scholarship to College of the Pacific; we discovered that my mother had diabetes. When I saw the unexplained hole between one of her outer toes, I became alarmed and decided to attend Compton Community (Junior) College in Compton, California. I played football, which accounted for my first airplane ride. We flew United Airlines to Boise, Idaho on a Friday morning. The following day we participated in the Boise Junior College (BJC) Homecoming Parade. We played BJC that afternoon. There were eight Black players on our team and none on BJC's. An employee at the hotel told us there were only three Black couples in the city. It was a new experience being in a city in America and seeing Whites who had never seen a Black person up close. We were treated nicely and with the utmost respect. When conversing with a couple, it appeared as though their carefully selected words were chosen in a manner, not meant to offend us in any way.

Compton College offered classes in golf, archery, modern dance, gymnastics, swimming, diving, fencing and almost every sport one could imagine. I learned to play golf, once off-limits to Blacks in Mississippi, and archery.

VI

AFTER FOOTBALL SEASON at Compton College, I worked part-time
for Pep Boys Auto Supply in Bellflower, California. I was transferred the
following year to the Downey, California store. Downey was an all-White
suburban city east of Los Angeles. One day while riding through South
Gate, California, I was falsely arrested by two young White South Gate
police officers; while returning from work at Pep Boys in Downey, in a
car driven by my co-worker. The officers stopped us on Firestone Boulevard in South Gate. When my co-worker asked why had we been stopped
and if we had violated any law, the older of the two officers advised that
we were being stopped for "Highway Mopry", a non-existent charge.

They ran record checks on both of us, which revealed a traffic warrant
for my co-worker. I heard their dispatcher advise, "No wants or warrants
for your subject John Sutton." The younger officer told me he wanted
to give me a field sobriety test. I agreed and advised him that I had not
consumed any alcoholic beverages. He said, "Okay, then do you know
your constipational [sic] rights?" I responded, "I know my constitutional
rights." His partner then asked, "Is Mickey Mouse a car or dog?" I replied,
"Neither, he is a comic mouse." The other officer stated, "Let's take him
down to the station anyway." My co-worker and I were handcuffed and
transported to the South Gate Police Station, where we were placed in a

61

booking cell. I was kept in the booking cell for approximately two hours. I asked the jailer several times why had I been arrested, and further related that I had overheard the dispatcher state that there were no wants or warrants for me prior to my being arrested. After a short while, a White lieutenant came and unlocked the holding cell and told me that he would transport me back to the car. En route the lieutenant held a non-specific general conversation, never mentioning the false arrest. He had an aura about him that indicated he was worried, but did not want to reveal that his two officers had made a mistake.

After I completed Compton College, George Phillips, the area general manager (AGM) promoted me to a full-time salesman position. George was a southern White male who had relocated from Texas to California about the time I had arrived. He was a high-energy workaholic that took a lot of pride in his work.

Unquestionably, he was an organization man. When fall came around and I was preparing to attend college full-time, the AGM convinced me to attend college part-time and to work for Pep Boys full-time. He related he was grooming me for a manager's position with Pep Boys. He stated that I had more formal education than any of the current managers and related that I would go places with the corporation. According to the AGM, he had discussed me with Moe Strauss, the only survivor of the Manny, Moe and Jack founders. By this time, I had been writing half the weekly order (approximately 5,000 different items) and assisting the assistant manager with auditing and balancing the daily books. The AGM made arrangements for me to write the whole order (over 10,000 different items) and to do the entire audit and balancing of the books daily.

The corporation hired shoppers to monitor our compliance with policy, procedures and guidelines. I was always rated the highest. About two months after I took over auditing and balancing the books, the cash registers consistently came up short, almost daily; sometimes as much as $50 and $60.

Trainers were sent to our store; one was a con artist with various tricks. One trick involved flashing a large bill, then changing it to smaller bill when passing it to the salesman. Another trick involved having the salesman count his return change back by placing it into his hand. He would keep his palms up with the money, secretly conceal a bill in the fold of his thumb and advise that you did not give him the correct change. The salesman usually reaches into the customer's hand to retrieve what he thought he had placed there.

The AGM started visiting our store twice weekly unannounced. At no time did he ever indicate, insinuate or give any indication that he thought I was responsible for the shortages.

When I was promoted to the position of salesman, I felt a lot of pride and always arrived at work 10 or 15 minutes before opening. One Monday I arrived about 20 minutes early a few seconds ahead of the AGM. After he parked, he asked me to join him for breakfast across the street from the store. When I tried to refuse, advising him that I wanted to be at the store when the manager arrived, the AGM advised me that I had forgotten the hierarchy. I relented and joined him for breakfast. After completing our order, the AGM went into a discussion about thieves, thefts, pilfering and how despicable some thieves are in their acts. He then told me that I had always been an ideal salesman and that I should go a long way with the Pep Boys Corporation.

After this big diatribe, the AGM told me something that I will never forget. The AGM related that he was very curious as to why I did not apply for a salesman job when I first applied for employment with Pep Boys. He answered it by telling me that I had done so because I thought my chances for employment with Pep Boys would be greater at the level to which I'd applied. He further related that I was one of the most honest and self-assured persons he had met in a long time. Yet it still puzzled him why I had not applied for a salesman position. [He knew that I was honest because I always look into his eyes without shying away, talk without stuttering, stammering or poorly selecting my words.] The AGM then stated, "I want you to know that when the registers continued to come up short and especially shortly after you started doing the audits, you were never a suspect even though you were in a catbird seat where you could steal. I want you to know, I never considered you a suspect and I told them at headquarters that you were not the thief."

After breakfast, we walked over to the store, where he called the manager and assistant manager into the rear office. When they came out, the AGM gave me the keys to both the store and the safe, along with a brown Pep Boys paper bag containing the store's bank deposits for Friday and Saturday, approximately $10, 000 in cash and $7,000 in credit cards and checks. He advised that the two managers were going downtown to corporate headquarters; I was given authorization to make payouts for returns up to $100.

Later that afternoon, the AGM and assistant manager returned to the store. The AGM had me join him for a slight repast at the bowling alley. He related that the manager was the thief and that he had also been photographed writing sales receipts, tearing them up and placing the money in his pockets. The AGM was very angry with the manager and related that he had stolen enough money to buy a service station franchise, which was $10,000 at that time.

The City of Compton, incorporated in 1888, had three high schools and a junior college. For years Compton held one of the largest track meets, The Compton Invitational, that attracted athletes from all over the world. It had a population of approximately 100,000 inhabitants, approximately 15 percent were Blacks and 10 percent were Hispanics.

At that time there were many all-White towns in Southern California: Bellflower, Downey, Lynwood, Maywood, Bell, Vernon, Torrance, Inglewood, South Gate, Paramount, Bell Gardens, Whittier, Garden Grove, La Mirada, Claremont, Upland, Montclair, San Dimas, Azusa, Glendora, Fullerton, Brea, La Habra, Huntington Park, Santa Monica, Redondo Beach, Gardena, Hawthorne and others. While Hispanics inhabited Covina, West Covina, Alhambra, El Monte, Montebello, Monterey Park and other cities, some tracing back to the fifth generation.

VII

AFTER WW II, Russia divided Germany with its allies and kept East Germany under Soviet rule. In 1961 they built a wall around East Berlin and restricted passage between East Berlin and the American sector of West Berlin. They further restricted travel between East and West Germany, which was independent and allied with the United States and other countries.

In July of 1961, several East Germans were shot trying to escape from East Berlin into West Berlin. The United States, involved in a Cold War with the USSR (Russia), strengthened its alliance with West Germany. About the 15th of July, I was drafted into the armed services along with former classmates and others in my age group.

We appeared at the U. S. Army induction station in downtown Los Angeles where we were sworn into the army and given a physical examination. I noticed that the doctor had written pes planus on my physical exam. It sounded like a serious disorder or disease to me and I asked him what it meant. The doctor chuckled and said, "Flat feet, that's what it means. Don't be alarmed, all you guys (Blacks) have it," motioning with his head to three Blacks in front of me. He assured me that it was an asset and meant that I would make a good foot soldier.

That evening around 8:00 PM, we were placed on a troop train at Los

Angeles Union Station. The train did not depart until 10:45 PM. En route there were guys from all over Southern California, sprawled in the aisle, some shooting dice, drinking whiskey, wine, beer and using profanity as though it was the language of the day. A Specialist 4th Class (Spec.4) came down the aisle several times stating, "Excuse me gentleman! Pardon me, may I pass, thank you?" He was extremely apologetic and got cursed out with every passing from his second trip on throughout the night. I was curious why he made so many trips to and fro about every twenty minutes. Most of the guys, like I did stayed up all night enjoying our first train ride.

About 5:00 AM that morning I dozed off. Approximately 30 minutes later, the train stopped on the base in Fort Ord, California. I looked out the window as the Spec. 4 disembarked and stood in front of a military band. He picked up a megaphone and screamed, "Every motherfucker and his brother get off this motherfucking train now, now before I kick all of your asses, did you hear me? Now, now, now, all you cocksuckers get off this goddamn motherfucking train!" When he paused, the band started playing "You're in the Army Now." The band played "El Capitan" as we hurriedly gathered our few belongings and got off the train.

The Spec. 4 had us, about 400 inductees, line up abreast three deep. He walked up in the faces of several inductees and screamed, "You are in the motherfucking army now" accompanied by threats to "beat the living shit out of approximately 20 men". We stood there unknowing if he was real or acting; allowing his rants and raves to continue unchallenged.

Basic training was quite an experience to behold. We were taught how to make a bed (cot) hard enough to cause a dropped quarter to bounce. Perhaps most importantly we were taught good hygienic habits, stern discipline, teamwork and survival skills. We were also taught that the basic job or duty of a soldier above all is to kill, kill the enemy with such quick dispatch that there is no time for remorse or vacillation.

At the end of basic training, we were given our Advance Individual Training assignments. Some in my company were sent to Ft. Hood, Texas; Ft. Leonard Wood, Missouri; Ft. Chaffee, Arkansas; Ft. Carson, Colorado; Ft Polk, Louisiana and Ft. Benning, Georgia. I was assigned to Ft. Sam Houston, Texas. We were given leave over the Christmas holidays.

My next airplane ride was on a Continental redeye flight from Los Angeles International Airport to San Antonio, Texas on New Year's Eve,

1961. After midnight, the Captain gave all adult passengers two complimentary cocktails. When we arrived in San Antonio, I was hungry and went into a restaurant in the airport to have breakfast. I became aware that I was again in the South where there were segregated facilities. While wondering if I would be served, I recalled that a federal law had been passed prohibiting businesses from refusing to serve Blacks. This included all businesses engaged in interstate commerce the catchall being if they sold coffee they were included since coffee had to be shipped into the states. I was served without incident. I was assigned to Brooke Army Medical Hospital and trained to be a Medical Specialist. My first trip to downtown San Antonio was quite an experience. I saw signs in businesses on Commerce Street marked "Whites Only" or "Blacks".

One weekend I attended a dance on base at a club called The Snake Pit. Bobby Bland was performing with a mixed crowd that was packed to maximum capacity. It was a frame building and the dance floor made creaking noises. Three soldiers in my Company were engaged. Two had fiancées that visited several times while we were there.

During one of the training sessions, a drill sergeant gave us the definition of a latrine and asked us about twenty times to define a latrine. I still recall today that a latrine is "fifty feet of non-porous canvass."

During reconnaissance training another sergeant taught us how to immobilize a charging dog. He explained that a dog would lunge for your upper body. He showed how to extend your forearm to receive the bite and simultaneously grab the dog's testicles and twist them hard while yanking them forward, which will immediately immobilize the dog. After teaching for a week, the sergeant again asked how to immobilize a charging dog and four soldiers gave him the answer. A soldier, who had been sleeping a lot in class and made to stand up where he also went to sleep, raised his hand. After the sergeant recognized him, he said, "Sergeant can I ask a question?" The sergeant responded, "Yeah shoot" he said, "Sergeant I don't think that will work all the time." The sergeant stated, "Don't worry about it trooper. It has been tried and tested thousands of times. Take my word for it, it works." The soldier then asked, "What if it's a female dog?" The sergeant became nervous and angry and gave us a 20-minute break. He left the class and never returned.

A week before the end of training we got our new assignments. While we were in formation one soldier got assigned to U. S. Armed Forces

Europe; he went into a sort of daze and walked out of formation toward the hospital. He was picked up two days later walking aimlessly around the base.

I got the same assignment and was shipped to Ft. Dix, New Jersey and transported to Ft. McGuire Air Force Base. I boarded a military jet with other soldiers and we were flown to Nova Scotia. We were put on board an old DC-9 type airplane with rear-facing seats. We departed Nova Scotia around 10:00 PM for Scotland. About two hours over the ocean, I looked out the window and saw fire and smoke coming from both propeller engines on the port side. I then went to the right side of the plane, looked out and noticed one engine was also on fire. I told the military flight attendant what I had seen and she told me not to worry that this was normal for that type of airplane.

We arrived safely in Padwick, Scotland early that morning. Without deplaning, we flew to Frankfort, Rhine Main, Germany. All I could see below was a blanket of snow that covered the ground. We were told that Germany was experiencing the coldest winter that Europe has had in 100 years. It was piercing cold outside, colder than I had ever experienced or imagined. We were bussed to a U. S. military base and briefed. The next day we were put on a train bound for our duty stations. We had our watches synchronized and were told the trains in Germany are accurate within one minute. We were then given a specific time to disembark and warned that if we did not get off at that time we would end up in East Germany and the East Germans and Russians would line us up against the wall and shoot us. We were advised that we did not hear this type of information in the States. We were further advised if we ended up in East Germany that there was nothing the U.S. could do.

I arrived in Bamberg, Bavaria, Germany in the afternoon, was picked up in a five-ton military truck and transported to a U.S. military base in the inner city. It consisted of numerous two-storied brick buildings with the resemblance of a prison. I was assigned to a medical unit in the headquarters of an Eight Inch tow-type howitzer battalion. I was issued bedding and advised to come back in the morning for the rest of my gear.

While exhausted and in deep sleep, about 2:00 AM, a soldier ran through the barracks shouting, "alert, alert, alert, alert." Everybody in my room jumped out of bed and started putting on their clothing and rushing about the place.

One of the soldiers told me I had to leave the building, to follow them. I put on my dress uniform and my winter overcoat and followed them to the motor pool. I got in the back of a five-ton canvas covered truck and we rode for about three hours, ending up in a forest somewhere in Germany. The three canon batteries set up in the forest with 18 howitzers pointed as though aimed at a target. Somebody screamed "Fire Mission" and the cannoneers moved about the howitzers simulating firing. It was piercing cold and I felt as though my face was freezing. We stayed in the field several hours until the march order was given. I rode back on the same truck and got so cold that I trembled and ached. It was extremely cold and the wind swirling under the canvass caused ice to form on my mustache from my breathing. It was so cold, the only relief I got was through praying and asking God to spare me. I thought I was going to freeze to death. When we arrived back at the motor pool, I had to be helped off the truck. There was a sheet of ice on the metal bed of the truck.

After checking in, I was issued field equipment and assigned to the Battalion Aid station. During debriefing, I learned about the alerts and our responsibilities during the alerts. There was a special responsibility for a Scarlet Alert: a notification that the war had started and to get combat ready. Due to the threat of a possible war with Russia and satellite countries, there was a curfew requiring that all U.S. soldiers be back on post by midnight unless on authorized pass or leave.

Sometimes when we went on regular alerts, lunch trucks would join us in the forest and sell snacks and beverages. We went on long field exercises some covering three weeks performed as though we were in a real combat situation. On occasions we went to the large artillery training camp in Graffenwehr, Germany. All 18 cannons would be placed in positions aimed at the impact area, with a forward observer placed at a position near the impact area where he called in the artillery rounds. They fired all night, often continuously for 72 hours.

I observed these rituals from a field ambulance. I was always thrilled at the battalion barrages when all 18 guns were fired simultaneously. The most exciting was seeing the process of handling and firing a simulated atomic round, using a 4-2-4 charge. When the landyardist [sic] pulled the cord, an extremely loud noise would sound causing the rear legs of the cannon to jolt out of its trenches accompanied by a large fire ring exiting from the mouth of the cannon. When the rounds landed in the impact area two or three miles away, they sounded like gigantic rumbles of thunder and the ground would shake as though from a major earthquake.

The Army Times highlighted the cold spell, relating that it was one of the coldest winters that Europe had experienced in 100 years. The ground in the field, motor pool and around the barracks was frozen solid; there was solid thick ice everywhere, even on the rooftops of buildings.

Inside all of the buildings in our battalion there were almost human-size placards explaining why we were in Europe. They depicted a White American soldier standing in a crouched position with his rifle, bayonet affixed and thrust forward in a fighter's stance. Across the top read, "Soldier Why are You in Europe?" The answer at the bottom read, "To fight, if necessary, for the rights of free men in a free world."

When I initially saw the placard, I became stunned and started recalling how I had witnessed Blacks from the Jim Crow South go to fight the Germans in WW II only to return home feeling like aliens or otherwise unwanted persons. That even I had experienced a type of racial hurt that can never be erased. I recalled Blacks from my neighborhood who were killed in Germany during the war. Perhaps most disappointing was that I was in a foreign country freezing and prepared to fight for the freedom of an ex-enemy when in reality I and other Blacks were not so free in America, our own country. I became bitter, knowing that nothing was being done about it, especially having had two brothers serve in wars and both returned home unable to find meaningful employment.

A month later, we went on a two-week field exercise in the same cold. It was somewhat bearable then because I had been issued my cold weather uniform and thermal boots, known as Mickey Mouse boots that actually warmed your feet when you walked. I also had a facemask and cold weather mittens. I later learned that the gun-bunnies thought they were keeping warm by secretly drinking alcoholic beverages when in the field. When their booze ran out, they came to the Aid Station where I was assigned and coughed, wheezed and gasped for breath asking for Elixir Terpin Hydrate with Codeine (G.I. Gin).

After we returned from the field, I went on leave in the city and walked into a bar in Bamberg called the Black Bear where I was denied service by a German waitress because I was a Black man. A little White soldier in civvies advised, "Yeah this is our place. Y'all got your places on Eber Strasse" and told me how to get there. He recommended that I take a taxi relating that they were cheap.

It was difficult to believe what I had just experienced. I took a taxi over to the Black section. I saw a German lady driving a yellow Opel back and forth on the street as if she was looking for someone. Before I could enter the first Gasthaus, a Black male exited a Gasthaus a few doors down, walked up briefly to the right side of the Opel. The Opel then took off with the Black male running behind it. After about two blocks, the Opel stopped and the Black male got in and they drove away.

I entered the Gasthaus and using the little German I knew, I ordered a cognac and coke. Two Black soldiers who observed that I was new in Germany joined me. We chatted and drank. When I told them about the refusal to serve me at the Black Bear, they advised that it was a club for rednecks. They said that Germans, like a lot of Americans were very biased toward Blacks. They advised that it existed all over Germany. When I explained the situation with the yellow Opel, both laughed. They related that the driver is a whore called Ten Mark Annie and that is how she operates. When a John approaches her for a date, she tells him the price is ten marks (the equivalent of $2.50 U.S.), followed by instructions for the John to follow her as she drives a few blocks. She then stops and lets him in the car. They drive out to the boonies where they consummate the sexual act. When he pays her, she brings him back.

After a while, we were joined by three local frauleins (females). We drank cognac and coke, beer and "Steinhager." After a while, the frauleins suggested we go to a Gasthaus down the street with a dance floor and dancing. We left the Gasthaus and started walking in couples down the street. About midway to the location, my date told me to wait. We stopped and she walked between two buildings immediately off the sidewalk, pulled her dress up, removed her panties and squatted and urinated. After she finished, she joined me and related that it is common for women to do what she had done. She further related that it was common for German women to walk arm-in-arm.

I learned that prostitution was a necessary profession wherever soldiers were housed, that the U.S. Government actually condoned it, as well as, provided soldiers with free little soldiers or raincoats (prophylactics) and stressed the avoidance of venereal diseases.

I thought the incident at the Black Bear was an aberration, although my Gasthsus buddies had stated otherwise, only prevalent in Bamberg.

After talking to other Black soldiers, I was advised that many had traveled to various cities in Germany and had encountered the same problem.

Some advised that they had reported it to their Company commander. As a result, some of the reported places were placed off-limits to U.S. soldiers, but most had no action taken against them.

While on duty in the Aid Station, a sergeant, of Filipino extraction, came into the office and related that I was supposed to fill out his medical discharge forms. After checking the in box, I found a manifold-type medical form utilized for soldiers being discharged from the service. When eliciting the biographical information, I detected that the sergeant seemed angry and disappointed. When I noted that he had 22 years of service, I told him that he would be getting a good pension for the rest of his life. I added that he would find it easy to get a job because of his military background. He doubted it and remarked, "I won't get a fucking thing, and they are not going to pay me shit for all these years." When I asked him why not? He told me that many artists, painters, sculptors, authors and music writers produce lots of artwork and things, and are not often considered to be an artist. He further related that some of the most famous artists only became famous posthumously, but he is now being labeled a "cocksucker" based on only one purported act. When I asked if they were calling him a homosexual, he screamed, "they're calling me a cocksucker man, a cocksucker, can't you hear what I'm saying, a goddamn cocksucker!" He broke down, cried and related that while drunk he had been accused of trying to orally copulate another male who turned out to be an undercover Criminal Investigator from the army Criminal Investigative Division (CID). While sobbing intermittently, he related that a CID report classifying him as "a cocksucker" had been prepared and is now being used to force him out of the army on a Dishonorable Discharge (DD) after all his years of service.

According to the sergeant, he was a highly decorated hero and had fought at Guadalcanal. He showed me two wounds on his left lower leg, relating that he had been awarded the Purple Heart medal. The sergeant was emphatic in his belief that he was being given the DD to prevent him from receiving a government pension for the rest of his life. He backed up his belief by telling how many military officials, from non-commissioned officers to field grade officers, easily lie to you and demean you whenever they can.

The sergeant described an incident that I also recalled, when we were at the motor pool performing daily maintenance, when a new recruit was sent to the quartermaster for two 16-ounce cans of muffler blast. The quartermaster advised him that he did not have any and sent the recruit to Service Battery; Service Battery sent him to Headquarters and Headquarters sent him to yet another location.

Unable to obtain the muffler blast, the recruit returned to his sergeant and reported that all the units in the battalion were out of muffler blast. When the sergeant had the recruit describe muffler blast, he realized he had been made a fool.

After chit chatting for a while and finishing the medical form, the sergeant broke down and cried again. He later regained his composure and left weeping. It was sad seeing an adult cry, sadder seeing a decorated American soldier cry, especially knowing that there was nothing I or anyone else could do to help.

Five other soldiers came into the Battalion Aid Station (dispensary) to be processed for discharge from the army. One was seeing an imaginary man flitting about his wall locker; one had a habit of walking up toward the opening of an 8-inch howitzer during a fire mission; one was hearing voices when in the field telling him to yell "march order"; one had started speaking gibberish, incoherent words; and the other soldier was a chronic bed-wetter who took it a step further by leaving a pile of feces in the hall outside of his room on several occasions.

After completing their medical manifolds, as ordered, I drove them in a military ambulance across snow-laden Germany from Bamberg to the U.S. Army Hospital at Wurzburg for psychiatric evaluations. The howitzer incident soldier rode up front with me. He was tall, muscular and stinky. His record indicated that he had a habit of wearing soiled and dirty uniforms. It was reported by his unit that he had started sleeping in his fatigues and rarely took a shower or shaved. During the almost two hour ride, he never uttered a word and looked straight ahead with a fixed gaze for long periods.

On occasions, saliva drooped from the side of his mouth and snot drooped from his nose in long strings and fell on his fatigue jacket, for which he displayed no concerned. I was convinced that he was the sickest of the six soldiers.

I sat in with the military psychiatrist during each interview. Some of his questions were centered on their dreams, home life, siblings, friends, girlfriends, favorite color, favorite foods and their aspirations. The Filipino sergeant was the last interviewed. After he finished, the psychiatrist asked me to bring them back into his office. We took seats in a semicircle in front of the psychiatrist. He called each of the six soldiers by name and talked briefly about something they had discussed in their initial meetings. The psychiatrist stood up and said in an even monotone, "Your trip to see me is for me to make a determination whether you are fit mentally to serve in the U. S. Armed Forces, especially here in Germany, so far away from your family and friends. It is quite an adjustment, especially with the very cold weather we're experiencing." He gesticulated with his hands, pointing them outward with his palms up like many ministers and how Christ is often depicted. His calm talk went on for about ten minutes and ended with descriptions of beautiful, calm, pleasant, peaceful, serene places in the states. He talked about fly and trout fishing in serene babbling streams on quiet days in pristine parts of beautiful parks.

We became very relaxed. I saw two soldiers briefly nod off to sleep. The psychiatrist sat down momentarily with his hands clasped for a few minutes then jumped up and screamed loudly, "What the fuck am I doing in this lousy-ass motherfucking army." He screamed, "w-o-o-o-o-o-w, get me outta here, get me out of this crazy motherfucking place, get me out now." He kicked his desk, pulled his military dress jacket off, threw it against the wall, ran over and kicked over a metal trashcan and continued yelling and ranting as though he had lost his mind. Then he jumped upon his desk and started stomping his feet yelling something indecipherable. We were all taken aback, so stunned at his behavior, we didn't know whether to leave or stay. He continued this act for about five minutes.

All of a sudden, he stopped and made a brief telephone call. In a few minutes, his secretary brought him a container of water and a towel. He toweled his face for a few minutes, regained his composure and calmly advised, "I hate this army just as much as you. I have always hated olive drab green color. This is a game. I have learned to play it and so should you. Now all of you, except the sergeant, go back to your units and soldier, be good troopers and soldier, learn how to stand at attention with your thumb and index fingers along the seams of your trousers with snap, precision, pride and dignity...soldier, be good soldiers. My report will state that you are well, able and fit for duty tomorrow. Y'all go back now and soldier!" The psychiatrist winked and smiled as we were leaving his office.

About 15 minutes into the return to Bamberg, the howitzer incident soldier sat up erect from his slumped position and said, "You know that psychiatrist back there is the craziest motherfucker I ever saw. The army has up and given that crazy son-of-a-bitch captain's bars. Can you believe that shit? And they've given that crazy son-of-a-bitch authority to judge others."

The medic duties in the Aid station were easy, interesting and a challenge. When undergoing training, we were emphatically told not to make medical diagnoses. Instead we were trained to put the caveat "possible" in front of all of our assessments. We kept certain narcotic controlled substances in our regular inventory and were allowed to dispense them at our own discretion, from our inventory, without a doctor's prescription. We gave all kinds of required shots such as: flu, typhoid, diphtheria, yellow fever, typhus, polio and other shots the military deemed necessary for a soldier. On occasions, a colleague surreptitiously gave 500,000 units of penicillin to certain soldiers with a social disease.

On my first pass away from Bamberg, three Black soldiers and I rented a car and drove to Nuremberg, Germany for two days. It was exciting placing our shoes outside of our rooms at midnight and seeing them placed in front of our doors all shiny by morning. The next day we went to TWIST- TWIST- TWIST, one of the largest nightclubs in the city. It was crowded with three dance floors. We sat at a horseshoe-shaped bar and were refused service. The waitress told us she was sorry that she could not serve us because we were Black. We were shocked speechless and stared at her for minutes until we regained our composure. A large White guy sitting at the bar said, "I heard what that fraulein bitch just said to you guys. I'm from Florida. I don't give a shit. I'm with you guys. If you want we can tear this mothafucka down. Y'all game?" Collins, from our group said, "No man, we don't want to cause any trouble we just wanted to have a few drinks," and we left.

As a child, I had always been fascinated by castles and had never seen one. We went to a large castle located in the Civic Center of Nuremberg and walked around the front. We went to a restaurant in the area and had a heavy German meal consisting of beer and Sauerkrauts. We wanted to sense the eeriness of the castle at night and decided to walk around the back at night. As we approached the back we heard a lot of noise. We continued until we saw eight lines of White males: several lines were nine and ten men deep, awaiting their turn. There were eight windows with two and three prostitutes per window waiting for potential customers to quote their price by flashing five fingers at a time, indicating five marks per flash. The prostitutes spoke English and were articulate in the use of various American phrases and sayings. The going rate for most of them was 25 marks, the equivalent of $6.25. One of the whores asked, "What do you Schwatzamen (Black men) want?" Collin yelled, "Pussy, just like the White boys here. How much?" The whore yelled back, "I am sorry we don't screw Black men here." That was the ultimate insult, being denied entry into a whorehouse. For some consolation, I remembered my mother's story about The Fox and the Sour Grapes and laughed.

The next day we toured the city and noticed certain Germans, both males and females, shunned us as though we had leprosy. We went to a Gasthaus on the outskirts of Nuremberg where we ate and drank beer. An old timer enjoined us in a conversation in regards to how did we like Germany. When we related that we did not and why, he told us numerous stories. One reason certain Germans did not like us was a result of the war. He explained that during the war, the German theme was "Deutschland, Deutschland Eber Alles" which meant, "Germany, Germany Over All" with the ultimate goal of obtaining a pure super-race. During the occupation, there were large numbers of Black-German babies born; in almost all cases the fathers were Black males. Most of them were transferred to some German island. I did not know whether to believe him or not and did not care. It was very disturbing finding Jim Crow thousands of miles away from home; the feeling was indescribable. It was very disappointing learning of the ongoing racial struggles and fights back home; especially reading about the police actually attacking and beating Blacks for merely marching for justice. The police violating the Constitution by actually beating citizens that the Fourteenth Amendment was ratified for them to protect; Constitutional protectors beating those they were hired and sworn to protect.

Early one morning after returning from a drinking spree in the Black section of Bamberg, I was in deep sleep, having successfully fallen asleep to avoid regurgitating, when a runner ran through the barracks screaming "Scarlet Alert, Scarlet Alert, Scarlet Alert." the signal that war was imminent or had started. We ran helter-skelter about grabbing our full field packs, rifles, and helmets. Several soldiers from Service Battery came into our room handing out ammunition. I was given something I had not seen since Basic Training, hand grenades. After receiving the ammo and grenades, other soldiers came thru the room and marked cabinets, wall lockers and footlockers with "destroy by fire." Two other Service Battery soldiers were lugging large wooden boxes with highly flammable symbols. One of the soldiers remarked that he would "torch all of the west and south wings on command" and stood by with a two-way communication unit.

We hurried down to the motor pool, where we started all of our battalion vehicles. We were instructed to camouflage all the medical units bearing the medical symbol (an ambulance, a jeep, a quarter ton truck and a five ton truck). While we were mustering, the 4th Infantry unit on base had assembled; an Armored Calvary Unit was readying armored personnel carriers for deployment; a self-propelled eight-inch howitzer battalion located at the other end of the base had mustered into a convoy and was exiting the east gate.

Our Battalion exited the west gate and drove for hours using cat eyes, following the direction of military police that were all over the place. The Autobahn and secondary highways were loaded to capacity from the movement of military units and equipment. There were 280-millimeter guns battalions, La Crosse Missile battalions, armored personnel carriers, tanks, jeeps, fuel trucks, tank retrievers, and Corps of Engineering Units all over Germany. On occasions we passed German units and U.S. infantrymen on foot. We set up camp inside of a forest at an unknown location. All 18 howitzers in our battalion were set up in a zigzag pattern with the muzzles aimed in the same direction.

Immediately behind our medical units, four armed guards marched around a "Swell Van," a steel-wall laden van that housed nuclear warheads that could be fired from eight-inch howitzers.

We were given briefings that this was the real thing, but none of the officers, including the commanding colonel, were sure. We were advised that as soon as the colonel knew anything; we would be immediately notified. We were further instructed to carry a minimum of 200 rounds of ammunition, six grenades and our gas mask at all times.

We remained in this readiness position until about 2:00 PM, not knowing what was transpiring or about to transpire. A German drove up to our area in a lunch vending truck. The battalion commander allowed him to enter our camp. The commander was the first to purchase a bag of pork skins and a coca cola. The vendor remarked, "We admire you guys for what you are about to do." When the battalion commander curiously asked, "What is that?" The vendor related that the U.S. was about to go to war with the Russians over Russian intercontinental ballistic missiles found in Cuba and three Russian ships sailing toward Cuba with additional missiles. President John F. Kennedy has ordered, "Stop them, search them or sink them." Premier Khrushchev has threateningly responded, "Don't stop them, don't search them, and don't sink them." This situation eased only after the Russians diverted the missile-laden ships. Our battalion commander later advised us that this was how he had learned the reason why we were on Scarlet Alert. We also had not been apprised that an American pilot had been shot down over Cuba by a Russian missile. It is understandable that a soldier, whose primary function is to kill, cannot be in on all secrets or all undertakings in crisis situations.

President John F. Kennedy was projected to be one of our best presidents. He was articulate, charismatic, rich, handsome, had a beautiful wife and two cute children. Blacks took to him like ducks to water. Four of the most frequently found pictures in the homes of many Blacks were pictures of: Jesus, Abraham Lincoln, Dr. Martin Luther King Jr., and President John F. Kennedy.

Shortly after the missile crisis, as a gesture to further show West Germany the United States' resolve in insuring their freedom from Russian intervention; President Kennedy took a trip to West Germany and spoke to the German people. In front of a large crowd, he shouted in Dutch "Ich bin ein Berliner." The German television station showed West Germans jubilating and lauding what a great person Kennedy is "Herr President Kennedy es ein primer man." They made references to his statement that he is a Berliner that he suffers the same plight as the East Germans isolated from other countrymen, including relatives, friends and acquaintances. I realized that he was another president fully cognizant of the U.S. Constitution and when sworn into the Office of the President that he had sworn "................preserve, protect, and defend the Constitution of the United States."

Blacks, who voted for Kennedy en mass, honestly believed that he would ensure that Blacks would be treated within the realm of the U.S. Constitution, especially in compliance with the Thirteenth, Fourteenth, and Fifteenth Amendments of the U.S. Constitution.

Kennedy failed to adequately support Black causes and the law. He failed to provide adequate protection for the freedom riders in Mississippi and Alabama. President Kennedy, like many of his predecessors, forgot about the basic rights of Blacks and did not do what was legal and expected, but what they thought was politically correct to do. They appointed department heads with the authority to correct the disparate treatment of Blacks; however, only the head of the Department of Commerce had the intestinal fortitude to ban segregation involving Interstate Commerce. He did so under pressure.

VIII

THE FEDERAL COMMUNICATION Commission (FCC) has long had the authority to curtail or stop the media from communicating racial hatred. There are many federal agencies that could have better supported civil rights. The U.S. Attorney General's Office could and should have been more sincere in ensuring that Blacks were treated fairly, the Department of Housing is another one. Instead, Kennedy and many of his predecessor's selected department heads that were spineless and did not want to, in any way be controversial.

Perhaps the most egregious federal agency was the Federal Bureau of Investigation (FBI), an agency with the responsibility to investigate Civil Rights violations and crimes involving interstate, political corruption and other federal crimes. Under Director J. Edgar Hoover, Kennedy and some of his predecessors, allowed the FBI to be selective in their cases. They allowed the FBI, which by law is an investigative agency, to conduct smear campaigns against many participants regardless of their race. They conducted numerous unwarranted investigations against civil rights activists, regardless whether they were Black, White or other. They mirrored the habits of the KKK. When they saw White civil rights activists working with Blacks, they were quick to label them communists and smear their reputation.

I went on leave to various cities in Germany and Copenhagen, Denmark, Malmoo and Stockholm Sweden, and Brussels and Amsterdam. While on leave, I found the Norwegians very friendly, caring and sympathetic. They showed an extra fondness for Blacks, especially the women. In Copenhagen, I drank a beer called elephant that was thick like molasses. When mixed with lime juice it was delicious. In Amsterdam, I went native and ate fresh sardines from a metal pail. I was taught how to pick one up by the tail, tilt your head back and bite half of it at one time. I road a boat in the canals of Copenhagen, visited the little mermaid, Tivoli's Garden and ate at fancy restaurant in downtown Copenhagen. In Copenhagen, I ate one of the most delicious soups, which consisted of two raw eggs cracked and poured whole on a bed of hot onions. I ate several meals in Denmark and Stockholm that were cooked in rich butter. I rode a hydroplane from Copenhagen to Malmoo and saw it dodge the numerous small rock islands. On the ferry from Germany to Copenhagen, I ate pieces of different species of fish from the North Sea.

I saw the beautiful Rhine, Blue Danube, Black Forest of Germany and the beautiful cities of Heidelberg, Hanover, Bremen, Hamburg, Kiel, Essen, Dusseldorf, Mannheim Cologne, Bonn and many smaller cities, towns and hamlets in Germany, each unique in itself and almost all with a local beer brewery. I toured a mansion, "The Mission Villa Hugel" belonging to the Krupp steel magnate family and saw their valuable art collection; read articles about the Krupp steel mill having made the stainless steel used in the Empire State Building and reportedly inventing the motorcycle. I saw ragged and partially destroyed buildings in Dusseldorf and Essen that had been hit by bombs during the war and had not yet been removed or rebuilt. I saw the beautiful Rhine Valley, picturesque mansions and homes on beautiful mountains and hillsides; the beautiful Oktoberfest in Munchen (Munich), where a comrade accurately identified Americans in attendance from their haircut, clothing, chewing gum, hands in their pockets, joviality and the main clue, their numerous trips to the bathroom. In a small hamlet outside of Munich, a German lady who apparently had never seen a Black person before stared at me unendingly and followed me with an astounded look on her face. After I spoke to her in German, she smiled walked up and rubbed my face with both hands and looked in her palms to see if any black came off.

When I began to identify disparate treatment of Black soldiers in

Bamberg and requested that the Army place racist establishments off limits to all soldiers, I was targeted as a rabble-rouser, investigated for being involved in some kind of movement. With only six months left on my tour in Germany and in the Army, I was transferred from Bamberg to Ansbach with no reason given. My new unit commander inadvertently let me know why I had been transferred when he advised me if I encountered German establishments that would not serve me because of my race to let him know; that he would immediately put the establishment on the Off-Limits list. The transfer prevented my promotion to the next grade.

I recalled something my mother once told me about not getting depressed, sad, not to hate and certainly not to take revengeful actions. Her panacea to all problems was prayer. She often talked about venting anger in positive ways and how to reassess a bad situation and turn it into something positive.

She gave examples of how several successful people had sunken to the bottom only to create or found an idea that made them prosper.

While sitting in the barracks drinking one weekend, I overheard a White soldier state that when he was in kindergarten he lived in Germany and was in Hitler's youth corps. He showed us a little routine where he would walk into a room, click his heels and scream "Achtung, Achtung, Sieg Heil, Sieg Heil."

We concocted a scheme. I shaped my mustache like Hitler's and my new German/American friend and I got a weekend pass. We selected a busy Gasthaus. My friend hurriedly walked in and clicked his heels loudly and screamed, "Achtung, Achtung, Sieg Heil Sieg Heil," leaving the front door partially opened. I then entered quickly and clicked my heels loudly and shouted, "Sieg Heil, Sieg Heil." Some of the old-timers, under the influence of liquor, actually stood up. They were really puzzled when they saw me with my Hitler-type mustache. We got a lot of free drinks performing that little skit.

In Ansbach, there was no main dispensary on base. As a result, medics had to man the Aid Station on base. In case of emergencies, we would call the doctor on-call. We wore a white medical smock at the Aid Station. One Sunday, while on duty a heavyset White female was brought in complaining of intense pain, so severe that she could only mumble. I took her vital signs and immediately called Dr. Robert Barth, the on-call doctor. He was at home at the time drinking and barbecuing. Dr. Barth came in and read the lady's medical chart and examined her, placing his hand and his stethoscope on her stomach. Dr. Barth looked under her dress and asked her about the pain. She mumbled something and pointed to her mouth. Dr. Barth then advised her that we still had time and that we would transport her to the U.S. General Hospital in Nuremberg. Dr. Barth made arrangements for her admittance to the hospital via telephone. He then questioned me regarding if I knew when delivery was imminent. I told Dr. Barth the symptoms are when pain comes every two or three minutes and lasts for a minute and the water breaks. He stated, "That's correct, I have given her a mild painkiller that should help her relax and manage the pain during the trip."

We placed the lady in the ambulance in a supine position with her legs pointed to the rear. I sat next to her facing the rear. We rode for about two hours. She slept the entire time until we pulled onto the hospital's lot. When she came out of the sleep and saw me, she fainted. I broke an Ammonia Nitrate ampoule and placed it closed to her mouth and nose. When she came to I timed her pain and asked her if her water had broken. She looked at me oddly and asked, "Why in the hell would you ask me if my water has broken?" I asked, "You're pregnant, aren't you?" She then broke out in laughter, and laughed so hard that she got red in the face. I gave her some water and she laughed again. When she calmed down, she said, "I thought that doctor was kinda drunk, looking at my health records and under my dress. He must have forgotten; he delivered my baby almost this time last year, hell the only way I can be pregnant is by getting pregnant on my way up here. Hell, I have an abscess in my tooth."

Each time I saw her thereafter on base, she would yell, "Hey Sutton, I ain't pregnant, not yet" and laugh.

The Vietnam War was escalating and the U. S. was becoming heavily involved. There was a dire need for helicopter pilots. The Army Times, Radio and Television ran ads encouraging volunteers. Battalion recruiting officers stepped up their efforts by reviewing personnel files for qualified candidates, calling them in on a one-on-one basis explaining the program and the benefits. They offered up to a 30-day pass plus up to $10,000 cash depending on the number of years volunteered. Upon acceptance and completion of a 44-week course, the candidate would be given a Warrant Officer's commission.

Several soldiers volunteered for as many as five years, and were paid up to $10,000 cash. They went on leave to Paris, Madrid, Denmark, Sweden, Norway, Austria, Holland, Belgium, Amsterdam, and still some back to the states. A few purchased cars.

I was ordered to see the recruiting officer. When I went into the meeting, I was to be interviewed by an old Black sergeant, whose claim to fame was that he was on "Pork Chop Hill where the gooks were placing mortars in our hip pockets. I was scared shitless, but I eventually walked up out of that motherfucker on both feet without a scratch. I lost a lot of my buddies on that hill."

When I entered his office, the recruiter was sitting with folders, leave forms and an approximately eight-inch stack of $100 notes. After exchanging pleasantries and sitting down, the recruiter let me know quickly that he knew a lot about my background, knew my army GT score and that two of my brothers had been in the armed services and both had been injured and were "Purple Hearters". He initially tried to encourage me to re-enlist for five years, $5, 000 cash, and a 30-day pass. When I refused, he raised the cash bonus to $10,000. He then gave a broad account of what would be expected of me and assured that I could pass all of the requirements without any difficulty. Each time I refused, he gave another spiel and on two occasions shoved a wad of $100 notes toward me stating "That's your money; take it, that's your money." This went on for about 30 minutes. He would not relent.

After a while, the recruiter stood up got a cup of coffee from another room and brought one for me. He looked inside of a folder and shook his head slightly up and down. The recruiter then said, "Sutton, I know you can complete this course and I want you to take this opportunity. Opportunity only knocks once. We don't have many Blacks in this program and I am making a special effort to put as many Blacks in this program that I can. You're not a white cap and I don't see LWW in your file." When I asked him to define white cap and LWW he laughed.

The recruiter related that persons unknown to him and others refer to a Black man with a White wife or White girlfriend as a white cap. He added that LWW is a carryover from when Black soldiers were in Germany during the war, some officers would write LWW in their file, which indicated loved White women. They were little tidbits some commanders wanted to know when it came to promotions. The recruiter also added that, "the door swings both ways you know. Take for instance, if a White guy likes Black women, they call him a black top and put LBS in his file which means loves brown sugar.

It was hard to determine if the recruiter was for real or just "shucking and jiving." The pile of $100 bills he had in front of him was a strong indication he could be real, could really have the authority he was professing to have.

After conceding that I would not volunteer, the recruiter asked me to think it over and said he would call me in a few days.

A few days later, I was again ordered to see the recruiter. I went to his office and found him sitting as before, with a large stack of $100 notes on the desktop in front of him, except this time he had an undated 30-day pass filled out in my name. After sitting in a chair in front of his desk, the recruiter shoved a stack of $100 notes in front of me and handed me the 30-day pass saying, "Here Sutton, that's yours. That's your money. All I need you to do is sign on the dotted line. That's your money." When I refused to volunteer, the recruiter became emphatic and stated, "Hey Negro, I know you like the pink toes, just think how much white pussy you can get with all that money, $10,000, it's yours." When I again emphatically stressed I was not interested, that I had been drafted into the army and just wanted to do my little time and get out, the recruiter shouted, " Get the fuck outta my office you're wasting my fucking time you no good son-of-a-bitch."

I left his office more disappointed and angry with the army for entrusting such a fatuous and feckless person with that kind of money and authority. I found his demeanor analogous to that of a used car salesman who is fully aware the car he is trying to sell is a piece of junk. I had other reasons to distrust the army and his little escapades merely fortified them.

Fifteen soldiers on base volunteered for the program and awaited orders to commence helicopter pilot training. As I had expected, they never came. The Army Times had an article relating that they had filled all of the helicopter pilot vacancies and encouraged those not selected to apply for Officer Candidate School (OCS). Thirteen of the candidates applied for OCS. Not one was selected. Several had as much as six years left to serve and no recourse. They had taken the leave and the money. In reality, they had signed a contract that the government would not honor. Since it involved the Department of Defense, there was nothing they could do. One day while at the main gate seeing one of our friends rotate back to the states, a soldier asked another soldier, "How many more days?" He answered, "29 and a wake-up." Another soldier screamed, "I got 13 and a wake. I am going to kneel and kiss the ground when I get back to the world (states)." I saw a soldier walk from the area staggering slightly and fall. I ran over and saw him gasping for breath, salivating and cyanotic. His body started to tremble and shake. I noted his tongue was blue and stuck between his teeth. I took a pencil and pried his mouth open on the side, elevated his feet above his head and sent a friend to get the ambulance. I removed his wallet and wedged it between his teeth and tongue and told him to breathe through his nose. I then tilted his head back, noting that his tongue was sliding back in his mouth. I took a safety pin, stuck it through the tip of his tongue and pinned it to the collar of his fatigue shirt. The ambulance arrived shortly and the medic placed a plastic pharyngeal tube in his mouth. In a short while the soldier felt better, started breathing normally, sat up and was taken to the Aid Station for examination and later released. The sick soldier was one of the volunteers for the helicopter pilot school.

The 10th of September 1963 was Christmas to me. I had completed my two-year military duty, was transported to Bremerhaven and placed on the U.S. S. Upshur en route to New York.

I felt a sigh of relief leaving a country where I'd felt unwanted, where I had experienced Jim Crow, where on Sundays I had often been awakened by the continuous ringing of church bells; their ringing was sad and depressing for it reminded me of a funeral procession en route to the interment spot in the cemetery. I was glad to leave a place where I had seen beasts of burden, (oxen) that I had never seen before, yoked and pulling a container of one of the foulest smells I have ever encountered—the honey wagon.

It was a most welcome feeling to leave a foreign land where things were very different, people that were different and seemed to look at you with disdain. Some would stare at you for long periods as though you were from another planet. In the army, there is no room for thin-skinned or timid soldiers; but there should always be room for kindness, civility and human decency. It made me realize how expendable I am and many people are; merely parts of cogs in a humongous machine that even the operators did not really understand or care about. It seemed the whole

Cold War was about former allies, who in their quest for world supremacy, were trying to outdo one another, without regard for the lives it cost.

The U.S.S. Upshur was a rust bucket utilized for the transporting of troops overseas and back. It was a calm, cloudless day when we put out to sea. We were placed in crowded hatches, with canopy beds stacked three high, and so close you could hear and feel your neighboring soldiers breathing. It reeked from the smell of urine, vomit, body odor and soldiers exuding gas. It was a pig's sty in every sense. We mopped and cleaned the floor in our area every morning and after each vomiting incident, merely to have a seasick soldier regurgitate again.

It was a seven-day voyage from Bremerhaven, Germany to Ft. Hamilton, New York. I had conditioned and convinced myself that I would not vomit, that I would keep food in my stomach, by diverting my mind to the anticipated homecoming, doing breathing and meditating exercises and staying topside as much as possible.

The third day at sea we encountered a violent storm. The ship rolled and yawed, completely floundering. Almost everybody was vomiting all over the hatch, on topside and those brave enough leaned over the railings.

I ran up on topside and stood trying to settle my stomach. It was difficult trying to determine if you were being bombarded by the huge swells or a combination of seawater and vomit. The tail fan rising and falling 20 feet or more made me sicker. I vomited uncontrollably, emptying all of the food in my stomach. For about an hour I vomited, seemingly expelling all the liquid I had in my body. Then I experienced vertigo; it lasted for hours. Not since my childhood bout of tetanus could I have imagined it was possible to feel sicker than I did at this moment being jostled by the sea. I had never been in such a filthy place and certainly did not expect it being a soldier. So sick, I began to think that if death were the only cure that I would welcome it. The storm raged on with no easing in sight. Lifeboats rocked, metal chains and ropes beat against the walls, and large surges of water came aboard and quickly rolled off the deck, taking all the contents of my and my fellow soldiers stomach's, back into the sea. It was pitch-black and on frequent occasions in the distance lightning ignited the sky, followed by the loud roar of thunder, with strong gusts of wind filled with water. The sky continued to light up in large swaths in several places and almost immediately the thunder would jar, roar and crack as though in an artillery impact area. Since there were no announcements on the public announcement system, it made the storm seem worse. It was then that I remembered my mother's solution for all problems, I prayed. I stood reeling, holding the stair railing and prayed silently and aloud. About two hours later it abated. We sailed into the calm, an area that was as clear as a cloudless sky at noon. It took a while before the sickness passed.

When we anchored a few miles from the New York shore at midnight, like me, almost all of the returning soldiers remained awake. We stood crowded at the railings topside staring at the skyline of New York City all night. It was a wonderful sight. I overheard numerous soldiers promising that their first act upon landing would be to drop to their knees and kiss the ground.

After pulling into the harbor, we were ordered to wear military dress uniform and gathered on topside with all of our belongings in a very crowded formation. I was in the third disembarking group. As we stood quietly, crowded shoulder-to-shoulder preparing to disembark, five White male civilians were behind our formation chatting despite the sergeant's orders to be quiet. One, in an effeminate voice stated, "Motherfuck this guy, he ain't got no fucking authority over us; what is he going to do, throw us off the boat." They chuckled and continued chatting. From the gist of their conversation, they were Americans who were traveling over various parts of Europe and ran out of funds. They went to the U.S. Embassy, explained their plight and were provided transportation back to the United States via the U.S.S. Upshur. The irony of it was they all appeared to be draft dodgers and had been provided better accommodations on the ship than the soldiers.

Prior to the order to disembark, an effeminate voice to our rear position loudly proclaimed, "I bet there is a mile of penis on this boat." A soldier shouted loudly, "Shut the fuck up, you faggot motherfucker! We're trying to get off this ship and go back to the world. We don't need no shit from you or your kind. Shut the fuck up." Two other soldiers then yelled in unison, "Yeah, shut the fuck up!" When we came on shore, it was amazing how polite and courteous the navy personnel were to the five civilians, addressing them as mister and answering with a sir attached to their replies.

IX

WHILE EN ROUTE to Los Angeles, there was a news reports describing the bombing of a Black church in Birmingham, Alabama that resulted in the deaths of four young Black girls. The suspected bomber was reportedly a member of the KKK. I felt a lump in my throat and a strong sense of sadness, grief, sorrow and disappointment upon returning home to such racial violence. I wondered who could harbor hatred so intense; they would be inclined to kill people in a place as sacred as a church. I was extremely angrier realizing that the reason I had been drafted into the armed services was to protect a country, West Germany, that had been at war with many countries in the world; a country that was responsible for the deaths and maiming of millions and the destruction of many countries.

There were reports of other Blacks being killed and assaulted by racist policemen whose duty required that they provide protection to all U. S. Citizens. I saw several television reports of firemen turning their hoses against peaceful demonstrating Blacks; and policemen directing attack dogs on innocent Blacks and beating some with nightsticks, beating Blacks who were merely trying to be free in the sense of the U.S. Constitution.

I started reflecting again on President Kennedy's trip to West Germany assuring them of the U.S.'s resolve in sustaining their freedom and wondered what, if anything, he was doing to protect Blacks in America from the unending violence perpetrated by racists, some policemen, firemen, angry crowds, KKK, and opportunists, all encouraged and supported by elected public officials. I saw the misuse of the National Guard by governors in the South further denying and prohibiting Blacks of their rights.

I had a strong desire to join some of my former friends and classmates who were quitting their jobs and traveling south to participate in the Civil Rights Movement. I felt a very strong urge to do so, since I had spent 18 months of my life as a soldier in West Germany preparing "to fight if necessary for the rights of free men in a free world." I felt an indescribable sickness realizing the complicit nature of my role as a loyal American, serving my country as a soldier overseas; only to return to such widespread racial hatred and violence against my kind in my homeland of the free. I became sicker seeing the perpetrators, of the violence and hatred, being those whose responsibility was to protect and ensure the rights of all citizens. Money and the need for a higher education, the means to earn a living, prevented me from joining the Civil Rights Movement.

President Kennedy, could have wrested authority and power from the governors to violate the U.S. constitutional rights of blacks by doing what his predecessor President Eisenhower had, federalized the National Guard. It is very sad when politicians and elected officials vacillate on the side of evil, unlawfulness and violence in order to be politically correct. Since Kennedy had disengaged himself from an earlier failed coup d'etat in Cuba he was basically walking softly. In that aborted invasion, he claimed he was unaware of the entire endeavor.

One of the biggest violators of Blacks civil rights was the Federal Bureau of Investigation (FBI) Director J. Edgar Hoover, a lifetime political appointee. The FBI headquarters located in Washington, D.C. is named in his honor, when in reality he committed or caused the commission of many criminal acts against Blacks. One of the FBI's major objectives involved the investigation of civil rights violations. In the Birmingham, Alabama church bombing that killed four young Black girls in 1963, the FBI withheld crucial evidence that could have been used in the initial prosecution of the suspect who was later convicted of lesser charges. It appears that under his direction, there were numerous unauthorized wiretaps, eavesdropping, burglaries and other crimes committed against Blacks and Black organizations by the FBI. It is glaringly apparent that Hoover spent an inordinate amount of resources suppressing the rights of Blacks, more so than he did ensuring what his duties required. It is also apparent that he was a very racially biased person with a penchant for supporting his racial hatred. It is pathetic that this racial despot was appointed for life and allowed to violate the rights of persons his duty demanded he defend with impunity. Unquestionably he was a major detractor of the Civil Rights Movement and its leaders, whose committed acts, if truly revealed, will disclose how warped and deceitful he really was. After learning of Hoover's Secret Files, one U.S. Appellate Court Judge described Hoover as a "sewer that collects dirt" and as one of the worst public servants in U.S. history.

I started thinking about the German prisoners of war that were housed behind our house in Mississippi during the war, specifically the ones that escaped and came to our house. I surmised that they are now enjoying a lifestyle in America better than any Black person.

After my arrival in Los Angeles, I visited a few haunts, chatted with old friends and neighbors and learned they all had changed. Several were "breaking camp in California" and heading south to join the Civil Rights Movements. A few had dodged the draft and lost themselves in the Civil Rights Movement. America had changed a lot while I was away. There were all kinds of movements afoot. The malls, airports and some heavily tourist areas had several groups of weird people, the flower children, acidheads and a purported religious group that worshipped Satan.

It was strange returning from the edge of a combat zone on foreign soil and seeing so much: hatred, divisiveness, lack of communication and draft dodgers assuming the identity of deceased and older persons to avoid the inevitable draft and the possibility of being sent to Vietnam. I had experienced our military deception before and felt compassion for some of the Draft dodgers.

After being home for a while, I went to the Tulsa Barbecue Restaurant in the Firestone Park area to chat and visit with my old friend Errol Drew's parents. After I entered the restaurant, I saw his father bussing dishes from tables. When he went behind the counter, he acknowledged me and said he would be back. He had a sad, dejected aura about him that made me think he was about to cry.

When he joined me at the counter, he immediately told me that Errol was in prison. Later in the conversation he related that he and his wife had lost their business, along with their savings and their home trying to keep Errol out of jail. Mr. Drew's eyes welled with tears, but he had too much pride to cry. He excused himself for a while, returned and advised that he had gone from a prospering owner of a business to a busboy, all in trying to help his only son. After chatting for a while and preparing to leave, Mr. Drew remarked I always told my wife that I wished Errol was as good of a kid as you. I felt sorry for Mr. Drew. I realized that there were insufficient words to describe the love many parents have for their children, despite how bad, evil and violent that child might be.

I decided I no longer wanted to be a teacher and changed my major from elementary education to criminal justice. I re-enrolled at California State College (now University) at Los Angeles (Cal State) as a full-time student. I again noticed that people and things had changed a lot while I was away. It seemed as though everybody in college was protesting about one thing or another. There was a generation gap between parents, politicians and young Americans that grew to a level where the older population became almost completely out of touch with the young. Their clothing was different, hair longer and students and non-students were protesting everything, from old politicians, politics, and the undeclared war in Vietnam to the draft, processed food, homosexual rights, animal rights and the legalization of marijuana.

LSD had hit the streets, the Beatles had landed in America and heavy metal rock groups were cropping up all over. Young Americans became more defiant of authority, including parents and older adults. Many had lackadaisical attitudes, were free-spirited, developed a dislike for compliance and took a fighting stance merely for the pose. They dressed differently, took up strange hygienic habits and some went back to nature and lived in communes with an unexplained restlessness that befuddled academicians, parents, politicians, clinicians and law enforcement. They established communes in Laguna Canyon, the Big Bear Lake area, Lake Ellsinore, in secluded spots in the Hollywood Hills, in caves in national and state parks; some raised their own vegetables and planted marijuana on state and federal lands. The smarter ones cooked their own drugs. At the universities and colleges, speakers came from all over and gave talks on various topics and subjects, ranging from Margaret Meade to The Mattachine Society, the latter espousing gay rights.

Students demonstrated on many college campuses in California. Some of the demonstrations were very violent and resulted in arrests, while others were peaceful. The students had a major riot at the University of California at Santa Barbara and pelted law enforcement with loaded bags of human excrement. Some used slingshots and hurled steel balls at the police.

The Free Speech Movement was at its peak. There were takeovers of administration buildings. Mario Savio and the likes were gaining national attention spouting their dislike for a system that had left them out of the loop. There were sit-ins and sit-outs, with groups singing We Shall Overcome, as an anthem motivating their cause. They reversed a patriotic saying and started shouting; "I'd rather be Red than dead." It was considered, in today's terminology, nerdy not being a part of some movement or protest or marching to express some point. Cal State had its share of dissidents. One was Jerry Farber, who had written a book with the word nigger in the title. One day on passing, I spoke to Jerry calling him by his full name. A few days later, I was approached by an investigator who, would not identify his agency, questioned me about Jerry. He tried to elicit information about Jerry being a member of a suspected Communist front organization. He refused to believe that I was being candid when I told him I only knew Jerry from seeing him on campus. I suspected he was a CIA agent conducting domestic intelligence. He described Farber as a little wiry rabble-rouser that was causing all kinds of problems. Because of the widespread unrest on college campuses, there were a lot of CIA operatives on many college campuses around the country. Some eventually transferred to the FBI, DEA, ATF, and other federal law enforcement agencies.

I was in the library on November 22, 1963, when a group of girls came in crying and relating that Kennedy had gotten shot. The library activated several televisions. Students came en mass and watched the newscasts. It was a sad day for all. I had, despite the Berlin incident, grown to like Kennedy. He was one of the first presidents to utilize Black Secret Service Agents on his protection detail.

It was purportedly because of President Kennedy having a Black Secret Service Agent on his Protection Detail, that I was given an applicant interview with Guy Spaman, the Special Agent in charge of the Los Angeles Division of Secret Service; also called "the Eliot Ness of the West". I thought I had aced the interview, but was never contacted regarding failing or passing. Secret Service at that time, was like many federal law enforcement agencies, had almost no Black criminal investigators.

The Black Muslims, an organization espousing that "the White man is the devil," was increasing in size and expanding in many heavily Black populated states. The organization became splintered after Malcolm X described the Kennedy assassination as an "example of the chickens coming home to roost." Although Kennedy, during his short tenure, had done nothing significant in promoting Black causes; Black Muslim leader Elijah Muhammad Poole liked him. Malcolm X broke from the Black Muslims and formed the Black Nationalist.

Shortly after the Civil Rights Movement, Hoover, utilizing FBI resources, initiated his own program of disinformation and suppression of Blacks seeking equal rights, which was later, coined COINTELPRO (counter intelligence program). Hoover was a master of deceit and ran this and other programs under the guise of fighting Communism. It is my strong belief that a very close scrutiny of FBI records during his tenure would disclose that Hoover was one of the most adamant White persons in power involved in disenfranchising Blacks of their civil rights and exposing him as a major perpetrator of uncivil, heinous and criminal acts against Blacks and Whites associated with the Civil Rights Movement. He garnered power and leverage over many politicians via his agency's responsibility for conducting background investigations of presidential appointees. He conducted his personal, private investigations of political figures under the guise of fighting Communism, un-American activities and espionage.

Organizations with little to no communist affiliation were called "Communist Front Organizations." From Hoover's viewpoint, almost all Black organizations were in some way tied to one or both organizations.

Under Hoover, the FBI utilized numerous confidential sources of information. While most were utilized to infiltrate organizations and to garner intelligence, a number of them were utilized as Agents Provocateurs. It is strongly believed that they actually engaged in the assassinations of certain dissidents. It has long been highly suspected that the

94

FBI contrived and concocted the disinformation and circumstances that resulted in the assassination of Malcolm X.

When President Lyndon Johnson was sworn in as president, his being from Texas caused many Blacks to feel further alienated and left out of mainstream America. Blacks had viewed President Kennedy as being sensitive to Civil Rights and believed that he had really espoused a need for Black inclusiveness in the American Dream. His statement, "Ask not what your country can do for you, but what you can do for your country," was a major Kennedy catch phrase. Blacks began to reverse the phrase to "What can my country do for me."

In turn President Johnson did more for Civil Rights than any of his predecessors. He appointed the first Black federal judge. It was under his administration that the Civil Rights Act (CRA) of 1964 was passed. Although there were efforts afoot during Kennedy's tenure, it was made more meaningful during President Johnson's first term in office. The CRA of 1964 is an oxymoron. It really does not cover anything that is not covered in the aforementioned Thirteenth, Fourteenth and Fifteenth Amendments to the U.S. Constitution, but rather stresses what all presidents over the last ninety plus years should have ensured based on what they swore to do when taking the oath of office for president.

When President Kennedy selected Lyndon B. Johnson as his vice president, he was cognizant that he also had the killing instinct required of that position.

During my last semester at Cal State, I took a 500 level English class with the intent of elevating my grade point average and to review the various parts of speech and learn more about clauses, independent and subordinate clauses, prepositions, prepositional phrases, metaphors, similes, diphthongs, etc. There were over 160 students in the class, which was held in a large lecture room in North Hall. On all prior occasions, I'd always read the first chapter of the textbook before attending the class to impress the professors. This was one of the occasions I skipped that procedure. Dr. Thompson came into the class, introduced herself and after a few minutes told us to turn to chapter 1. She then started lecturing stating, "There are 24 phonemes in the English language. Phonemes are the sound features and morphemes are the meaningful features. Syntax is the arrangement of morphemes to form clauses, phrases and sentences. She discussed labiodentals, bilabial, aspirated, unaspirated, fricatives and voiced-slit fricatives sounds. Rolling air across the tongue as in the letter L, she explained, produces a dorso vela sound. She further talked about alliterations in morphophonemic changes and voiced slit fricatives. I heard one classmate state, "I better slit fricative myself out of this class." Unbeknownst to most of the class, we had enrolled in a graduate level descriptive linguistics class.

Many of my classmates knew we were in trouble when they noted that, a person, known as the campus class curve-setter, had dropped the class on the next class session. Most of my classmates had a graduate degree and unknowingly enrolled in the class, as I did; as a refresher course. After four class sessions, we were down to 16 students. I spent an average of 18 hours per week to keep afloat in that class.

About a year after I was discharged from military active duty, I received a letter assigning me to an army reserve unit in the San Francisco area. I made several telephone calls regarding living more than 300 miles from San Francisco; exempted my requirement to report to duty and I quoted a section from papers I had received when I was discharged. I later received a letter reducing my grade; with a threat that if I missed another meeting I would be called back to active duty for 45 days. I was further threatened that I would be incarcerated if I failed to report to duty. I was later advised that the military had made an error and I was then ordered to report to a reserve unit in Bell, California, about 30 miles from my residence, which I did. I was unable to attend one Thursday night meeting and telephoned to advise the unit. As it turns out, being sick was no excuse; I was then called to active duty for 45 days, two months before I was scheduled to graduate. The only consideration I was given by the army was an extension of my reporting date. I knew many young men who fled to Canada, Mexico, Europe, and Costa Rica, going underground, dodging the draft during this period. Some, who were drafted with me and had left no forwarding address for military contact, were never required to join a reserve unit. When I brought this to the attention of the military, I was advised that I was being assigned to an active reserve unit because I had completed a critical Military Occupational School (MOS).

When the 29th of January 1965 came around and I received my Bachelor of Science degree, I jubilated. Being the first of my immediate family, excluding my parents, to receive a college degree was an achievement. I immediately pondered pursuing a graduate degree.

I prepared a nice resume and forwarded copies to 63 federal agencies. I only received two responses. I also forwarded numerous copies to state and local agencies, with few results. I filed an application for a law enforcement position with the city of Compton, California. Before I went into the service, Compton had a population of approximately 100,000 residents: 70% White; 15% Black; 10% Hispanic and 5% Oriental [sic]. However upon my return the Black population had reached 60% while the white population had dropped to 10%.

Several older residents related that young Jewish salesman named Theodore (Teddy) Flyer initiated a major blockbusting project that caused the population shift. In the process when Blacks moved into the area, south of Rosecrans Avenue to Compton Boulevard and east of Wilmington to Willowbrook Avenue, it became known as Henrietta's Kitchen. Blacks then moved east of Wilmington to Atlantic Boulevard and then throughout the city in a short period, almost within three years. They also purchased homes in Victory Park and Richland Gardens.

I took and passed the written, oral, physical fitness and physical examinations for a police officer position with the Compton, California Police Department. I, along with approximately 30 applicants, then took the Minnesota Multiphasic Personality Inventory and the Rorschach Inkblot Test. After the test, we were called in individually to a room for an interview with the psychiatrist. After 15 applicants had completed the psychiatric interview, two White applicants came out with red faces and related that they thought they had failed. When I went into the interview, the psychiatrist talked in generalities about my having experienced a well-rounded family life and made a declarative statement that I thought my parents were a little too strict on my sisters, to which I agreed. He related that I had never had any real problem with my mother and repeated the same about my father, to which I also agreed. He then casually asked a shocker question, "How many times have you had the Clapp?" After the interview, he advised that I had done well.

The CHP officer who stopped me when Joe Jr. was smoking marijuana and the LASO deputy I encountered with Leotis, Lil Will and Henry were strong influences that led me to a career in law enforcement. I wanted to be, as they were to me; mild-mannered, sensitive to the feelings of others, not easy to provoke and possessing the ability to treat everybody I encounter with kindness, courtesy, dignity and respect. Another major influence was my White friend Jack from the armory, located behind my childhood home. I wanted to always emulate him, to be in an authoritative position one day where I could have in my life unpopular, unattractive (in the biased minds of others), unloved friends and acquaintances that I could treat, as he treated me: with care, concern, love, acceptance and fellowship.

Shortly after I was offered a police officers position with Compton Police Department, I was re-drafted into the army for 45 days. I was assigned to the U.S. Army Hospital at the Presidio of San Francisco. I saw many soldiers from various U. S. Military branches that had returned home from Vietnam with amputated limbs, burned and scarred tissue, some who would never walk again, and some who could never really work a meaningful job again; even a soldier being treated for syphilis. It was ironic, that the syphilis patient had more visitors than other patients.

I worked under the supervision of a White female nurse, who was unlike many nurses. She had no compassion for the soldiers and treated them like she was doing them a favor. In some instances she talked to them as though it was their fault they were there, that they had done something wrong. The only decent thing about the place was that it was clean and served decent food. From this brassy nurse, I developed a strong appreciation for our veterans, especially those who had no choice but to serve because they were drafted. I developed a lot of compassion for those disabled veterans, some with a variety of amputations and the small amount of their pension, having to eke out a living, especially having given a part of their body in protecting our country. I also admire those career soldiers often degradingly called "lifers and losers" because I know they are loyal Americans willing to put their lives on the line for our protection.

I pat myself on the back for being one of four brothers who served in the U.S. Armed Forces; prepared to fight or fighting for freedom, when I as a Black person was not yet in essence free almost 100 years after the amendments to the U.S. Constitution had granted it.

Airplanes flew in daily, transporting injured almost dead soldiers. I saw several soldiers with a kind of spasm in their legs and arms commensurate with deep stomach pains. I suspected they were heroin addicts drying out cold turkey.

I saw a televised report featuring a double-leg amputee, wheelchair-bound Vietnam veteran explaining his arrival home. When he arrived at the airport terminal in a wheelchair and was proceeding through the terminal, one of his best friends ran up to him and two of the first questions he asked about Vietnam were, "How was the dope? How was the pussy?" He was dismayed that his friend had asked such questions.

A day before I finished my 45-day tour of duty, the Watts Riot broke out. As the United Airlines pilot activated the fasten seatbelt sign, he advised we were making our final approach into the Los Angeles area where a major riot was in progress. After a few minutes I looked out the window south of city hall, the ground below was covered with buildings burning in patches; large stacks of smoke billowed up into the sky. After we banked right and flew into the Los Angeles International Airport landing zone, the smoke below looked like a war zone. There were hundreds, possibly thousands of smoke stacks that covered the whole South Central area making it resemble Ploesti during WW II. Fires blazed like napalm in sporadic patches. As we descended lower, black and white police units in tandems of five raced up and down the street, some followed by red fire engines.

My sister met me at the airport and recommended that I change into the civilian clothing she had brought along. Shortly after we left the airport and crossed Western Avenue on Imperial Highway, police cars, from both the LAPD and LASD sped down the street and others crossed our path at various intersections. Bands of Black looters in cars, trucks, on bikes and afoot crawled over the streets like army ants, looting and destroying every non-Black business in their path. I saw two mobs of looters converge on each other, one shouted, "Watts" and the other group held up two fingers and shouted, "Vernon" in unison.

As we arrived at Avalon, the south wall of Volume Food Market exploded, blowing the entire south wall into splinters onto Imperial Highway. There were a number of smaller explosions from the floor area of the building. I felt very sad because I had shopped there many times with my uncle and two aunts and knew the White husband and wife owners as wonderful, kind considerate and compassionate people. They had done something no other business in the area had ever done; employed local residents. When we got caught at the light on Central Avenue, a mob of young Black youths stormed our car carrying unlit Molotov cocktails and hollered, "Where're you from?" My sister raised three fingers and shouted, "Compton." The mob told us to move on for they had some "burning to do." There was something strange about them. They did not appear to be from any of the areas in Los Angeles we knew. Although in riot mode, for some reason, their odd demeanor made it obvious they were not from California. The sounds of fire engines, police units, ambulances and horns and, black smoke filled the air.

As we drove south of Central, we saw several mobs coming out of the Nickerson Gardens Housing Projects walking toward Central Avenue on both sides of Imperial. The sight of smoke stacks billowing upward all over the area could be seen for miles north, west and east. The Watts area grew from the original Central Avenue east to Alameda, Century Boulevard south to 108th Street to encompass all of the main Los Angeles Black Belt, the area from Pico Boulevard south to Rosecrans and from Crenshaw west to Alameda.

The riot started as a result of the California Highway Patrol attempting to arrest Marquette Frye, a Black male, on Avalon and 116th Streets; assisted by LAPD officers. Frye resisted, and a scuffle ensued requiring the use of force to subdue him. Onlookers, some under the influence of alcoholic beverages, drugs, or a combination of both, believing that force was excessive, formed a mob and moved against the police. They started attacking the police, Whites in passing cars, and neighborhood White-owned businesses.

They entered businesses and looted them of goods, liquor and money. They made Molotov cocktails (a mixture of rags, sand, or sawdust stuffed into a bottle and mixed with gasoline with a part of the rag protruding out as a wick), ignited them and hurled them at buildings, passing cars occupied by Black, White, Brown or Yellow riders. Law enforcement caught off guard by the surge and unequipped to make mass arrests, provided psychological encouragement for numerous onlookers who willingly joined moving mobs and rioted.

They looted White-owned businesses and torched them in their wake. Black business owners reinforced their ownership by painting "Soul Brother" in the windows.

A Black Los Angeles disc jockey, The Magnificent Montague, urged call-ins to "burn baby, burn" as part of his broadcast, which meant dance baby, dance. Shortly after the riot began, the rioters adopted the slogan "burn baby, burn." The disc jockey was taken off the air.

As the night came on you could see flashes like lightning, similar to strobe lights flashing in a pitch-black darkroom, new buildings burning, silhouetted against a partially smoke-filled sky. Gunshots echoed sporadically into the night, sirens whirred in yelping monotones, ascending, pausing and descending in the night. The drone of the four barrel carburetor emanating from police units could be heard rolling through the streets, accelerating and decelerating in rhythmic unison, the fire trucks racing with their mighty sirens, mighty horns and mighty roaring engines; all mixed with the sight of embers ascending into the night air, flickering in the midst like fireflies made it difficult to sleep at night. It was an unwelcome feast for the senses.

The Monday following the onset of the riot, I and another Black male were sworn in as the 11th and 12th Black police officers in the Compton Police Department. There were 12 other officers in our class. We were taught basic procedures during the day and paired up with a senior officer and rode as back up until midnight. The third day on duty, my partner and I drove up Central to Imperial Highway, where we saw soldiers, in armored personnel carriers, barricaded behind sandbags with rifles in ready fire positions. Large smoke stacks continued billowing skyward and police and fire engines raced noisily through the streets with emergency lights, sirens and horns blaring incessantly. Gunshots rang out frequently. Rioters shot at the police cars, ambulances and fire engines; chaos. As a result, firemen and emergency treatment teams refused to answer calls without police escort. All Blacks seen on the streets during this time were presumed rioters by law enforcement and the National Guard (NG) units patrolling the streets. A 10 PM curfew was imposed on the city, limiting workers from going to and from work. If they were caught on the streets during curfew they would be arrested.

All Los Angeles area television stations ran continuous news footage of the riot. On one station I saw a black couple exiting Gold's furniture store, laboriously carrying a nine-foot crushed velvet sofa. After exiting the front, they sat for a few minutes then carried it across Washington Boulevard, barely escaping through the onslaught of passing cars.

They showed a black male walking away from a store carrying about

100 suits. The bundle was two times wider than his body. The aerial shot made him appear like an ant carrying a piece of food four times larger than its body.

The Compton PD watch commander reported a potpourri of crimes that had occurred in the city. There were a significant number of armed robberies; almost all had been committed by a "male Negro wearing a stingy-brim hat, who fled on foot with no vehicle seen or heard. Each watch was extended to 16 hours, overlapping shifts, in preparation of the riot possibly entering Compton.

The watch commander emphasized a sudden rash of burglaries that were occurring in the city. Since many were occurring during the day, he instructed us to be especially alert for rioters and to check cars carrying furniture and appliances. I was paired with a seven-year veteran, Ray, who had a sense of humor. We were designated as Unit 5, the roving midtown felony unit.

Ray designated himself as the driver. He was quite a character and often said that he would rather fight than have sex. While fueling, Ray stated, "there are about 100,000 suspects out there, let's see if we can go out there and get us some."

Immediately upon departing the lot, I grabbed the mike and advised, "Unit 5, 10-8." The dispatcher acknowledged, "Five clear." We proceeded eastbound on Myrrh Street to Willowbrook and when turning north onto Willowbrook, we saw a 1964 Chevrolet with the trunk ajar full of clothing and a television, in addition to articles of clothing piled on the back seat and rear deck; reverse from a driveway and speed northbound. A man ran out of the house screaming to us to "stop that car, stop that car!" There were articles of clothing strewn on the porch and lawn. We followed the speeding car across Compton Boulevard to Arbutus. Per Ray's instruction while en route, I activated the emergency lights and advised the dispatcher that we were in pursuit of a 4-5-9 (burglary) suspect. We stopped the car at Arbutus and Oleander. I radioed the station that we had the car stopped. Ray approached the driver cautiously with his .357 Smith and Wesson magnum revolver drawn as I obtained a felony car stop position on the right side of the police unit. Ray then placed the barrel of his revolver in the left ear of the male driver and shouted, "Place your hands on the dash board and don't move!" The driver complied. I got on the P.A. system and ordered the female passenger to exit the car with her hands in the air and to walk back to the police unit and obtain a front-leaning rest position. She complied. I then learned a new verb from Ray when he shouted in an authoritative manner ordering the driver to "Okay, un-ass this car motherfucker!" When the driver appeared confused, Ray shouted, "I said un-ass this fucking car!" The driver then complied and as instructed kept his hands high in the air. I handcuffed both subjects and placed them in the rear of the police unit. I admonished them of their rights by reading from a card. Ray then grabbed the mike and advised the station that we had two burglary suspects in custody. He requested that a unit transport the victim to our location. A few minutes later a unit arrived with the victim.

Ray told me to fill out the burglary report as he chatted with the sergeant who had also arrived. The victim thanked us for catching the suspects, I said, "Yes sir, we try to stay on the ball, the idea of these people burglarizing your place almost directly across the street from the police station." The victim stated, "Burglary, what burglary! They ain't committed no burglary."

I called Ray over and told him we had a problem. Ray asked, "What's the problem?" and turned and explained that we needed to take certain information for the Burglary Report. The victim stated, "They ain't committed no burglary." Ray then asked, "Then why did you tell us to stop this car?" The victim stated, "Hell this asshole is running away with my wife." Ray disgustingly advised, "Mister running away with a man's wife ain't no crime." The victim then asked, "Then what in the hell are the police for?" Per Ray's instructions, we unarrested [sic] the subjects.

Under California law, a policeman could not make an arrest for a misdemeanor not committed in his presence. When handling domestic calls, we could not blankly ask a couple if they were married. When we asked how long had they been married, on occasions they would give an approximate year. To further discern if they were truly married, we would ask the name of the church where they got married. At this point, we were able to distinguish a marriage from a cohabitation, which was needed to determine if a woman with scars or bruises was a victim of California Penal Code Section 273D, felony wife-beating. If it involved cohabitation, it was a misdemeanor. To alleviate not being able to arrest for a misdemeanor, on occasions we would instruct the female mate on how to execute a citizen's arrest. Domestic disputes were hard incidents to handle.

One day Ray and I were dispatched to handle a domestic call involving a fight. The police had been out to this location numerous times, sometimes as many as three times on the same day. After we arrived and conversed with the couple, it became obvious we were not making progress and there was the likelihood that they would make additional calls after we left. Ray decided to grant them a divorce:

"Mrs., what's your name?"

"Sally Mae Johnson."

"How long have you lived together?"

"Six years."

"How many children do you and what's his name have?"

"We have three boys, the oldest boy ain't his"

"What's your, his name, your ah, husband?"

"Billy Jackson."

After obtaining their ages and dates of birth, Ray asked Sally if she had a Bible he could use. She left momentarily and returned with a large Bible with a white leatherette covering. Ray then, in some kind of ritual motion, waved his hand over the heads of Sally and Billy and had them stand facing him. He told them to put their left hands on the Bible and raise their right hands. Meanwhile, I stood to their right completely dumbfounded and without a clue as to what Ray was doing.

Ray then said, "It appears to us that after being here almost a half hour, that we cannot solve your problem. If we took Billy to jail you would probably not file charges, be lonely and come down to the station begging us to let him out. I came back here three times one day when you and Billy were fighting, and after I got off, another officer had to come back two or three times." After more discussion, Ray said, "Okay Sally and Billy, keep your right hands raise and your left hand on the bible. I am sure both of you know your constipational rights, don't you?" Both replied in unison, "Yeah." Ray then stated, "As a police officer for the city of Compton, California in the county of Los Angeles and in the state of California and by the powers invested in me by the State as an officer, I now pronounce both of you, Sally and Billy, to be forthwith divorced. Further orders of this divorce proceeding are; Billy you are ordered to pay Sally $250 per month child support, and both of you are to refrain from annoying each other. Billy you have two weeks to move from the residence. You are allowed visitation of your children to be carried out outside of this residence. Is that clear?"

Sally and Billy responded, "Yes", and looked at each other in disbelief. Billy asked, "Honey you don't want to be divorced do you?" Sally responded, "I don't know."

Ray then added, "This divorce shall be deemed complete and final if the police have to come back when you two are fighting, is that clear?"

When Sally and Billy removed their hands from the Bible, they walked over and sat on the couch holding hands and talking lowly.

When we departed, I told Ray that that was an awful thing he had just done. Ray remarked, "Aw what the hell, you don't understand. They will be making love in a little while and they will still be living together. I bet we won't have to go back there again. What you bet, besides you can't divorce someone who isn't married, right?" I agreed.

Some of the jokes some White officers played on the Blacks were too embarrassing to relate to, especially seeing them take advantage of the uneducated. I saw some give drunks the "Lie Detection Test" wherein they'd ask a question and have the subject answer into a non-keyed mike. They would turn the squelch sound on as an indicator that the person had lied. Some officers not only performed divorces, but performed marriages of drunks and people under the influence of drugs.

One White officer had a penchant for finding "peter parties" in the drive-in theater. Prior to searching for them, he would go to the snack bar and immerse his Kel-Lite flashlight in the ice container, spin it around like one would spin wine in a container. He would then drive around through the drive-in until he saw a car shaking and no visible heads could be seen from outside. The officer would sneak up to the car and rub the cold flashlight down the bare back of the male. After the couple gained their composure, he would threaten to jail both of them for indecent exposure, which would require that they thereafter register as Sex Offenders.

The officer seemed to relish having an advantage over the couple. He would then lecture them for a while, fill out a field interrogation card and threaten to jail them if they were caught again. I knew then that police work would be challenging.

On the fifth night, my partner and I joined five Compton PD units in the Rosecrans Plaza strip mall on Central Avenue pursuant to a tip that the rioters were planning to loot and burn businesses at that location. With the exception of a large supermarket, all of the businesses at that location were Black owned.

We conferred with the owners. Most of them had armed themselves and their employees with shotguns, rifles and pistols. About 10:00 PM, a large group of rioters in cars, trucks, on motorcycles and on foot converged on the mall. One of the sergeants shouted on a megaphone, "This is an unlawful assembly. You are ordered to disband and leave the area immediately. If you do not leave in five minutes you will be arrested, all of you disperse!" The mob started chanting, cursing and threatening to burn the plaza down, but had not crossed Central Avenue. About a minute later the order was repeated. Then five officers fired shotgun blasts in the air and the sergeant on the megaphone screamed, "Get the hell outta here, we're not going to let you burn anything down here, do you understand?" The would-be rioters left the area almost as fast as they had arrived.

The weekend came around and we were assigned 12-hour day shifts. Fourteen looters stormed a convenience store on the northwest corner of El Segundo and Central, across the street from the Compton city limits. My partner and I and another unit stopped them with aimed shotguns as they ran out of the store and around the corner with cases of liquor, cigarettes and other items. With our shotguns drawn we placed 12 looters in front-leaning rest positions against the wall and handcuffed the two would-be torchers together to the door of our police car. We radioed for assistance from the Los Angeles Sheriff's Office (LASO) Firestone Park station. A few minutes later five black and white LASO patrol cars arrived, looking like lowriders. Twenty-five big muscular deputies got out. The lead deputy asked my partner, "What have we got here?" My partner replied, "14 rioters and their loot." The deputy said, "Cut them loose. Let 'em go. We are the Special Enforcement Detail (SED), we can't move on a crowd of less than 100 participants." The deputies got back in their patrol cars and like lowriders sped from the area eastbound toward Willowbrook Avenue.

The National Guard manned most of the main intersections in South Central Los Angeles. LASO and SED roamed the county dispersing crowds and arresting rioters. Their LAPD counterpart, Metropolitan

Enforcement Detail (MED) roamed the city arresting rioters. SED and MED were crack enforcement units specially trained in riot prevention and control. Their initial requirements were: you had to be at least six feet tall, minimum 200 pounds and in good physical condition. When they wore their special unit uniforms, the crash helmet made them look at least seven feet tall. The curfew remained in effect.

X

ONE LATE EVENING shift, my partner and I drove north on Willow-brook Avenue to El Segundo Boulevard in the county. As we were approaching with our amber lights flashing the NG checkpoint on the east side edge of the railroad tracks, we saw rifle flashes and heard several sounds like flying jets whizzing by our black and white police unit. My partner screamed, "What the fuck, they are shooting at us." I grabbed the spotlight and aimed it at the barricade as my partner grabbed the speaker and yelled, "stop shooting, we are the police."

When we contacted the sergeant in control of the checkpoint, he apologized for the shooter. The shooter, a young NG trooper, nervously explained that when he saw the flashing amber lights of the police unit, he assumed rioters had taken it. After my partner gave them a barrage of profanity, we drove back to our district in Compton.

Even as a policeman, I had angst of traveling during curfew hours despite wearing police uniform. The NG checkpoint incident was hard to forget. After 11 days, the Watts Riot, one of the worst disasters in Los Angeles' history, ended, with a once beautiful city scarred, full of debris, rubble, charred buildings and smoke and showing strong signs of destruction. There was an indescribable feeling seeing the National Guard patrolling city streets in a law enforcement position. The LAPD-MEG and LASO-SED were direly needed and performed heroically, especially since it was their purportedly abusive action that precipitated the riot.

There were many reports of White males , non-police types, who traveled in the riot torn area unmolested, not harassed as though they were perpetrators or managers of destructive activities. There were a number of groups of Blacks seen on the streets looting who were not Californians. Rumors flourished that the riot was a major CIA undertaking; a CIA major activity.

One of the most important lessons learned from the Watts Riot was a need for community relations and sensitivity training in law enforcement. Another lesson gleaned shortly thereafter, identified certain levels of job related stress that befall officers, some so severe and if not treated properly, can make an officer a threat to the public. Another lesson indicated a need for increased diversity on the police departments. At that time, Los Angeles had a sworn police population of about 7,500 officers, of which only 250 were Black and only a handful of Black Firemen. Blacks had just begun to find employment with the yellow cab company.

There were many lessons gleaned from the Watts Riot. Perhaps even the rioters learned that they must be law abiding and let the Police do their job without outside intervention; that an arrestee does not have the right to resist an arrest by a police officer, whether the arrest is legal or not. Our city fathers and other state and federal officials need to ensure fairness and bridge opportunities for communication between the police and the public in a non-hostile way.

The military in a law enforcement position or peacekeeping position in our own country, although is different from overseas situations, gives a sense of dictatorial rule, a very unpleasant sight in America.

After the riot ended, I drove over to my parents' house in uniform. My mother smiled more than she did when I got my degree. I surmised she felt that as a policeman, I would unlikely go to jail or end up running from the police. Shortly before I became a policeman, my youngest brother Samuel was drafted in to the army, resulting in all four of my mother's sons serving in the U. S. Armed forces. All of her sons had served their country well, all received honorable discharges and two were awarded the Purple Heart Medal. When Samuel was drafted, there was a large number of Americans dodging the draft. When Samuel returned from the service, like his brothers before him, he found it difficult to get a job.

After the Watts riot there were talks of an anniversary riot in August of 1966. Prior to the riots and shortly thereafter, there were dissidents all over America complaining, marching, and protesting some issue. Many students, both Black and White, were reading Chairman Mao Tse Tung's Red Book espousing for the workers of the world to reunite. The Freedom rides in the South were in full force. People, seemingly were all over America marching for some cause. The Black Muslims, The Black Nationalists, The Black Panthers, and other groups were trying to change a system they thought direly in need of repair.

In addition, Cesar Chavez was hard at work in the San Joaquin Valley pursuing equality for migrant farm workers. The Black Panthers were patrolling neighborhoods armed with hunting rifles. In Compton, we had a contingent of the Black Nationalists party headed by Hakeem Jamall. They strutted around with holstered guns and long rifles. They were within the law as long as they were not loaded or discharged within the city limits.

Local law enforcement agencies in the area went on alert the first week in August. We were tasked to gather information from various sources regarding the possible anniversary riot. We talked casually to citizens, business owners, cooperating arrestees, established informants, passersby and students.

In conferring with several Compton College students, they were of the opinion that there would not be a riot. One student believed that there were several military bases in California already prepared for detention camps to house Blacks involved in any future riot. He mentioned the marine base at Twenty-nine Palms and a large military base called Fort Hunter Ligget.

Another student did not think there would be an anniversary riot in Los Angeles because the dissidents only had a few guns, Molotov cocktails, sticks and stones for weapon. He related that the government had tanks, grenades, airplanes, rockets, napalm and the atomic and hydrogen bombs.

A group of Black militant males often approached Black police officer and posed the question, "Where will you be brother when the Revolution comes; yeah when the revolution comes?" They had a tendency to debate or argue any response you gave. After the argument, they would depart referring to the Black officer as "a Black uncle tom motherfucker."

During the alert period, my nephew ran out of gasoline on 103 Street west of Wilmington Avenue, the heart of the true Watts area. He walked to the service station and was given a 1-gallon jug that did not have a top. He purchased a gallon of gasoline, placed a paper towel over mouth of the bottle to prevent spillage and started walking back to his car. En route, he was arrested by LASO Firestone Park deputies for possession of an incendiary device. There were many Blacks arrested on similar charges during that time. Throughout South Central Los Angeles the SED and MEG displayed a strong presence. Instead of having anniversary riot in August, they had a "Watts Parade" followed by a large picnic and festival at Will Rogers' Park.

XI

WHEN I WAS hired by Compton PD, I was one of three policemen with a college degree; Chief William K. Ingram and Captain John Start were the other two. Compton policemen, like many other policemen, had never received community relations or sensitivity training and consequently treated Blacks with a high degree of disrespect and disdain. Some officers often planted evidence on suspects when they flunked the "Police Attitude Test." There were officers, Black, White and Brown that had a strong penchant for beating suspects for little or no reason.

A Black officer named John had a penchant for beating arrestees; only Black arrestees. John was a light complexion Black, that would have been passé blanc if it would work for him. The White officers treated him for what he really was, an extraordinary Ninja. In the presence of other Black officers he would often remark, "Look at this stupid nigga mother f——-r."

One day while working the jail, John arrested a young Black male and placed him in the booking cage. He remarked that the arrestee had failed the "Police Attitude Test." John started an argument with the arrestee, then went into the holding cage and told him to spread out on the wall. He pulled the arrestee backward; with his legs spread apart and started taunting the arrestee about not being a badass now. John then took his

Gonzalez sap (a thick leather sap with lead inside) and struck the arrestee several times about the head and shoulders. When I screamed for him to stop, he struck the arrestee several more times, turned and looked at me as though in anger.

I met John on my lunch break and told him what he had done was a violation of the law, that there was no valid reason to strike the arrestee because he was already in custody and was not a threat. John disagreed. John then voiced his suspicion that I was an FBI plant in the department. As we were leaving, John smiled and remarked, "I hope you ain't an FBI plant because if you ever get into a shootout, you will have to wonder who is shooting at you, the crook or police."

I then realized that John was a very sick person, full of anger, hurt, evil, venom and animosity. I suspected his career, as a policeman, would be short-lived.

One night while patrolling District 2, I was given a call to assist another one-man unit on Rosecrans west of Wilmington. Upon my arrival, I saw the Unit-5 White officer standing in front of a Black male. As I got out of the car, the Black male quickly pushed the officer backward with his hands. The officer grabbed the subject. I ran up and assisted in subduing and arresting the Black male.

This officer had a high arrest record, which was suspect to me because they consisted of an inordinately high number for resisting arrest and assault on a police officer. Albeit, this was a time when policemen were not too popular, nevertheless, to me, it was unusual for a policeman to get assaulted for mere traffic stops.

One night the Unit-5 White officer invited me for coffee and donuts at Winchell's donut shop on Alondra Boulevard. When I drove onto the lot, he joined me carrying two coffees and four glazed donuts. After we chit chatted for a while, he asked me if I knew how to make an arrest for assault on a police officer. He then explained the following: "When you stop a Black guy that you don't like, get his driver's license and stand close, facing him, when you see your back up unit arriving, slowly step on the guy's right outer toe. All Blacks have corns on their feet and the one on the right outer toe is usually the most painful. When you step on his toe, he will instinctively push you off his toe. Your back up will see him assault you. That way it won't be just your word against his."

I found it unbelievable what this idiot brother policeman had just explained to me. I felt sorry for the man I had assisted him in arresting. Perhaps more puzzling to me was, why anyone would or could perpetrate such an act on another person; the thought that a policeman could was reprehensible. Although we patrolled bordering districts, I decided to avoid him as much as possible.

One night I brought an arrestee into the station and placed him in the holding cell. The jailer was not at the counter. I heard someone being struck and crying and pleading. I walked back to the area and saw a Black teenager handcuffed to the cell being beaten and kicked by K. R., the jailer. When I screamed, "What the hell are you doing?" He answered, "This little Black mother f-----r won't shut up, he has been crying and hollering every since he was brought in here."

Despite K.R. being a more senior officer, I told him he was wrong and had no reason to strike an arrestee in custody and certainly not a juvenile. I also explained that he had booked the juvenile into the adult section of the jail, which was a violation of the law. K.R. tried to be apologetic and asked me to have lunch with him.

When I met with him later that morning at Jerry's Barbecue, he brought a tray of barbecue ribs, fries and cokes over and joined me in my patrol car.

The first question he asked, "You are not going to drop a dime on me are you; you're not going to rat me out are you?" He then remarked, "I know you are a standup guy." I intentionally did not answer him yes or no. K.R. then related that there was scuttlebutt around the department that I was an FBI plant working undercover.

For several weeks K.R. called me inquiring, if he was in trouble or if I had ratted him out. I never responded to his inquiries and always diverted the conversation from the issue. About a month after his last call to me, K.R. was dead from a fatal heart attack.

The "Bush" or "Afro" hairstyle became famous. Heretofore, most all Blacks wore their hair cut close to the scalp. Some particular singers, actors, musicians and those "in the fast life", preferred the Process also referred to as, "he Doo or the Marcel." The Process involved using various types of lye to straighten the hair to give it the "White boy look." Some of the Compton officers adopted a habit from LAPD. When they wanted to punish an undesirable or a crook, they would find out from informants when the crook was cooking (processing his hair). They would execute his arrest after he had placed the caustic solution on his hair. They would use the burning pain from the solution to convince the arrestee to cooperate. Once he agreed to cooperate, they would allow him to wash the caustic solution from his hair. They called it "developing informants".

The Compton police hired several new officers, sent to them to the LASO Academy, and assigned them to senior officers for on-the-job training for six months. Jim Worsham, a Black officer was assigned to two White training officers for two months. He wore a neatly trimmed Afro. When he was assigned to ride with me, the watch commander called me in and insinuated that Jim was a militant. He remarked, "Look at his hair; what do you think?" I responded that Jim's hairstyle was not an indication of militancy, but merely a fad in the Black community. Jim turned out to be a fine officer. He later transferred to the Inglewood Police Department and become the first Black officer on the IPD

There was never a dull shift. There were a few calm nights and other nights we ran from one felony call to the next. We handled calls ranging from pet cats in a tree to homicides and other major felonies. One of the interesting and stranger calls involves death notifications (DN). The first DN I was involved in was shortly after the riot. My partner and I were given a DN regarding the death of a young man, in Cleveland, Ohio, whose parents resided in Compton. When we drove to the house and knocked, a large irate middle-aged Black male greeted us with, "What in the fuck do you pig motherf------s want knocking on my fucking door, harassing a good citizen like me? You should have your fucking asses out there recovering some of that stolen property that was taken during the riot!"

My partner said, "Sir I am Officer Smith and this is Officer Sutton, are you Mr. Ronald Jackson?" He replied, "I can see who in the fuck you are. What do you motherf-----s want?" My partner asked, "Sir are you the father of Ronald Jackson Jr. of…" Before he could finish the question Mr. Jackson interrupted with, "Why motherf----r, what if I am and what if I am not; why in the hell do you want to know? Anyway he ain't here motherf----r!" Officer Smith replied, "Sir we are not looking for him…" my partner attempted to advise when again was abruptly cut off. "Then why in the fuck are you cocks------s knocking on my door?" he yelled. After battering back and forth, my partner advised, "Sir, we are merely here to deliver a message."

Mr. Jackson continued to spew profanity at us. He finally conceded by stating, "Yes, why motherf----r, why?" he bellowed. My partner looked Mr. Jackson in the face and stated in a low monotone, "We were sent here to tell you that the little cocks----r is dead. He was shot to death in Cleveland, that little bastard. Here is the telephone number for the police in Cleveland."

On my last DN, I was a one-man unit in District 2. I knew from the order to land line the station the task I was being assigned: to notify a Mr. and Mrs. Riggins that their son had been killed in an automobile accident in Detroit, Michigan. Except from rescuing an old lady's cat from a tree or an eminent threat, DNs were one of the most humane duties that police officers performed for the people, but were not glamorous because it made the officer the bearer of very sad news.

I drove over to a nice neighborhood in east Compton and rang the doorbell. Mrs. Riggins, a matronly Black lady approximately 50 years old, invited me into the residence without asking what I wanted. She offered me a cup of coffee. I decided to chat for a while rather than break the sad news to her right away. We talked in generalities about the weather and other non-essential things. I noticed she dabbed her eyes occasionally as though secretly removing tears. I pondered making the notification when her husband, who had gone to the store, was home. When I stood up and started to tell her that I would come back later, she stood up, put her hand on my right shoulder and stated, "Please Officer Sutton, it is okay. Sit down for a few minutes more please!"

Mrs. Riggins went into the kitchen returned and refilled my cup. She pulled her chair up in front of me, placed both of her hands on my leg, looked me in the face and asked, "When did it happen?" I replied, "About 3:30 this morning mam, are we talking about the same thing? Did someone call you mam?" She asked, "It's my son isn't it; he is dead isn't he?" I answered, "Yes mam, he is. It happened this morning just outside of Detroit."

When Mrs. Riggins stood up, I embraced her, patted on her back and wanted so badly to ask how she knew her son had passed. I offered my condolences and assistance and left.

This incident was one of several DNs that I was involved in, where the mothers actually knew that their child was dead before being officially or unofficially notified.

I am convinced that there are types of nonverbal communications that mothers often get regarding their children that are inexplicable.

Shortly after I got married in 1966, my wife and I drove up to Bakersfield, California where she had relatives. It was in late summer and many residents in that area were suffering from Valley Fever, which made them tired, lethargic, sleepy and weak. We visited an old man (OM) who wore a string around his neck with a small makeshift cloth ball attached to it that had a strong pungent odor.

The OM related that he had lived in Bakersfield for a long time and has never had Valley Fever. He related that the stuff in the cloth ball prevented him from being bitten by the many large mosquitoes in the area. According to the OM, he had learned it from his parents; former slaves. The OM, after learning that I was a police officer, took a liking to me and wanted to personally prepare a meal for me.

He had just killed a turtle and was going to cook it later that evening, but decided to cook it for his newly found friend, the policeman. He placed the turtle in a large black cast iron skillet and turned on the gas burner. I watched the turtle cooking for at least 10 minutes noting how the meat was moving in the skillet, as though still alive. I painstakingly advised my new friend that I did not eat turtle. He apologized and told me he should have asked me if I liked it before he started to cook. I then accompanied him out to his backyard where he grabbed a black and white, feathered chicken he called a domino. He swung it around several times and took a knife and whacked its head off. The headless chicken ran a few steps, dropped and wiggled for a few seconds and stopped. He did the same ritual with a rust feathered chicken he referred to as a Rhode Island Red.

I watched him pour hot water over the chicken and helped him pluck feathers from them. When he cut and eviscerated them, I suddenly developed a weak stomach from the smell. I watched him make dumpling, the OM smiled in the process and appeared to enjoy preparing a special meal for his new friend. As a child, I had never liked chicken and dumpling, never developed the taste for it.

I knew that I would, despite my angst, eat the chicken and dumpling, especially after my friend had put forth so much effort in its preparation. While eating, the OM told me that he was a little boy in Lawrence, Kansas when Jesse James rode into town one day. The OM also told me that he was in Lawrence when an Engineer named Buck White brought a train into Lawrence, Kansas. He was with other town folks admiring the train up close. Engineer White was the focus of attention, standing on the platform talking about specifics of the train. He had on bibbed overalls, a red bandanna and a black and white striped engineer's cap. On occasion, he would climb into the cab, let off steam and sound the horn.

When a lady asked White if he was afraid of such huge machinery, he said, "No mam, I take the Number-1 out and bring the Number-2 in." When asked by another lady if he was afraid White stated, "No mam, I take the Number-1 out and I bring the Number-2 in; whether it is God's will or not." According to the OM, that very day Engineer White took the Number 1 out; at the end of the line, the engine blew up, killing Engineer White. The next day the Number 2 brought Engineer White back into Lawrence.

I learned from the OM that various parts of the pig such as: chitterlings, feet, ears, tail, brain, ham hocks, snout and testicles, also known as mountain oysters; were the throw away parts of the pig Black slaves often had to eat.

I learned humility from the OM; learned to make myself unpleasant for the sake of friends striving to make me happy. I also learned that you are what you eat and that when someone prepares food for you as a guest, it symbolizes a profound friendship; almost equal to saying I want you to be a part of me. I further learned from Engineer White's incident, that there is no man greater than God. Since that time I have seen and heard of numerous people putting themselves equal to, or above God only to be shown in the end who is really in command. I also learned that the little pungent smelling ball around my friend's neck was a makeshift insect repellant; it was the first I'd ever seen.

There was a liquor store in my district, District 2, on the corner of Wilmington Avenue and 134th Street. The owner, Gus, as he was known in the neighborhood, had a semi-circle scar on his forehead and an aura about him that indicated he was in fear or had lived a very fearful existence. One day out of ignorance, I asked Gus why he had numbers tattooed on his right forearm. He related that he had served in a Jewish concentration camp during WW II and was one of the few survivors. I subsequently made frequent stops to check on Gus or his employees during my shifts.

About a block and a half down the street from Gus's Liquor Store lived one of the meanest Black men I've ever met: Ernest Chappelle "Butch" Gloud. Everybody knew that Butch's elevator did not go up to the top floor. The entire neighborhood and most people that knew him were afraid of him. I had cautioned Butch several times about threatening Gus. On one occasion when I advised Butch that Gus had been a Jewish, German prisoner, he expressed compassion and promised to never harass him again.

Butch often had fistfights with his father and he always won. On one occasion, he was fighting his father so viciously; his mother suffered a fatal heart attack. I answered several calls involving Butch trying to evict his father from their home. It was highly believed that Butch needed clinical treatment, but trying to get him in the system was always an imbroglio.

Butch had a reputation for carrying a shotgun underneath an overcoat he wore, even in the summertime. He would get off the Red bus at 134th Street and walk toward home in the middle of the street. Most neighbors that knew him would pull to the side and let him pass, for those who did not, Butch would fire a few shotgun rounds into the air. Some drivers parked to the side, others reversed their cars and went in the opposite direction. When neighbors saw him coming down the street, they hurried their children into their houses.

One summer evening Butch got off the Red bus on Central Avenue at El Segundo. A short time later I received a call that the bus driver had just let a passenger off at that location, whom he suspected had a shotgun or weapon underneath his overcoat. The subject was walking eastbound on El Segundo. A few minutes later, I contacted Butch and arrested him after finding a 12-gauge shotgun concealed under his overcoat.

About six months later, I got a call that Butch was fighting his father and had put the word out that he was not going back to jail again. When I responded to Butch's residence, backed up by another unit, Butch came to the door with a pistol and started firing into the air. We took protective positions between the doors of the police units with our service revolvers aimed at Butch. When he ran out of bullets in the revolver, we charged Butch and arrested him for discharging a firearm inside of the incorporated city limits. When my back up told Butch that we should have killed him, he remarked, "What for, I wasn't shooting at y'all; why would you want to kill anybody just for that?"

White Front was a major chain of discount stores located throughout California, similar to: K-Mart, Wal-Mart and Sam's Club. During routine patrol, I met a Black manager (BM) of one of White Front's stores, who lived in Compton, at a restaurant inside of the Woodley Lewis Bowling Alley on Central. When I advised him that I was a police officer, he started eliciting information regarding thefts from businesses. The BM was concerned that his store, located in the heart of South Central Los Angeles, was experiencing an increase in thefts of: radios, shavers, mixers, and other small electrical appliances.

When the BM asked what I would do in such a case, I mentioned casually that I would hire a few rent-a-cops (Security Guards) and related that their hourly rate was inexpensive, certainly less expensive than hiring an off-duty police officer. I noted that he was writing something down on a pad as we talked.

The next time I saw the BM about three months later he was very happy, thanked me and told me what a big help I had been to him. According to the BM, he wrote a proposal, an employee suggestion, regarding the hiring of security guards to prevent property loss. White Front's corporate office accepted the suggestion, and as a result gave him and his wife a one-week trip to Hawaii. Additionally, he was given a $10,000 bonus for his innovative Loss Prevention idea.

Uncle Nick in his Navy Uniform circa 1944

My mother, father and youngest brother Samuel circa 1945

Left to Right:
Oldest sister Daisy, cousin, Uncle Nick and Aunt Evelyn circa 1984

Author with childhood friend Norman Smith, circa 2006

Author's first kill (deer), circa 1990

John P. Sutton

Ova Miller, Executive Director of BASIC
St. Louis, MO and New Orleans, La., circa 1994

XII

I LEARNED FROM the incident with Butch that many people are killed by the police, for merely discharging a firearm; although they were not aiming at the police or anybody; just shooting in the air. I surmised that there are and have been a number of despondent people who actually committed these acts with the intent that they be killed by the police, commonly referred to as suicide by cop. Some unable to take their own life, selected the police to do it for them. I further learned that it is very difficult for a policeman to restrain from killing a person when that person is firing a weapon. It is also difficult to discern if the person is shooting at you, or will immediately turn from shooting in the air to shooting at you or another person, requiring a split second decision of, whether to shoot or not to shoot.

Perhaps more revealing were the public sentiments regarding shootings. When an officer killed a person, after that person had fired a gun, there were seldom any doubts that the shooting was justified. However, after the Watts riot the public no longer believed or suggested that the police shoot a criminal in the leg or shoot the gun out of his hands as, often, seen in movies. Although the public hires policemen to enforce the law, sometimes they quickly forget that they're humans and capable of making honest mistakes in judgment. Often officers have been punished for honest mistakes in judgment. I witnessed officers obtaining a kind of unconventional insurance to compensate for those honest mistakes in judgment; they started carrying all kinds of untraceable throw down weapons (a weapon that is thrown near the body of a shot and oftentimes deceased suspect) to justify the mistake in judgment.

I never carried a throw down and tried my best to perform my duties as a policeman to the best of my ability. Some of the citizens in my district apprised me that a District Attorney's investigator was making inquiries about my character, asking for information about any criminal activities that I could be involved in that they knew about. Around this same time, I stopped a White male driver with a British accent for running a flashing red light on the corner of Alondra and Central Avenue. He smelled of freshly poured alcohol. When I asked him for his driver's license, he opened the glove compartment and several $100 notes fell onto the floor. He fumbled around inside and more money fell onto the floor. I assisted him in retrieving the money and had him secure it in his front pants pocket. I surmised he had approximately $10,000 in cash. The driver related that he did not trust banks, as his reason for having the cash.

I never had a desire to steal and was disappointed that some investigative agency sent a stringer to test my veracity. A short time later, a window smash burglary went down in my district. When I met the owner, I was made aware where he stored his receipts and cash. Ironically, within a few months, that same location was window smashed three times. I always arrived before the owner. I never went to his money stash and noted each time he joined me at the location, he asked if they had gotten his money. My answer remained the same, "I am not sure, I just checked for suspects possibly still in the building."

There was a White field sergeant, I will refer to as Sgt. W-----, who always entered burglarized locations and helped himself to items not likely to be missed like: cigarette lighters, cigarettes, fifths of liquor, etc. I never saw him take cash, however, I dreaded him coming to any burglarized crime scene I was handling.

One night, burglars hit a neighborhood grocery store, on north Wilmington Avenue, in my district. Sgt. W----- came to the scene and advised that the owner was en route with an expected time of arrival of 45 minutes. Sgt. W----- asked me for the keys to my police unit, which I provided, while remaining inside of the store assessing the damages, checking for prints and partially filling out the burglary report. After the owner came and we cleared the scene, Sgt. W----- told me that I had done well shopping; I didn't have a clue what he meant. He then asked if I had a spare in the trunk of my police unit. When I checked the trunk, it was packed with groceries: large sticks of ham, cheese, bologna, pressed ham, liverwurst, eggs, bacon, steaks and other food items, all packed neatly in boxes in the trunk. I suspected this thief was either setting me up or establishing an insurance policy. I did not think any officer would stoop to such a level to determine if I was, as suspected by some, an FBI plant (undercover agent).

I drove around the rest of the shift worrying that Sgt. W----- had somehow entrapped me. At 7:30 A.M. instead of checking into the station, I delivered the grocery to the storeowner and told him a lie that it had been found up the alley from his store by an unknown passerby.

The thought of what the Black officer had told me about wondering who would be shooting at me in a shootout caused me great concern. The prevailing consensus then, and likely now, in police departments being "you don't rat out your own"; often referred to in some police circles as "Blue Code". I remember what I had responded I would do, when asked during the oral examination, if I caught my biological brother stealing. I gave the expected and correct answer, that I would arrest him. Now, I had encountered a brother law enforcement officer committing the same offense and I failed to act. I thought of telling the chief, but hesitated when I realized that after being on the police force for three years, the chief had never spoken to me once, never returned my greetings, but merely walked by as though I didn't exist. I recalled speaking to him on several occasions when passing in the hall, in the training room and in the lunchroom; only to see him walk pass as though I was invisible.

Over the last two years, I had the highest felony arrest record and conviction rate in the department, yet when it came to officers being transferred to the Detective Division, I was never selected. Up to this point, there were no Black detectives in the division. It was commanded by Captain Thomas, then a purportedly John Birch Society member.

One day when preparing to go on my regular graveyard shift, 11:30 PM to 8:00 AM, I received a telephone call from Captain Start of the Patrol Division advising that Captain Thomas had advised him that the Detective Division had received reliable information that there was a Stop

Order for me, a contract on my life. When I asked Start who had issued the Stop Order or the source, he said he did not know and recommended that I contact Captain Thomas for details.

I met with Captain Thomas and found him extremely secretive about the source of the information and even sketchier about the details of the order. I found it most unusual and unprofessional that Thomas responded so negatively to me about the matter and offered no suggestions or indications that they were investigating it further. He proffered no advice and seemed to relish the fact that he held something of importance that he did not have to share with me.

That night after I left the station, a reserve officer and I made a bar check at the 339 Club, on Compton Boulevard, within one mile of the police station. Shortly after we entered the bar, a large Black male sitting at the end of the bar dropped a small aluminum package on the floor. I retrieved it and examined it, noting it contained four red seconal capsules known as red devils. The reserve officer and I arrested and handcuffed the subject and placed him into the police unit. Before we drove away, the arrestee said, "Hey Sutton, you can take the damn cuffs off now." He then related that he was the source regarding the Stop Order and gave specific details regarding how it was scheduled to transpire. The arrestee described the FBI agent he was working with and he described Captain Thomas as the person in on his interview. We released the subject. The following day, I wrote an Officer's Report and forwarded it to Captain Thomas with details of the information I had gleaned. I found it hard, unbelievably so, that a brother law enforcement officer would be that uncooperative with another officer.

One night when fog descended across the city, the visibility in some areas was limited to a few yards; even lights could not be seen until almost directly upon them. I was patrolling the southwest part of District 2 with my headlights out, when the radio dispatcher blurted, "4-5-9 (burglary) alarm off at Nancy's Boutique, in Rosecrans Plaza, units responding acknowledge!" After three units responded they were rolling from the east side, I advised that I was en route. I was one street north of the location and drove over quickly, unhampered in the thick fog. Upon arrival, I surprised a White officer who was at the scene placing articles of clothing in the trunk of a police unit. After I got out, the officer immediately approached and asked what size dress my wife wore.

I told him none from that boutique and asked him if he was booking the dresses in the trunk of his car as evidence and, if so, that I would help mark the evidence at the station. Instead, I assisted the officer in putting the dresses back into the boutique. He threw them on the floor instead of placing them on rack. I then left, leaving three back up units at the scene with him.

I began to think that there were a lot of crooked policemen in the department, but much to my surprise most of them were honest, hard working and duty-oriented.

A short time later, I took the Sergeant's Exam and believed that I'd aced it. It consisted of problems I had worked on in college and was very familiar. When the results came back, I was advised that I had missed the cutoff by one point. Like most police exams, there are answers that can be challenged. I was never afforded the opportunity to view the test results. I was confident, devoid of any doubt, that my test had been skewed. I knew it was time for me to make a career change. I thought of the numerous times my life had been threatened when handling routine police matters, the danger that the job exposed one to on a daily basis.

I recall responding to an apartment on Alondra to investigate a "Misc-Pub-Invest, Sick Cared For" call. Routinely, this type of call required an officer to: determine if an ambulance is needed or direct the family to the proper medical facility. This type of call is a one-man car call and rarely required a back up. When I arrived at the residence, a very calm lady admitted me in. She advised me that her husband was in the next room with a loaded shotgun and threatening to kill someone. Before I could ask her additional information, he called from the room asking, "Who's that out there with y'all?" The lady immediately became quiet. I answered, "Mr. Bailey I am out here. I am a police officer; do you mind if I come in there and talk with you?" He replied "Naw, I don't mind, come on in." As I opened the door and walked into the bedroom, Mr. Bailey was sitting on the edge of the bed with a shotgun aimed in my direction and his finger on the trigger. I walked over to him and asked if I could sit on the bed with him to talk. He agreed and motioned with the shotgun for me to sit down. I engaged him in general conversation about his health, the weather and eventually came to what was upsetting him. Mr. Bailey related that he did not know what was wrong with him. All of a sudden he had just gotten mad and wanted to kill someone. When I asked him if I could see his gun, he handed it to me immediately relating that he had a double ought buckshot round in each barrel. I unloaded the shotgun and asked Mr. Bailey to do me a favor. He agreed. I told him I was going to call an ambulance for him to go see a doctor, to find out what was making him so mad. He agreed and remarked that he had just felt like cutting somebody in half with the gun just to see if the double ought bucks could.

After completing that call, I went to Winchell's doughnut shop up the street and reassessed what I was experiencing as a policeman. I started realizing that a bad policeman is worse than the worst thug on the streets. If a policeman can steal or plant drugs or concoct charges on an innocent citizen, he could or would not hesitate doing the same to another officer.

The job was becoming very stressful fighting crimes on the street and seeing some purported crime fighters (policemen), actually committing crimes. It was alarming realizing that they would commit offenses in my presence; there is the likelihood that their criminal activities were much wider in scope than I imagined. I had long held a prejudicial thought about thieves: I could never believe they would ever stop stealing.

I was cognizant that when a policeman went against the "Blue Code" he was titled a: snitch, ratfink, songbird, sleaze ball or shit bird; impeding future employment with another law enforcement agency. This would also spill over into those private or government agencies that required a background investigation. I was at an impasse in my career.

I often visited my mother and father for relief. Often my father would opine that something was bothering me from the expression he apparently saw on my face. He would then ask me if I was keeping that special person, God, with me in the police car. When I first became a policeman, my father told me to always take God with me to work and on those not so busy moments to pray and thank him for keeping me out of harm's way.

On one occasion, I confided in him, without being specific, that there were things amiss with a few officers in the department. His initial opinion was that they were beating suspects and not telling the truth in their reports. My father, despite what he had experienced in Mississippi, always believed that there are 10 times more good Whites than bad ones. When I mentioned Mr. Alford, who had left money for him in his will, my father seemed somewhat upset, but as always, maintained his composure.

My father related that his father and his brother were born into Slavery. Their parents had acquired about 500 acres of land in Holmes County that was called Pinch Back. The two brothers, his uncle and dad, married two sisters from the area. While working the field during a storm, they, my grandfather and his brother, were killed by lightning. Some time after their deaths, unknown White men took Pinch Back from my grandmother and her sister on alleged tax delinquency and non-payment. According to my father, Mr. Alford had been somewhat involved in the unlawful takeover. My father believed the money he left him in the will was his way to make himself right with God; a kind of payback for what he had done involving the land.

Mr. Alford, on several occasions before his death, had stopped short of telling my father something that had long been troubling him. I will always admire my father, not for any perceived acts of cowardice, but for being brave and having the survival skills to exist during a time and in a place, so vehemently hostile toward Blacks. I often thanked him for his sage advice, support financially, spiritually, mentally and for always being there for me. I admired him for stepping down from a senior pastor position and moving our family to a safer part of the country, California, when he did. I further admired him for not having an attitude about the Senior Pastor at Belmont Baptist Church, on 92nd and Avalon, being paid more while being a less effective preacher.

Sometimes when I would visit him, I would lift him off the floor and walk carrying him to show him how strong I was. When he would state in his baritone voice, "Put me down boy," I would put him down immediately. Despite his small size, by comparison to mine along with the big gun I carried on my side, I always had reverent fear of my father's authoritative voice.

I applied for the U.S. Department of Justice, Bureau of Narcotics and Dangerous Drugs (BNDD) the predecessor of the Drug Enforcement Administration (DEA); and was offered a Special Agent position within two weeks, pending the completion of a full field background investigation.

While ending my last two weeks at Compton PD, I ran into the BM again in the restaurant at the bowling alley. He was dejected and sad. The BM related that at the onset of hiring the security guards, things progressed nicely with a major drop in thefts. About six months later the thefts skyrocketed, involving larger costly items: sets of tires, refrigerators, stoves, televisions, freezers, bicycles, and other more expensive articles. The BM related that the large thefts were perpetrated by or in concurrence with the security guards.

The BM related that the major thefts had caused a major loss in revenue resulting in the closing of several stores. He was of the opinion that, eventually White Front would declare bankruptcy.

After I reported to the BNDD office in Los Angeles, I was apprised that it was time for me to leave the CPD because I was working with a bunch of snakes. I was allowed to review part of my background investigation. When I read the comments that two White sergeants had made about me to the background investigators, I felt very sad, dismayed and never believed that they were or could be so vicious. I was mostly shocked at the comments of Sgt. G----, for he smiled all the time, was very friendly toward me and even walked up to me on numerous occasions and chit-chatted about many things, including: families, friends, dogs, certain movies to watch, fishing, baseball and other topics. He appeared to be a very fair person with the ability to perform well in a diverse work force.

I learned many valuable lessons while on the Compton police force. I learned that very often, the most qualified person does not get the promotions or good job assignments. There are many games played in the workforce. One of the most serious is termed "dirtying one up", which involves contriving, concocting and creating false statements and false acts against another person. While that person is under investigation, he/she cannot be promoted. When that matter is cleared up another false situation is contrived. Management is thereby provided a reason not to promote a certain person. In addition, management often will look at an employee who has had several accusations, despite being cleared of all, as possibly guilty of at least one and will unlikely consider that person for promotion.

The rumor mill is another game, wherein a rumor is spread that a minority has a particular job sewed up. The rumor circulates throughout the agency up to the deciding official. The deciding official will not select the minority applicant to alleviate any thought of pre-selection.

This works in reverse when the rumor involves a majority. Once it reaches the deciding official, it is used as fodder/fuel for his selection; in that the deciding official is likely to believe he is the agency's choice.

The most alarming lesson is when certain members are corrupt; they corrupt or attempt to corrupt others by involving them in their acts. Often they will utilize the newcomer as the scapegoat if suspicion arises. The corruptors are able to cast off the suspicion of their own illegal activities by placing it on others, by deflecting the focus away from themselves onto innocent coworkers.

During this period two of my most memorable moments involved Dr. Martin Luther King Jr. The first one involved shaking Dr. King's hand after his speech at Will Rogers Park on 103rd Street in Watts. The second, about a year later, involved calming an angry crowd of Blacks after a White Compton police officer shot and killed a 16-year-old Black burglary suspect in Compton, in the early morning hours, after Dr. King was assassinated. 1968 was a year full of turmoil and unrest. There were riots in several cities attributable to King's assassination and there were rumors of pending riots. In other areas, anti-war demonstrators were pitched to the edge itching for a riot. Some of their demonstrations resulted in riots, almost riots and arrests by various police departments. During the same year, presidential candidate, Robert F. Kennedy was assassinated. With the Vietnam War at its crest; Americans were being killed by the thousands. Those not killed were severely wounded and returned home with a variety of macabre and gruesome injuries. There were draft dodgers all over the place, many assumed fake identities and remained in the states, others pulled up and moved to: Europe, Canada, Mexico, Costa Rica and various South and Central American countries.

There were many public outcries about the "war in Nam" and whether it was worth the U.S. efforts. Several news media even featured news stories of other countries displeased with the war. The U.S. Allies became scarce to none. Many scaled back their support, leaving more American soldiers fighting than South Vietnam, the country we were purportedly assisting.

The war protesters staged a major riot at the Democratic National Convention in Chicago, Illinois in August of that year. Some of the major protesters, some who were arrested and those not arrested, went underground and conducted a kind of domestic guerilla war against the war for a long period.

President Johnson apparently had had his fill of killing and seeing Americans killed for a piece of land not really worth fighting for in the first place, however; like his predecessor he did not want to embarrass or disclose mistakes made by his predecessors. He not only continued the war, but escalated it. Exhausted from the killings that later resulted, President Johnson did not seek re-election.

An aspiring presidential candidate Richard M. Nixon, during his campaign, promised the American people, not to end the war in Vietnam, but if elected president, "I will bring the North Vietnamese to its knees."

One early morning while patrolling the neighborhood west of Central Avenue at 135th Street with my lights out, I observed a man walking behind another man down an unlit section of 134th Street. The man in the rear had something in his hand extended toward the other man's back. The man in front casually looked over at my black and white police car, and immediately ran toward the car screaming, help me please, help me. I cast the spotlight on the other man and ordered him to freeze. The man who'd screamed for help began hugging me, telling me that he was being robbed. I had to fight him off in order to deal with the robber. I ordered the robber to raise both hands high above his head and to walk to the police unit. It was then I noticed the robber had a sawed off shotgun in his right hand. After I handcuffed him to the rear and secured the shotgun; I learned that it was my old high school classmate, Leotis Sanders. I had not seen him in several years and had been told that he had gone to jail several times for small stretches: a year or two at a time. After he recognized me, Leotis remarked, "I had an idea it was you cause I was told this was your beat. I started to spray the hell out of your police car with the double ought bucks, but I didn't want to hurt an old friend like you. I know you're going to give me a light ass-whipping and send me home huh?"

"No, I don't think so Leotis. I have to take you in just like any other arrested person," I advised. Leotis then started being Leotis as I remembered him 14 years prior. He started calling me a slew of profane names and threw in one I had never heard, "You Black Bitch Ass Motherf-----".

It was a sad, but sweet occasion; in that I prevented an armed robbery and actually rescued a terrified man in the process. The victim related that he thought that Leotis was going to kill him. He further related that after he exited Woodley Lewis's Bowling Alley and walked to his car, Leotis jammed him in the ribs with the shotgun and threatened to blow his brains out if he made a sound or did not obey his directions. Leotis marched him across Central Avenue into the dark residential area. He surmised if he only intended to rob him, he could have done so at his car. Leotis later pled guilty in Superior Court and was sentenced to 10 years.

One day while driving eastbound on Imperial Highway crossing Wilmington Avenue, I saw my youngest brother, Samuel, walking north-bound from Imperial in an area called the front, a noted drug trafficking area. When I confronted him about it via telephone, he related that he was meeting a friend whose car had broken down in that area.

About a month later while on patrol, I made a traffic stop of a young Black male driver and saw him toss something on the curb. I examined it and noted that it was a heroin kit, consisting of a spoon, rubber band, matches and a needled affixed to an eye drop syringe. I arrested the driver for violating California Health and Safety Codes, possession of heroin paraphernalia. The driver remarked, "You know having a Jones is not a crime. Haven't you heard of the Jones Miller Act?" I advised him that he was correct, but possession of a heroin kit was a crime. The driver then remarked, "You ought to be arresting your brother Samuel. He's got a stronger Jones (heroin addiction) than me." I felt my heart beating fast in my chest, my mouth immediately turned dry and I was rendered temporarily speechless by his words. I had the driver repeat his accusa-tion and asked him specific questions about Samuel that he answered correctly. They had been classmates in high school. I released the driver and tossed his heroin kit in a sewer. I was very sad and disappointed. I prayed that the allegation was untrue. I was cognizant that a heroin addict is a very dangerous person. Heroin addiction makes the addict a slave, who would do anything to free himself from the severe agony and intense pain, resulting from the need of heroin. I was aware that even rich heroin addicts often go to jail. I could foresee my mother really dying if her baby went to jail or god-forbid to prison for any length of time.

Samuel, a baby boomer, was born when my mother was 43 years old. As the youngest, naturally he was treated royally and allowed more rein than his seven siblings. He was spoiled rotten. My parents relished in doing all they could for him. The more they did for him, the more he demanded. Samuel volunteered for the army after high school, which did not curtail our parents continuously giving him money. They sent him money on a monthly basis when he was in the army. I remember telling my mother and father that they were spoiling Samuel, making him think that the world owes him a living instead of having to work for it. I remember my mother's frequent admonishments, "John, you are singing to the choir."

Immediately after terminating my shift, I made an unannounced visit to Samuel's residence and questioned him about his reported heroin use. He related that he was just chipping (experimenting) with heroin but was not addicted. Samuel claimed that he had developed a drug habit in the army while stationed in Germany. He promised to quit all drug use before my scheduled completion of the Federal Bureau of Narcotics and Dangerous Drugs Academy.

I could not imagine telling our parents of his plight. I felt very disappointed in Samuel for stooping so low and allowing himself to get addicted to something that now controlled him. I was fully aware that there's no such thing as experimenting with heroin, which once ingested you became an instant slave and heroin became your new slave master.

XIII

AFTER BEING SWORN in as a federal narcotic agent, I spent one week in the Los Angeles office before being sent to Washington, D.C. for 12 weeks of basic agent training in September 1969. Seeing the beautiful buildings in our nation's capitol was awe-inspiring. Being employed by the United States Department of Justice was more than awe-inspiring, eclipsing a level beyond a dream coming true. Although I took a $10,000 pay cut, accepting the position, I believed it was well worth it, especially with the realization that I would no longer be a part of the shenanigans that were going on in the Compton Police Department. I no longer had to think about whether the chief spoke to me or not. Today, many years later, I am at a loss for words regarding his attitude toward me. Perhaps he also thought I was an FBI plant or maybe he had a type of color blindness that prevented him from seeing Black.

There were 32 basic agents (BA) in my class, BNDD #6; nine were Black. All BAs had a degree from various colleges and universities. We were housed in the Manger Hamilton Hotel at 14th and K streets in Washington, D.C. The BNDD headquarters was located at 14th and I streets, a few blocks away. The area was typical east coast with old brownstone buildings mixed with a few modern buildings with various types of glass sides. There were numerous buildings some concrete, some marble, early American and European architectural styles and some with verdigris domes. There were beautiful statues of noted historical figures.

St. Thomas Circle, a few blocks up the street from our hotel, was the beginning of what the locals referred to as: whore stroll. Sometimes during the day a few prostitutes strolled the street, but at night there seemed to be a whore convention in the area. They were all over: streets, cafes, hotels, drug stores and other businesses in the area. They were very aggressive and some followed guests into the lobby of our hotel plying their wares; talking loudly about what they do in their trade.

There was an inexplicable aura about D.C., the seat of our national government. All of the federal buildings seemed majestic, spotlessly clean, with carefully manicured lawns, lawns that were devoid of leaves that had fallen. There were taxis all over the place. During my first taxi ride, I was impressed by the zone-based fare system. While riding in a taxi, the fare could calculate the cost by reading the zones listed on the back of the driver's seat.

It was impressive seeing so many Black taxi drivers, especially since there were so few in Los Angeles and other cities. It later became depressive seeing them because of their habitual refusal to stop for Black fares. I later found most of the Black taxi drivers were foreigners from Africa, South and Central America and the Caribbean islands. Their refusal to pick up Black fares, reportedly were based upon a number of robberies many had experienced on the part of Black fares.

All of the passersby wore nice clothing and seemed busy; hurrying to get to a certain destination. Many had an aura of being someone of importance. There were homeless people that camped out on the grates of numerous federal buildings; they picked special spots where the heat and steam from the boilers kept them warm during the cold winter days. The police seldom bothered them because the prevailing sentiment was; the buildings were public buildings and as such were equally owned by the homeless, as well as the gainfully employed.

One day I took a tour of the city and ended up in the really bad part of town "ghetto", in the area of 14th Street where U & T streets cross. At the intersection of 14th & T streets I saw three paintings on sections of a protective wooden construction fence of a Black arm with the needle of a syringe stuck in the ventral fold with "Slave 1969" written on the side.

I had been cautioned not to display any large bills when making a purchase, as not to entice the robbers. A couple of Black agents and I took a taxi from our hotel to the Southern Diner on Florida Avenue, where we relished eating a good southern cooked meal, topped off with a slice of peach cobbler with a scoop of vanilla ice cream.

After the meal, we walked outside and found that none of the taxis would stop for us. After about twenty minutes, a taxi dropped a fare off at the diner, when we attempted to get in the driver sped away with the rear door open, leaving us at the curb. Luckily a taxi driver stopped for a carryout meal and we were able to get a ride in his taxi.

The food in the area near the hotel was mostly fast food, not very tasty or selective and consisted mostly of carbohydrates, pastas, hamburgers and fries; with little to no, raw or cooked vegetables.

There were hordes of busloads of children from all over on field trips to D.C. On several occasions the nearby cafeteria ran out of food completely and closed before the evening meal. About that time, in mid-November, D.C. was invaded with over a half million Vietnam War protesters. The food supply dwindled for three days. I had seen the crowd at the Rose Parade in Pasadena, but never a crowd this large. They were on foot, bikes, motorcycles, cars and buses moving over parts of the city like army ants. Some carried guitars, tambourines, maracas, horns and other musical instruments. The stench of marijuana filled the air for days. Taxi transportation was the most convenient. There were excavations in many parts of the city for a rapid transit train system. We knew that we were going to have to do a lot of walking if we wanted to get around in the city. We were cautioned about bad areas of the city, where the crime rate was high.

There was something different about D.C. residents. Those not working a government job had to work a full-time and part-time job to exist. I had never seen so many people working both a full-time and a part-time job than in D.C. Some worked two full-time jobs.

After completing Basic Agent Training, I was assigned to the Los Angeles office. At that time there were a few Black supervisors, although not many Black BNDD, FBI, ATF, Secret Service, Immigration and Naturalization Service agents or U.S. Deputy Marshals.

As a result, I was asked to work in various cities in the United States, especially where there were limited Black agents. Although it provided opportunities for travel, it was hard on the family life.

One of my most memorable moments occurred, when I first went on temporary assignment to Detroit. The office was located in the Federal Building downtown. One day when another agent and I were exiting the building for lunch, we passed Rosa Parks as she was entering. There was an aura about her that seemed magical even before I was told who she was. She was working for Congressman John Conyers, whose office was also in the Federal Building. Later that day, I went up and introduced myself to her and thanked her for her refusal to sit in the back of the bus. She smiled and talked about many things, other than the incident as though she wanted it to be behind her, to be forgotten. I admired Congressman Conyers for hiring her, especially since she could not get that type of job or any decent job in the South.

After I left, I thought of Ms. Parks as a hero and admired her mostly because of her small size. I then thought of an expression my football coach had often preached, "It is not too important how a dog fights but what is very important, is the fight in a dog." I thought of the number of people, Black, White or Brown, who passed her often without knowing who she was or what she had done.

I reflected on my life in the Jim Crow South, in particular on the Paramount Theater in Greenwood, Mississippi where I had witnessed a White lady letting her dog drink from a fountain that I was not allowed to use because I was Black. Many thoughts flowed through my mind projecting her as a Saint; for being small in size and standing up to a principle that even giant Black men dared to do.

On every opportunity I had while on temporary assignment in Detroit, I created opportunities and situations to be in her presence. When Congressman Conyers had a reception in his office, I arrived there ahead of time and was in the last group to leave. In reality, I was a stalker, but my reasons for stalking were honorable, done out of reverent admiration and awe.

While back in the office in Los Angeles one day, I received an anonymous telephone call from a White male alleging that there were three kilograms of cocaine in a specific office building on Hollywood Boulevard, diagonally across the street from a hotel that had a long history for being utilized by drug traffickers. My partner and I went to that location to conduct an investigation. After entering the office, we contacted the Black secretary and requested to see the manager. A tall, medium-dark complexion robust man with a distinctive baritone voice came out and greeted us. Immediately, I recognized he was Civil Rights Activist James Farmer. We identified ourselves and I advised him of the purpose of our visit. Mr. Farmer smiled and seemed unshaken by our presence. He offered coffee, which we accepted. I informed Mr. Farmer that I was aware he had been one of the main founders of the Congress for Racial Equity (CORE) and also aware that he had initiated the "freedom rides" in the South. Mr. Farmer advised that he was in the freedom business, not the drug business or any other illegal business. He then advised that we could search the entire office if we were not convinced.

I noted during the entire conversation, Mr. Farmer never shied away, appeared deceptive, or ever at a loss for words at any time. I did not view his search offer as false bravado to mask deception. We chatted about numerous projects afoot designed to enhance the Civil Rights Act of 1964 and subsequent amendments. After about an hour, we exchanged salutations, shook hands and my partner and I left. We noted that all during the conversation, Farmer never pointed an accusatory finger at any particular person or group when mentioning it is the price you pay when you are constantly in the public eye.

It was awe-inspiring meeting a man of Mr. Farmer's position, especially a person giving his all for change, a person not easily thwarted in achieving a set goal. Perhaps more importantly was meeting a real Black man, one with the gonads and intestinal fortitude to fight for equality, especially at a time when doing so often resulted in violence.

During one of my job related travels, I was perplexed at what the bartender told me at The Red Lion Inn bar in Seattle, Washington. It was a cold, wintry December night and I had returned from testifying in the U.S. Court. I stopped in after dinner to have a few drinks before retiring for the night. There was a group of about 20 customers in the corner of the room bantering with one another. After the bartender served my drink, he told me I would be surprised to know what the group was discussing. He related that they were discussing committing suicide because they had been laid off from Boeing Aircraft. The bartender related that he believed they were very serious in their discussion and he was concerned that they would really commit suicide. When I related that they appeared to be just talking in generalities, he was adamant about his belief.

We chatted for about an hour. I was impressed being apprised by the bartender that in the United States, most suicides are committed during the winter months with December being the peak month. The bartender did not have to remind me that there is nothing in this world that is important enough to cause a person to commit suicide.

In recalling my initial arrival in California, I wanted to continue my faith in God, continue going to church and learn to live a godly life. It seemed as though all new arrivals in California immediately forgot about God and looked at California as some kind of heaven on earth. Uncle Nick, a man of high morals and ethics, was not much of a churchgoer. Some of my relatives voiced that he did not attend church because they took up collections; in some churches as many as five during the regular service. Uncle Nick was too frugal to get involved.

The nearest church to our house was Faith Tabernacle Church on Central Avenue and 114th Street. One Sunday in late 1955, I attended Faith Tabernacle Church and enjoyed the choir, sermon, friendly atmosphere of the members and the structure of the building. I was strongly concentrating on joining the church. On my fourth attendance, I was insulted by the head pastor, Reverend Douglas F. Farrell, in regards to how much money I had placed on the Bible during collection time. His insult was piercingly cold in that he wrongly singled me out as a grown man; without any knowledge of my age or financial condition at the time.

Perhaps the fact that he was touting the church to buy him suits to attend a convention that day triggered my anger. It was heightened in remembering that this minister had a tryst with his secretary, which resulted in his divorce. Reverend Farrell changed my whole outlook on certain religions and ministers. He had such a negative influence on me that I became like my Uncle Nick, a non-churchgoer for a long time. The negative impact remains indented in my mind. Now I almost automatically have a tendency to dislike seeing ministers living opulent lifestyles while their churches are doing nothing for the community it purportedly serve. I learned a lot from Uncle Nick: how to quickly discern the real from the unreal, how to improvise, how to utilize almost every ancillary thing you acquire, such as: grocery bags, rubber bands from newspapers, glass containers from fruits, vegetables, jams, jellies, etc.; and a host of other items including: newspapers, coat hangers and the plastic wrappings from dry cleaners. I mentioned earlier how Uncle Nick began walking daily after finding money. I learned to walk frequently, like him, but for healthful results. At the age of 17, I learned from my uncle how to really brush my teeth using toothpaste mixed with baking soda; how to brush horizontally and vertically on both sides of my teeth; how to floss my teeth with a piece of thread; how to pick my teeth after every meal, if toothpicks weren't available, how to use a straw from a broom; how to change: a carburetor, fuel pump, muffler, tires, brakes, tailpipes, manifolds, spark plugs, oil, seats, seat covers, batteries, my clothing daily; use a clean towel only once, irrigate my ears with peroxide or peroxide and soap solution; how to use a trashcan liner as a poncho or raincoat; how to keep my fingernails clean and a host of life skills not mentioned. A very important thing I also learned from him was to always appreciate the cook by telling them how much you enjoyed their meal; at times eat those meals that are not tasteful, but were prepared for you.

In our family, the frugality of Uncle Nick was often topic of discussions. Initially I thought it was an exaggeration when I was told that he squeezes dollars when paying for an item. I watched him one day as he peeled off several dollars and how he rubbed each to see if they were stuck, then he popped them for further assurance that none was stuck.

Uncle Nick was very secretive about his financial affairs. Long after I had moved from his home and when I had gotten married, I was the only relative he would take to his bank, or let see his bankbooks. In his household, he assisted my aunt in the paying of all bills. He was a laborer, employed by a drum recuperating company in Vernon, California. Uncle Nick was a good planner; always seemingly prepared for unexpected events. He even planned his own funeral. He is buried in a crypt in Inglewood Cemetery, wearing his old Navy double-breasted black dress suit.

Although not too formally educated, Uncle Nick was one of the sagest [sic] of sages I have ever known. He was an important influence and major Difference Maker in my life. I learned from him, how to be a good: father, provider, husband, son, uncle, friend, neighbor, and relative; in addition, how to be reliable, honest, civil and responsible.

Seeing him kowtow to the Texas State trooper years ago when we were coming to California never caused me to loose respect for him, conversely I admired him more for his physical restraint; how he accepted racial humiliation and denigration in the presence of his family without an equivocal response, any protest or violent reaction. My admiration and love for him deepened. I realize that he did what many men vacillate to do, that is, he took the responsibility of including me in his family when he already had two children.

My love for my mother is indescribable. I remember times when she had a tendency to be fussy. Even during those fussy snits, when I would ask her for money, she continued fussing while shoving me the money. She came along during the peak of segregation, lynching, and overt disparate treatment of Blacks on the part of White America. She hailed from the family of Walter Smith, a large Black landowner in the Durant/ Lexington area who was born into slavery. Her father, my grandfather, had sharecroppers on his place. The property was eventually lost after he remarried and had another family. Like many Blacks during those days, few if any knew anything about wills, codicils or keeping good records. Most of the properties were lost due to alleged delinquent or non-payment of taxes; consequently they lost their lands to unscrupulous Whites. My mother started teaching school in 1925 in Mississippi, 10 years before the advent of Social Security. She taught for 31 years. When she reached 62 and was eligible for Social Security, she was living in California. The Social Security Administration advised that no record could be found indicating that she had ever paid into the system.

Despite all the storms my mother experienced in her life, she never faltered from a strong belief in God; never expressed or showed hatred toward anybody or the system. She was the first person to tell me that all the things on earth were "things loaned to us for a short while." My mother was a staunch believer that evil and ungodly people will suffer the mighty wrath of God. I remember her telling me how during that period that stones would fall out of the heavens striking them unmercifully and that God himself would jubilate from their sufferings. Despite my mother's strong religious convictions and continuous prayers that none of her children would get arrested and incarcerated, the inevitable happened. My youngest brother, Samuel, was arrested and convicted on a drug charge and was sentenced to prison at California Men's Colony in Chino, California. The name was far removed from the prison or penitentiary my mother was familiar with, nevertheless, it was extremely painful that one of her sons, her youngest son, was in prison.

During one of her many lectures to me about prisons, she related in detail how she, during her early teaching years, had roomed with a family that lived close to a prison. During those days they beat the prisoners.

My mother related the horror of hearing leather strike the flesh of the prisoners and the attendant screaming, squalling, whimpering, begging and crying for mercy.

It was difficult understanding how she could hold such pain and fear for so long. I was certain the arrest and incarceration of my youngest brother would be more than her kind and tender heart could bear. I knew she had given him the same lecture but it fell on deaf ears.

It was painful to see her in such intense pain, sorrow, and agony. In a conversation with her one day she asked me if I really thought that my brother Samuel was ever on drugs. After I told her yes, she then lectured me about talking negatively about my brother. Perhaps it would have faired better had I lied and told her that I did not know. I learned that most mothers have an intense love for their children that is indescribable. They will support them when right or wrong, and will give their all, for their well-being and comfort. I could not brace myself to tell my mother that during all the numerous times she was telling me not to get arrested, that as a Black man regardless whether in Mississippi or California, my chances of being arrested were more than eight times that of a White male.

After seeing prisoners in Mississippi wearing black and white striped uniforms with a metal ball and chain attached to their ankle; she started commiserating about her youngest son having a ball and chain attached to his leg. I tried unsuccessfully to convince her that he did not have a ball or chain attached to his ankle.

After discussing this many times and failing to convince her, I suggested we visit my brother. She agreed and I made arrangements to pick her up that following Sunday at 9:00 AM for the two hour drive to the prison.

At 6:30 AM, I received a telephone call from my mother complaining that I was late.

When I arrived at her house, she was dressed as though going to church, but was very nervous; her hands trembled like I had never seen before. On every occasion, she avoided looking me in the face, which I knew was one of her ways of hiding tears. I drove her to the prison and saw a sigh of relief when she read the sign California Men's Colony, Chino, California. When my brother joined us in the visiting area wearing blue jeans and a denim shirt, she seemed more relieved. About twenty minutes into the visit and after my brother had reassured her several times that he had never had a ball and chain on his ankle, my mother had him show her both of his ankles on three occasions. We visited for two hours. I watched my brother hug and kiss my mother several times, assuring her that he was doing okay, that he was in a men's colony, not a prison.

En route home from the prison, my mother remarked several times that she thought I had used my law enforcement influence to get the ball and chain removed from my brother's ankle prior to our visit. Despite the facility being called a men's colony, to my mother it was a peniten-tiary. It was sad seeing her cry, crying inside as though concealing part of her hurt that in reality was inconsolable. I watched my mother's, a non-drinker, hands shake like the delirium trembles of an alcoholic. I suspected that of all the things I could imagine that could kill her, the incarceration of her baby would be the coup de grace.

My mother's love reflected that she loved all of her children equally. She displayed the epitome of motherly love when she showed that weaker siblings required more of her attention, love, care, belief, trust and fi-nancial support. Although she lambasted me many times for speaking the truth about the criminal ways of my youngest brother, I know that she loved me unconditionally; there was never a doubt.

Despite all the other diamonds and pearls I learned from my mother, I learned to love my children equally and never to indicate otherwise. I also learned that the weaker or not so able or confident child, required more attention and support. I also learned to put their well-being foremost in my life. I learned that parenting does not terminate when children become adults and acquire their own families; it is everlasting.

Although I never became a minister, I did develop some of my father's God-given talents such as: the talent of giving, the talent of caring for others, sometimes almost more than myself, the talent of helping and fellowship.

My oldest daughter was born when my father was on his deathbed. His last words to me were, "Make sure you always take care of your family." He was an outstanding provider and I thank both of my parents for being together until their deaths.

One of the best coaches I've ever met was Mr. Butts, who lived on our street between Wilmington Avenue and Willowbrook. Mr. Butts was married to a Mexican lady and had two non-biological, beautiful daughters. I took his oldest daughter to the senior prom. He was one of those unheralded heroes in the Compton area. He coached little league and minor league baseball for years because he loved the game, loved involving young boys in the game. Mr. Butts was one of the most generous givers I had ever met; he gave a lot of himself. Although I never played much baseball, I am cognizant of the thousands of hours Mr. Butts volunteered assisting youth, mostly Blacks and Hispanics teaching them baseball and supporting their efforts. The number of professional players he developed ranges in the multiple hundreds.

Shortly after I was discharged from active duty, a Black doctor, Dr. Milton C. Woods, who had his office in a frame house on Avalon at 120th Street, treated me. It was my first experience with a doctor actually sitting down and explaining not only my ailment, but ways to stay healthy. I was very impressed with Dr. Woods and considered him my family doctor.

At that time, I had developed a habit of smoking. On one occasion, Dr. Woods showed me a picture of the lungs of a smoker and one of a non-smoker. I felt a little guilty every subsequent time I saw him and I had not quit smoking. I recommended him to many of my friends.

An old male friend, whose wife was a wayward woman, confided in me that there were questions in regards to him being the biological father of their two sons. I recommended Dr. Woods to him. Not knowing Dr. Woods, my friend requested that I arrange a blood test to determine if he was the biological father. I tried unsuccessfully to dissuade him from such a test. After making the appointment, my friend asked me to accompany them to Dr. Woods' office. When we arrived, Dr. Woods called my friend into his office and asked me to join them. Dr. Woods told my friend that he could discern that both of the boys were his sons devoid of any test. My friend was adamant about the test. He related if it was determined that he was not their biological father that he would never tell them. Dr. Woods continued to tell him that they were his sons but he was adamant about going through with the blood test. Dr. Woods drew blood from both of his sons and advised that he would have to get a sample of his wife's blood as well. When all of the required samples were eventually obtained, Dr. Woods again told my friend that he was certain that he was the biological father. He remarked that the blood test was merely an unneeded, additional expense.

About a month later, my friend advised that he had been to Dr. Woods' office and that the test was positive that he is the biological father of his sons.

I hesitantly referred a friend of mine, whose husband was in the Navy, to Dr. Woods. After the examination he escorted her back to the waiting room where I was seated. When my friend asked Dr. Woods how to avoid her illness from recurring, he took her back into his examination room for a few minutes. After we left his office, my friend related that she thought that Dr. Woods was somewhat displeased with her for some reason.

In a subsequent conversation with Dr. Woods, he indicated that he had a professional obligation to treat sick and injured patients, but he did not like to treat a man or woman for any illness derived from infidelity. Although he did not allude to my friend, I assumed he was talking about her. It was clearer now why she did not go to a military doctor where she did not have to pay.

Dr. Woods was a very intelligent man with very good communication skills. I saw him converse with the not so educated and almost illiterate, using words that they easily understood. He was unique from other doctors, in that he did not drive a fancy car. His consultation fees were $10 and $15 contrasted to the normal fee ranging from $20 to $50. One day I asked Dr. Woods why his fees were lower than other doctors.

Dr. Woods assured me that he earns about the same as other doctors, but he has to work harder. He related that he treats more patients, works longer hours and his overhead is less. According to Dr. Woods, after he graduated from college with a master's degree in Chemistry, the only job he could find in Philadelphia was as a janitor. When he was working, many of the Blacks poked fun at him because he had a master's degree and was doing the same kind of work as other janitors, some of whom had not completed high school. As a result of being mocked, he decided to become a doctor where as a Black man he would always be able to find employment. Dr. Woods related that he preferred to practice in the Black neighborhood to be closer to his patients. He further related that he could move to an office in a fancy building on the west side or downtown with high rent that would cause him to charge more for services.

A few months after that conversation, the Los Angeles Herald Examiner printed a list of the state and county funds paid to the top 50 doctors in Los Angeles County. Dr. Woods was in the top ten; listed as having been paid over $345,000 by the County. There was a caveat attached, advising that the article is not to be misconstrued to indicate that any of the listed doctors had done anything wrong or illegal.

One day after having been seen by Dr. Woods, there were three Black males sitting in the waiting room. One hollered, "Doc, what do you think is wrong with me now?" Dr. Woods smilingly looked at him and clapped his hands. He had a good sense of humor and seemed to know all of his patients by first name.

Dr. Woods' office was four blocks south of where the Watts riot started. I asked him if he was affected by the riot or by the increase in crime in the area. He related that outside of one minor burglary, he had not been affected. He had no intentions of relocating from the area.

One day while being treated, I saw Dr. Woods in the waiting room speaking Spanish to three Hispanic women with children. I noted he spoke rapidly and responded immediately to questions that the ladies posed to him. Dr. Woods advised that he had to learn Spanish because a large percentage of his customers are Hispanics now.

XIV

IN EARLY 1973, my wife and I purchased a new house in the 600 block of Hoss Street in Diamond Bar, California. At the time Diamond Bar was unincorporated and had a population of approximately 20,000 residents. The city was growing rapidly.

I enjoyed doing personal landscaping on my yard and over a few years planted numerous flowers, a beautiful guava tree, a fig tree, an orange tree and a dwarf peach tree. I copied my next door neighbor one day and rotor-tilled the front and back yards and installed a sprinkler system. I graded the lawn and planted Dichondra grass seeds. About a month later, we had the second prettiest lawn on our cul de sac.

I had been very active as a street agent and was in Detroit attending a trial when the BNDD was changed by President Nixon, rather had been merged with parts of U.S. Customs into the Drug Enforcement Administration (DEA). President Nixon was very enthusiastic about law enforcement and on an annual basis had law enforcement officers from all over the U.S., specifically his home state of California, come to the White House where he hosted them. My friend, Special Agent Joseph Gordon, had been to the White House on two prior occasions. One day I was called into the Regional Director's office and advised that I had been selected to attend the annual meeting with President Nixon in the

White House. I went to the Garment District on Los Angeles Street and purchased a navy blue suit, shirt, necktie and shoes. Later that week, I had my teeth examined and cleaned. I waited two days prior to the planned travel date and got a haircut. I spit shined my black shoes to a very high gloss.

The day before the travel date, the trip was canceled. I was very dismayed, but got over it. President Nixon was embroiled in the Watergate scandal. He had a frown and weary look on his face, as though he was being mistreated.

I suspected that his scary, weary, worn and dejected look was a result of some of the coup activities he had authorized that had resulted in the deaths of many innocent people; all under the name of furthering democracy.

Perhaps the death of Salvador Allende, of Chile, was the most troublesome for him. In the law enforcement arena, several officers/agents joked about President Nixon, relating how he was for law and order; but instead of leading a posse, Nixon had now found himself a few steps ahead of a fast approaching posse.

Despite my cancelled trip and never really caring for Nixon as a president; I became concerned that he was under scrutiny and felt sorry for him based upon the expression on his face. In a subsequent barbershop visit, I heard two Blacks discussing President Nixon. One stated, "Yeah them politicians are raking his white ass over the coals." Another man stated, "Yeah, they're cutting him a new asshole. He deserves all of it coming from an all-white town like Whittier."

I really wanted to meet President Nixon but realized that my opportunity had been zapped. The thought of meeting a president close up was unheard of and I dismissed the idea. I admired the photograph SA Gordon had on his desk, depicting him shaking hands with President Nixon.

About a year later, a new neighbor moved into a house across the street from ours. After they settled in somewhat, I walked over to meet them and to welcome them into the neighborhood. That is when I met Daniel (Danny) M. Ozeki, a Japanese-American male, his wife Yolanda, a Mexican-American female, their daughter Erica and sons Derrick and Daren.

Over a period of a few years, Danny and I became close friends and good neighbors. Danny owned an auto parts store in Orange. He liked to party and invite friends from his old neighborhood, as well as new acquaintances. Unbeknownst to me, Danny would time my arrival and would always be struggling with something in his yard. On some occasions, before I entered my residence, I would go and help Danny. He had a penchant for completely letting me finish the job alluding to how strong I was and constantly filling my cup with fresh coffee and giving me water.

On one occasion it rained continuously for three days, which caused the clay hill behind Danny's house to slide down toward his house. Danny ran over, told me what was happening and we went to Home Depot and purchased two large rolls of plastic sheeting. I put on my golf shoes and climbed the hill numerous times with the plastic sheeting and bricks. I rolled the sheeting from the hill down to the elevated flowerbed in the rear of Danny's house. I anchored it at the top with spikes and bricks and formed a trough for some of the rainwater to drain into the flowerbed. I formed another trough to divert the water spill into the street toward the sewer opening. Danny thought it was the cleverest thing he had ever seen.

Needless to say, I did the bulk of the work as Danny stood by inflating my ego about how smart and strong I was, simultaneously filling my cup with warm coffee. He and I were big coffee drinkers and we did not hesitate to drink a little brown water (alcoholic beverages) every now and then, especially on weekends.

On some weekends, Danny would throw a party. He was a very good host and liked to have a variety of foods ranging from Oriental, Mexican, Italian and Soul. Almost always the crowd at Danny's house was the most cosmopolitan that I had ever seen at a single family party. Sometimes his guests included Whites, Blacks, Hispanics, Orientals, Jews and Native Americans. Danny was always the perfect host; always assured that the attendees got enough food and drink. Ramona, one of our neighbors and friend was a petite blond divorcee. We often watched her consume large amounts of brown water without getting drunk or under the influence. We could gauge when she had consumed about six strong drinks by the change in her voice, from a high soprano to a guttural and raspy voice; somewhat like the voice of Suzanne Pleshette. Ramona would then start philosophizing. Danny and I were amazed at her ability to consume large amounts of alcohol without staggering, swaying or slurred speech. We often spoke of her having a hollow leg. Sometimes when Danny and I had poured on a good one, Ramona would ask if we had encountered some bad ice.

On one occasion while visiting Danny, I noted water oozing from the floor of his hallway. We conferred by telephone with several plumbers and were advised that most homes in California were built on concrete slabs with the plumbing encased in the concrete. Consequently, the plumbers advised that the cost to do a leak find was $1,200 to $2,000, which would likely involve digging into the concrete slab. They all advised that they would not be responsible for replacing or repairing the concrete slab. The repair estimates ranged from $3,000 to $4,500.

While standing out front chatting with Danny the following day, our neighbor Joe Hunter arrived home. We had been advised that Joe was a maintenance engineer for Western Electric in Lynwood, California. We had no clue what his job entailed. In South Central Los Angeles, Maintenance Engineer was a fancy title for a janitor. We approached Joe and advised him what had transpired. Joe told us he would freshen up, eat his dinner and meet with us in about two hours in regards to solving our problem.

Joe came over, assessed the problem and noted that the water was hot and coming from the hot water heater. We went up into attic with Joe and saw him measure several areas. When he came down, he went home and said he would meet with us later. When Joe came back he had a sketch of a plan to bypass the floor and re-route the water lines from the hot water heater through the attic. He had a sketch that included the type of copper tubing, quantity, couplings, solder, soldering tank, protective goggles and a cost estimate for the materials. Danny blew a sigh of relief thinking that Joe, as a good neighbor, would perform the work. Joe advised us that he had done his neighborly duties and related that it was not difficult to re-route the lines but we would have to do it. When he tried to explain how to Danny, Danny went into a confused state and repeatedly asked the same questions several times about how to do the soldering. I surmised that he was trying to dummy up to get Joe to perform the work with our assistance. Joe did not fall for the ruse and left advising that we could do it and if we ran into a snag that we could come and get him.

It was then that I realized that my friend Danny was lazy. I ended up doing the work with Danny keeping me company in the attic and bringing me coffee and water and acting as my assistant. Not only was Danny lazy, he was not a finisher. He had part of a car that he was building in his garage that he never finished.

Danny became so lazy that he stopped going to his business to work but went to the racetrack often. I never knew what actually happened to Danny's business and never asked. He was the type of friend that when you asked him a question that he did not want to answer he would divert your attention to something else. Danny stayed at home daily, smoked a lot and drank coffee all day.

Yolanda got a job with UPS and Danny stayed home like a househusband, except Danny did not believe in performing any house chores. On occasions I would visit with him for a few drinks and chat. Sometimes we stayed up until midnight chatting, drinking and watching television. Danny often checked his watch and related that it would be about 2:30 AM before his wife Yolanda arrived home. He often wanted her to make him an omelet, immediately after she arrived home from work.

If I were to stereotype Danny, I would say that he was the laziest Japanese man I ever met. He often marveled at some of the things I did around my house and sometimes would come over and watch me work. Danny was a skillful mechanic, knew a lot about cars, enough to partake building one from scratch. The only work I actually recall him ever doing was placing meat on a grille for one of his parties.

On many occasions, I conned him into taking his children down to the neighborhood park. I encouraged him to take them with me fishing sometimes; he never did.

One day his youngest son Daren was at my house playing with my daughter. On two occasions, I heard him scream, "O-o-o-o-oh caca." When I asked Daren what he was saying, he stated "caca." When I asked him what did caca mean, he advised that he did not know what it meant; other than it is a word you say when you are mad.

I took my daughter Heather and Danny's children Erica, Derrick and Daren fishing at a lake near the San Antonio Winery in San Bernardino County. They each caught three catfish. Their fish were weighed, eviscerated and placed in separate plastic bags with crushed ice. Erica, Daren and Derrick could not wait to show their dad the fish they had caught. Danny was in disbelief that they had caught them, especially in such a short period of time. Although they showed enthusiasm about fishing,

Danny never got the urge to take them or take them with me when I would go. There was no doubt about the love that he had for his children. He was a proud man and loved his children as much as the next father.

One Easter Sunday I was standing in my front yard with Danny chit chatting about sports, when his daughter Erica came out of their house wearing a yellow dress and black patent leather shoes. Danny remarked, "Man look at my little angel, isn't she beautiful?" I replied, "That she is," and added, "She will make you proud of her with her family one day, her husband and children." Danny agreed, and sadly remarked, "It bothers me a lot that one day, some man will ask my daughter to perform fellatio on him. It just tears me up, just the thought of it." I demurred, in relating that she might enjoy satisfying her husband, realizing that Danny was very serious about the issue. Instead I proffered, "Yes Danny, that is the sign of the times." Danny did not like my comment. He sucked hard on his cigarette and abruptly walked across the street to his house.

I saw my friend Danny madder than the proverbial wet hen one day. My wife and his wife had an appetite for take out Chinese food. Per my wife's recommendation, we placed orders for shrimp fried rice, sweet and sour chicken, sweet and sour pork, egg rolls, crab Rangoon and hot and sour soup at a restaurant in West Covina. Danny and I had a few cocktails awaiting the return of our wives with the Chinese food.

After they arrived, we set the table and sat down to eat. Danny found two cockroaches in his hot and sour soup and one in the shrimp fried rice. He telephoned the restaurant and talked to the manager. When the manager asked Danny if the roaches were sautéed, I thought he was loosing his mind. His face became swollen, eyes watery, and his complexion became a whitish gray. Danny salivated and when shouting profanity in the telephone large balls of saliva exited his mouth as though he was choking. When he finally calmed down, he went into his bedroom, returned shortly, grabbed the food and stated, "Let's go talk to this motherfucker. That goddamn chink motherfucker, who in the hell does he think he is talking to anyway."

As we were riding to the restaurant, I asked Danny if he had a gun. I relaxed when he assured me that he did not. Danny cursed the manager vehemently and threatened to call the health department.

The next time I heard the word chink, a White Kirby vacuum cleaner salesman came into the neighborhood and gave me a big spiel on the

Kirby vacuum cleaner. Despite being told numerous times that I was not interested in buying one and neither was my wife; he seemed to take offense at my knowledge that my wife was not interested. When he was leaving, I spoke to Danny in his front yard. The salesman then asked me if Danny was Chinese or Japanese. When I told him Japanese, he retorted, "That why I hate that little chink motherfucker, I thought he was a goddamn Jap. I hate all of those squinted eyed fuckers. He ranted on almost loud enough for Danny to hear him across the street how he hated him. The salesman ranted on about Danny being a Jap and married to a Mexican. "What a helluva combination." The next thing you know you'll have lowlife Mexicans moving up here and all over the place. It was apparent the salesman had forgotten whom he was talking to, that he was talking to a Black male.

I invited the salesman back into the house and asked him why he had made such statements about Danny. The salesman related that his father had been captured by the Japanese during WW II and was one of the prisoners in the infamous Japanese death march involving captured American soldiers. According to the salesman, his dad hates Japanese with a passion and has over years convinced him to do likewise. I never questioned him about his remarks about Mexicans knowing with certainty how he felt about me.

I could not muster enough courage to let him know that my friend Danny had endured living in the United States almost analogous to the death march. Danny was born in a Japanese interment camp in Colorado. Two of his uncles were part of the few Japanese Americans allowed to serve in the U.S. Army. The bad and poor living conditions in the interment camps were morbid chapters of our American life.

I could not muster the energy to further tell the salesman that Danny's parents were American citizens at the time they were placed in the interment camp. I knew it was useless to also tell the salesman that Danny's father had been killed while being robbed by Black robbers. I wanted so badly to tell him that of all that I have endured, Danny perhaps had endured the same or worse. Perhaps, the only consolation was that Danny was too young to really remember being born in an interment camp and the inhumane conditions that existed there. Additionally, he had received from the U.S. government monetary reparation for his short stint in the camp.

I never knew Danny to be religious or to attend church. On those occasions when I had mentioned God in his presence, he merely shied away or lost himself in something other than what was before him.

About a year and a half after I retired, I was notified by telephone that on February 29, 1996, my friend Danny had fallen asleep in the arms of Jesus. He was 53 years old at the time of death. I was deeply saddened that he had passed at such a young age.

Danny was small in size but will be remembered for having a big heart. His funeral program was 3.5 inches by 5 inches, the smallest I have ever seen. It was folded with an insert. The Lord's Prayer, 23 Psalm, was on the inside left page and there was no obituary. In the insert, I was listed as one of three speakers following mass. Without using notes, I spoke three minutes over the allotted two minutes about Danny's outstanding character and how he was a true American; how he loved all people regardless of race, color, creed, religion or national origin. Those in attendance were an attestation of his love for people from all walks of life.

The Memorial Chapel, completely filled with family members, friends and acquaintances, was as cosmopolitan as Danny's parties had been. Danny was interred in Rose Hill Memorial Park, 3888 Workman Mill Road in Whittier, California; the largest single plot cemetery in the world.

The most interesting thing I learned from Danny was how skillful some people are in putting the monkey on your back; to get others to do their work. Danny was a master. I surmised that Danny had a pain that no medication could ease, however; he never displayed it and tried to live his life to the fullest. I learned to have a cosmopolitan make up of friends and acquaintances and to take every day, make every day as happy as you can as though it is your last day.

XV

AFTER EIGHT YEARS as a street agent, I started applying for supervisory positions. I was denied on all occasions. There were many occasions when I did not even make the Best Qualified List. I was perplexed because there were no guidelines or criteria listing requisite knowledge, skills and abilities for promotions. At best the DEA promotional plan was like a crapshoot, any number between two and twelve could come up.

I had applied for close to 100 promotions and noted that they were given to non-Black agents with less seniority, less diversity in experience, less depth and breath of experience. Most of them were less formally educated. About that time it was apparent that Black DEA agents were on the receiving end of more severe punishment and for lesser infractions. Many instances involved unauthorized use of an official government vehicle. There was a clear and distinct pattern of disparate treatment of Black agents in the DEA, which resulted in two Black agents filing a suit, Henry Segar v. Attorney General Griffin Bell. The suit resulted in a Black Class Action Suit. I was very depressed learning that as Black employees of the U.S. Department of Justice (DOJ); the DOJ had to be sued for Black DEA agents to get justice. Perhaps more disappointing was that several agencies under the DOJ were blatantly subjecting Black agents to disparate treatment; years after the 1964 Civil Rights Act had been passed.

After applying for 102 promotions, I was finally promoted to a Group Supervisory position in Detroit, Michigan. I relished the promotion and the location because it would afford me additional opportunities to see Mrs. Rosa Parks.

While stationed in Detroit, another DEA agent and I traveled to Bangkok, Thailand. En route, we flew from Detroit to San Francisco then to Hong Kong with a one-day layover in Hong Kong. We then flew from Hong Kong to Tokyo, before heading to Bangkok.

My love for America strengthened seeing a crowded country, with toot toots, bikes, motorcycles, so many Japanese make cars on overcrowded streets, some almost running over others in a traffic pattern best described as a major imbroglio. Smog from the gas operated engines filled the air like a blanket and pedestrians walked the crowded streets almost colliding with each other.

I saw the snake farm with many dangerous cobras; the king cobras almost 15 feet long that raised part of their body to the height of some humans. Their sound, flared neck, evil eyes and hissing were fearful. There was a smaller snake, the banded krait that was reportedly more poisonous than the cobra. The Thais called him the three-step snake. Reportedly when bitten by the banded krait, you can only walk three steps before falling, then dying.

I saw a show involving a small Thai man wrestling with a 15-foot crocodile. The mouth of the crocodile was wide enough to engulf the small wrestler. He was a brave little guy who managed to taunt and tease the crocodile in various positions, frustrating the animal beyond his ability to catch his little teaser. In the finale, the wrestler maneuvered the crocodile into a position where he used the animal's own weight to flip it over onto its' back, then he rubbed the crocodile's stomach in victory.

While in a toot-toot riding down Sukhumvit Road, I saw a man get struck by a car that tossed his body high in the air. The impact was loud and sounded like metal hitting metal. Immediately, a group of people ran toward the fallen man. I assumed they went to assist him, but was advised by the toot-toot driver that they were huddled over the dying man asking him for the lottery number. There was a prevailing belief that dying persons possess the lucky lottery numbers. This was reportedly a common practice in Thailand. According to my driver, the driver of the striking car would probably settle with the victim's family at the scene or the next day by paying her several hundred dollars. If the driver was a "superbaht," a wealthy or not so poor Thai, the family could be paid as much as $1,000 for the victim's death. I was dismayed that there was an immediate monetary value that could be placed on the life of a Thai accident victim and that could be settled by the on-scene policeman. It left me to believe that in Thailand; there was no such thing as murder if a car intentionally strikes a person. It made me again proud to be an American.

The employees at the American Embassy confirmed that that was the tradition in Thailand. Often the payment is made at the scene of the deceased and sanctioned or authenticated by the police. From my first arrival in Bangkok, I immediately admired the copper-colored skin of most of the Thai people, their small size and the language. Seeing females bow, place their clasped hands under their nose and say "Sawatdee ka" was musical. The smiles on their faces indicated a welcome kind of friendliness.

While in Bangkok, I realized that there was a world currency that is highly preferred and spendable almost everywhere: the U.S. dollar.

The Americans, Canadians, British and French embassy personnel lived like kings and queens; they all had live in maids, some also had butlers and drivers, all living on the Thai economy and saving money in the process.

I was taken to Rajah the tailor, where after being measured I ordered six suits. When I wrote a personal check, I was startled that Rajah, the East Indian owner, accepted the check without any identification; something I could never do in America. Unbeknownst to me, the suits were tailored the following day in a sweatshop operated by Rajah.

During that trip, we were taken to the Therme and the Darling bathhouses; to Soi Cowboy and the Pat Pong areas of Bangkok. At Pat Pong, we ate freshly prepared Peking duck served on a lazy susan in the center of our table. After dinner, the Thai police treated us to a live adult show in the club section of Pat Pong.

Bangkok DEA agents took us to a supermarket, on Sukhumvit Road, where we ordered fresh, large, river-shrimp that was cooked and served to us in the restaurant section of the market. The next day, they placed an order over the telephone, and took us to a restaurant where we were served a little roasted pig with an apple in its mouth. One of the agents remarked, "When you guys go back to the world, you can now tell them we are really living high on the hog here." I agreed.

We were in Bangkok for 10 days. I enjoyed the trip, my first trip to Asia. I found the people very friendly; all seemingly catering to foreigners and making them feel welcomed. I missed America. Despite the good food I consumed there, I missed a simple McDonald's hamburger, French fries and a milkshake. I missed the unpolluted air, seeing some American cars on the road, the smiles on the faces of families out for a ride or going to and fro. I missed the athletic events on television, the morning news and weather forecasts, reading the morning newspaper while drinking coffee from South America and eating foods processed in America.

Although I enjoyed Bangkok, the thought that my life had little to no value in Thailand, was frightening. In conversation with Thai residents, they had a vision of America as the ultimate paradise. They asked questions about many places in America and seemed to imagine how beautiful they were. Two of the Thai Police Captains that escorted us were fluent in English; one had attended Michigan State and the other had attended the University of Michigan.

I was convinced that there is something extra special about America, after I was told that the King of Thailand, Rama XII, had a daughter attending an Ivy League college here.

I made two subsequent trips to Thailand on official DEA business. Although I enjoyed them, they made me love America more. Perhaps seeing the armed soldiers strutting around with assault rifles and bloused boots in the airports in Tokyo, Hong Kong and Bangkok, gave me a sense of how secure we are in America. En route back to America on my last trip, we had a four-hour layover in Tokyo. While walking around in the airport, we passed several African males dressed in bright colored clothing. I was standing at a coffee stand when a tall African male walked by wearing a beautiful green African suit, baggy pants tapered close to the ankles and a long dashiki, and sandals.

A White American tourist (WAT) stared at the African until he walked out of sight. He remarked and asked, "My-y-y.... that is some fancy outfit he is wearing. I wonder where he's from." I said, "Harlem" and continued drinking coffee. The WAT and his wife were pouring something out of a flask into their coffee. About twenty minutes later the African male returned back to our area. The WAT asked, "Where did you say he's from?" I stated, "Harlem." About five minutes later the WAT broke out in uncontrollable laughter, laughing so hard until he turned red in the face. When he regained his composure he stated, "Boy you really put one on me that time."

In Detroit, we worked joint investigations with the Royal Canadian Mounted Police and the Ontario Provincial Police across the river in Windsor. We had border day activities, picnics, and golf outings on both sides of the river. I traveled to Windsor via the bridge and the tunnel. I also traveled to Toronto and found both cities clean and beautiful; and the people friendly. I was puzzled for a long time, wondering why there was such a low crime rate in Canada. I later learned that area wise Canada is larger than the United States, but with about 1/5th the population. Additionally, it was difficult to get firearms in Canada and there were programs that really seemed to take care of the basic needs of its citizens, and too, there was legalized prostitution. I prefer America to Canada and dislike Canada for sending us those chilling Alberta Clippers and Siberian Expresses.

I found Detroit a very strange city, in that it had not changed much since my earlier temporary assignments there. Somewhere in my college days I recall reading an article about intelligent people residing in very cold climates. Part of the assertion made a reference to being confined indoors caused them to read more, than in Mediterranean-type climates of long hot summers and short dry winters. This was given credence from my stay in Michigan, where I found some of the most intelligent and formally educated Black professionals in Detroit. I met many doctors, lawyers, judges, politicians, engineers, architects and various other professionals. A large percentage of them came from blue-collar family backgrounds that worked in the automotive industry. Most of them had beautiful, new or late model American made cars.

One of the smartest was Dr. Ben Carson, a graduate of Cass Tech in Detroit. I read some of his accolades and several articles lauding his intelligence and medical prowess. It was interesting to learn that he came from a one parent, mother-ruled home; having emerged from such humbling beginnings to become a world-renown surgeon.

The mass movement of Blacks from the South to Detroit also encouraged non-Blacks to also move north. Although, many of the new arrivals were poorly educated; they were able to find good paying jobs either in the automotive industry or with an ancillary company. Many of the marginally educated, from both the Black and White communities, had difficulties finding jobs and resorted to criminal activities: some stole cars, operated chop shops and blind pigs, committed burglaries, robberies, arsons and sold dope.

I learned several unforgettable things while in Detroit. For instance, of all places, one would unlikely think that in Detroit, cars would be stolen and taken to a chop shop to be dismantled and sold for parts. Chop shops were widespread in Detroit, some actually ship car parts all over the U.S. and to some foreign countries. Reportedly, many of their clients were in Cuba.

I learned that a blind pig is not an animal, but an after-hours establishment or bawdyhouse where illegal things like: alcoholic beverages, drugs and sex are sold. Some blind pigs operated 24-7 and were seldom raided by the police; they were located in various parts of Detroit, especially in residential neighborhoods.

In Detroit, I learned the two definitive uses for a McDonald's spoon/ coffer stirrer— a small plastic spoon that could hold about two to five grams of powdery substance. Its' intended use was as a stirrer, to mix cream and sugar in McDonald's coffee. However, the dopers in Detroit used it to measure street quantities of heroin and cocaine. It became so famous in the dope trade that it cast a bad name on the restaurant chain. Today, the coffee stirrer is a plastic spatula. After the end was made flat, the dopers started using it as a dipper to ingest cocaine.

While in Detroit, I started doing something I never dreamed or imagined I would ever do: watching the fall foliage colors change throughout the state of Michigan, especially on the north, east and west coasts and the Upper Peninsula of the state.

In Detroit, I was able to visit with Rosa Parks on occasions and see her at Judge Damian Keith's annual Christmas luncheons.

I was fascinated to have the opportunity to shake the hand of Jacques Cousteau after he disembarked the Calypso at Hart's Plaza, came ashore and was given the key to the city by Mayor Coleman Young. Cousteau had returned from Lake Superior after underwater viewing the wreckage of the Edmund Fitzgerald ship.

I was transferred to Chicago, to a DEA Inspector's position, for two years. In that position, I conducted investigations involving misconduct; including criminal conduct on behalf of employees of the DEA. I also conducted investigations regarding compliance with DEA and DOJ policy, procedures and guidelines.

I had often read about the slums of Chicago and found them as bad as previously seen in books, magazines and newspapers. The city was extremely cold and windy. The people were less friendly, than I had ever encountered. Almost like Detroit, there was a kind of dreariness about Chicago, especially seeing the old water tanks on the tops of buildings and a cloudy gray sky about six months out of the year. The winter of 1981-82 was the coldest I had ever experienced, since Germany. The temperature was 40 below zero with a wind-chill factor of 80 below. It was so cold that ice formed on my scarf from exhaling. A few days when the temperature got up to 20 below, I drove over to Lake Michigan and saw the whole lake frozen. Seeing frozen waves was an indication as to how cold it was.

While in Chicago, another Inspector and I conducted an investigation involving a group of DEA agents reportedly committing perjury regarding the location of an informant in a DEA case that was tried in the state court. My partner and I had the opportunity to meet and interview, then, State's Attorney Richard M. Daley regarding the validity of the case. He was very uncommitted and did not give any answers as to the real facts of the case, or whether he would really consider the evidence in the case. I learned two things from the incident. The first is that a political aspirant will use or refuse to use logic in determining an issue, if it does not further his desires or goals. I further learned that sometimes a vacillator talks in generalities to prolong time, rather than make a decision at an inopportune time.

My partner Inspector, a White male, was immediately coined a "head hunter" without evidence to support it. I learned that not only, was he intelligent, but a very fair investigator who let the facts evolve, as they transpired, devoid of any embellishment or spin.

The main thing I learned is that there is a division between perception and the truth that can seldom be determined in a Polygraph Examination, that is; if an examinee believes he actually observed something, regardless if he actually did or did not, the test will likely favor his belief over fact.

Two years later, I was promoted and transferred to Puerto Rico to head the district office. Shortly after I arrived in Puerto Rico I was invited to St. Thomas, U.S. Virgin Islands to meet Wilbur "Bill" Plase, the agent in charge of the U.S. Virgin Islands Narcotic Task Force. It was a pleasure meeting Bill. Although I had not met him previously, I knew that he was once a DEA agent and had initially opened the DEA Office in Panama.

Bill was a very nice person with excellent managerial skills as previously related to me. It was apparent for he, an outsider and a White male, had been selected to manage the task force. I invited Bill over to San Juan to visit our office there and to extend DEA support to his task force.

About two months later, I received an invitation from Bill inviting me to attend a retirement function in his honor. When I arrived in St. Thomas, I immediately asked Bill if he had acquired another job or if he had been pressured to leave. When he responded negatively to both, I asked him why he was leaving the job. I had never met another person that told me what he did. Bill related that he was a quitter, had been a quitter all of his life and the only things he did not quit were drinking, smoking and college. He further related that he had in fact quit college one time but eventually went back. Bill had quit the DEA without enough time to get a pension. He did not have a single reason for quitting the DEA or the task force job. Bill added that it just came to him that it is what he should do, he should quit.

When I asked him what he planned to do after he quit, he had no answer and had not even thought about it. He related that he was not experiencing marital problems, or any other problem, that he was simply quitting.

The thought of what Coach Wade used to say came to mind and I was at a loss trying to discern why Bill was really quitting his job. I finally realized that there are people in life who are, in fact, just quitters. They quit those things that are important and meaningful to them absent any good reason. I talked to Bill over dinner for two hours and never came close to any answer for his rash decision; nor could I convince him not to quit. I learned from Bill that there are people who like to "do things my way." They make decisions on very important issues that also affect others, with the sole thought of "doing it my way." I further learned from

Bill to strongly consider the positive or adverse impact my decision would have on others before making a critical decision.

As the Agent in Charge of the San Juan District Office, I made liaison trips to St. Lucia, St. Vincent, St. Maarten/St Martin, Grenada, St. Barthelemy, Guadalupe, Martinique, Barbados, Antigua/Barbuda, St. Kitts/Nevis, Montserrat, the Dominican Republic, Dominica, British Virgin Islands and Haiti. All of these locations are beautiful vacation paradises, except Haiti. In Dominica, many tourists opined that if Columbus came to Dominica today he would not see much of a change. I enjoyed its tropical rainforest aura and the numerous rivers and natural spas. None of these locations could fractionally substitute for the beauty of America and what it has to offer.

I recall my first and subsequent trips to Haiti, accompanied by an agent from my office. From college studies, I recalled that Haiti was the second republic in the Western Hemisphere; a Black republic that had arisen from a slavery revolt; how it had been occupied by the U.S. Marines; how Papa Doc Duvalier, a U.S. Puppet, had taken control of the country and ruled it with terrorism and voodoo. His son, Jean Claude Duvalier, aka "Baby Doc", was currently ruling Haiti.

I had anticipated Haiti to be not as advanced as the United States but modern. When the Air France plane banked left over the mountains and made the final approach into Francois Duvalier International Airport, I noted that mountain on the west was almost treeless, with large patches of dirt and sparse patches of trees on both sides; it resembled remnants of an old forest fire with standing dead trees.

Upon arrival at the airport, I noticed that all employees and spectators around the airport were less jovial than I had ever seen as though laughter and smiles were prohibited. They conducted themselves in a business-like manner and were hesitant to talk; they only answered a few questions and never added additional information. I got the impression they feared talking to strangers and they acted as though they were being watched.

While on Harry Truman Boulevard en route to the U.S. Embassy, I saw a Black male pulling a make-shift cart fashioned out of the rear axle of a car with bags of grain stacked 7 feet high. He was barefoot and shirtless and toiling like a beast of burden. The muscles in his back and lower legs were tense as he struggled up the dirt road. Perspiration rolled down his back like water.

Beyond the cart puller, a crowd milled around a waterspout, surrounded by women, men and children who occasionally drank from the spout, filled plastic bottles and left. As others stood in line, little children ran in and out of the crowd playing. As we passed an old air force base on the left, we saw two attractive Dominican prostitutes poised on the corner motioning to incoming and outgoing traffic.

We came to the Iron Market, a shantytown, on the left with crude palm thatched huts, lean-tos, living quarters made out of cardboard, tin, wood, auto parts, grass, cloth and rags. From the road, the ground of the Iron Market was black and appeared wet and soggy. Little chimneys of smoke swirled upward from small pans surrounded by squatting poorly dressed women. In the middle of the Iron Market area, a woman clad in a ragged and dirty dress walked graciously carrying a large untied stack of wicker baskets, balanced on her head. Out front, little boys rolled tires down a dusty road. Big and small jitneys loaded with people ambled down the dirt road leaving large clouds of dust in their wake. The whole Iron Market area looked like a huge cesspool. The smell of burnt garlic, newspaper, oily and rubbery smelling smoke and funk filled the air. The only relief was a slight breeze that came in off the bay.

After meeting briefly with the Ambassador, Deputy Chief of Mission and a unique section of the Embassy, The U.S. Department of Agriculture, Reforestation Program, I was advised that a Cocktail party had been arranged for that evening, to introduce me to various Haitian officials.

I was then taken to meet Colonel Albert Pierre, the Chief of Police for Port-au-Prince and Chief of the Presidential Guard.

As we got out of the Embassy car and walked toward the police headquarters, two soldiers, apparently not fluent in English, aimed Uzi machine guns at our waist area. The Embassy official spoke French and we were escorted upstairs where I was introduced to Colonel Albert Pierre and his assistant Lt. Colonel Maunpoint. Colonel Pierre was approximately 5 feet 7 inches tall and approximately 150 pounds. He was very dark complexioned and had a mole about the size of a quarter on his face with hair growing out of it. Colonel Pierre had a Little Man's Complex, sometimes referred to as a Napoleonic Complex. He had an eerie aura about him and seldom smiled. Although he spoke moderate English, he preferred to speak in Creole and French. I was convinced that the embassy official with me was a CIA agent. I detected that he had some kind of managerial or superiority relationship with Colonel Pierre.

We had Haitian coffee and snacks and chatted about possible drug problems in Haiti and any assistance that the DEA could provide. Colonel Maunpoint was over 6 feet tall and thinly built. During the meeting, he seemed very nervous and afraid of Colonel Pierre. He stood at attention mostly with his hands nervously trembling and shaking along the seams of his trousers.

Later that afternoon we were picked up by an embassy driver and taken to the cocktail party at the Ambassador's residence. Two Haitian guards manned the entrance. As expected, the Ambassador's residence was elegant with waiters and servers all over the place. While standing in a huge party room conversing with an embassy employee, I faintly overheard a conversation going on outside. The embassy employee was apparently wearing a special hearing device. He remarked that the Chief had arrived, had an argument with the guards and walked away from them. I thought he meant Colonel Pierre, who I had met earlier as the chief.

I looked toward the doorway and saw a huge, Joe Frazier-like, Haitian male walk into the room wearing banlon type beltless pants. He had a .45 automatic pistol stuck in his waistband like a cowboy. For a Haitian, he was large, muscular, and clean-shaven possessing an aura that indicated that he was cocky, strong, confident, difficult to impress and that he would enjoy a good scrap, a good bar type fight. The .45 in his waistband sent a strong message, that despite being in the ambassador's residence, he was Chief of Police and was not relinquishing his gun; especially to a non-Haitian citizen or employee thereof.

The embassy employee introduced me to Acedius Saint Louis, the Chief of Police for Port-Au-Prince and Haiti. I was confused because this is how Colonel Pierre was also introduced. Saint Louis was a colonel and an educated Haitian who spoke French, Spanish, English and Creole. I immediately got the impression that Saint Louis was a "Spook" or a special U.S. Government employee. I later met Captains Andre, Baguidy and Jodesty and several other military and police officials.

Before the party was over, a request was made that the DEA conduct marijuana over flights, to determine the extent of marijuana cultivation in Haiti. Colonel Saint Louis requested that I come back to Haiti during the over flights.

The next day we drove down dirt roads through the downtown section of Port-Au-Prince and took John Brown Avenue to Petionville. There were beautiful homes on the mountainsides and foothills that resembled many of the affluent areas in America. It was amazing leaving dusty streets with dilapidated buildings, turning onto paved roads bordered by plush estates, laden with beautiful flowers, plants, trees and perfectly manicured lawns; further equipped with gardeners, maids, drivers and household workers. Most of the driveways were filled with luxury cars.

When leaving the inner city, we saw a woman on a hill urinating in a stream that flowed down toward the inner city. A few yards downstream, a woman hand washed clothing in the same stream. Where the stream flowed into a crossing stream at the bottom of the hill, we saw a woman dip water from the stream and pour it into a charcoal cooker where she cooked tidbits of food and sold it to passersby. Jitneys passed in both directions loaded to capacity, stopping at certain points. Clouds of dust rose and fell in their wake. The pedestrians on foot looked like dust monsters and it was hard to determine in the dust if they were male or female.

We drove through Petionville to the Baptist Mission operated by Dr. Wally Trumbull. We ate at the mission restaurant and looked out the window at the mountainside where the mission had taught the Haitians how to cultivate crops, to make marketable items for sale, to care for the sick and disabled, to vaccinate, and above all, how to believe in God and work toward being independent and self-sustaining.

I walked past the Medical Station to a house to visit Dr. Trumbull. An elderly lady immediately invited me into the house and offered food and refreshment before exchanging greetings. There was something angelic about her, possibly her faith, ability to discern good from evil, or her confidence and trust in mankind. After learning that Dr. Trumbull was off the island, I chatted with her in the shady comfort of the modest living room. I felt a strong sense of peace, calm, relaxation, acceptance, and affection; that I had never experienced before.

On J.J. Dessalines Avenue while en route back to the Royal Haitian hotel, a woman walked across the street in front of us that appeared inhuman. She walked on her hands with her knees striking the ground like a hyena. When she turned, twisted her body back and looked at us, her face seemed more animal than human.

The Haitian employees at the Royal Haitian hotel were extremely hesitant to talk and barely answered questions when asked, as though in fear. Nate, an American casino pit boss advised that Haitians are constantly watched by the Ton Ton Mercutes, the secret police established by Papa Doc (Baby Doc's father) and how their action mirrored that of Hitler's Gestapo.

On the next liaison trip, I went to Santo Domingo, Dominican Republic, located on the opposite end of the island of Hispanola with Haiti. The Dominicans, like Haitians, have heavy African influences. They were more talkative, friendly and outgoing. It was strange seeing men walking the streets with large wads of Dominican Pesos exchanging them for U.S. dollars at 4 pesos per dollar ratio. The pesos were spent as equal to the dollar in the businesses.

I consumed Dominican foods and walked the malecon (beach front), noting that the Dominican Republic was cleaner and more modern than Haiti. While in Haiti, I never saw a Haitian dance. In the Dominican Republic the people were gayer and danced the samba, merengue and salsa. Musicians played on the streets, in restaurants and bars along the malecon. While dining in a patio type restaurant on the malecon, prostitutes roamed the streets. I heard an American comment on how professional the Dominican prostitutes are, adding that he had heard they go to some school for prostitution and about their penchant for "leche especial."

At the same restaurant, I saw Nelson, reported to be the smallest living man. I took a photograph with him standing in my hand. He appeared to be less than two feet tall. After the photograph, Nelson advised me that I owed him $5 and remarked, "You don't expect me to pose for free do you?" Several tourists also posed and took photographs with Nelson for $5.

After arranging for the DEA Air Wing to conduct the marijuana over flights in Haiti, I was asked the seating capacity of the airplane, which was a total of four. When the DEA agent from my office and I met the DEA pilot at the airport in Port-Au-Prince, I was impressed.

The pilot, a sky cowboy, got out of the DEA plane wearing a Stetson hat, Ray Ban sunglasses, a cowboy shirt and cowboy boots with brass tips on the toes. The Haitian arrived with Captain Baguidy, a lieutenant and a soldier from their G-2 section. The DEA pilot realizing what was happening whispered, "I see what these assholes are doing to you John, I'll fix their asses. I'll have them puking their guts out after 10 minutes in the air." The pilot kept his promise. When they returned about 30 minutes later, the two military officers had vomitus all over the front of their uniforms. Captain Baguidy, the sickest of the three, had puked and re-ingested his own vomitus. He had a hangover and an askance look about his face, as though he was being mistreated. When the pilot advised he was ready to resume the over flight and said, "Let's saddle up and finish this, we only have about an hour more," they wimped out. The liaison DEA agent and the DEA pilot completed the over flights. I traveled to Haiti on about 10 subsequent occasions.

I made several liaison visits to St. Thomas, U.S. Virgin Islands, meeting frequently with the attorney general and the Narcotic Strike Force. Task Force Director Wilfred Barry challenged me to participate in their Carnival. After several requests, I finally gave in and "jumped up" in the Carnival in April of 1985 as Vision, a member of his 150-member troupe called the Raunchy Bunch. I saw huge woofers and tweeters, some taller than a man, on the back of flat bed trucks, beating loud enough to make your heart thump harder. In the village, vendors sold fungi, wilkes, salt fish, conch, crab cakes, rum and coke and a mean drink called "kerosene mint." Moki Jumbi (stilt walkers) stepped off the roofs of buildings and tied down their stilts and walked like giants down Main Street and Veterano Avenue. The parading troupes danced to the music of Bob Marley, Chalkdust, the Mighty Sparrow and various other noted Caribbean groups. Some sang "Soca Rock." The jump bands one on each end of Veterano Avenue brought the jubilators to a "Clash" at a center point where they danced against each other, with the loud music from both jump bands trying to play louder than the other. The array of colorful costumes and the music created an aura of magical awe, a feeling of relaxation, thrills, excitement and joy; it was like nothing I'd ever experienced.

I had a great time dancing the mile distance in the hot sun and eating bull foot soup for energy. Miraculously, a part of our troupe, which I was in, was photographed and the picture was used to advertise Carnival for the following year, in 1986.

XVI

WHILE RETURNING TO Puerto Rico from another Haiti trip, I was apprised that Maurice Bishop, the Prime Minister of Grenada had been assassinated. The next Saturday, I received a personal telephone call from Dominica's Chief of Police J. D. Blanchard inviting me to have dinner with Dominica's Prime Minister, Eugenia Charles and Commodore Diego Hernandez at the U.S. Navy base at Roosevelt Roads, Puerto Rico. I informed Blanchard that protocol required that I receive an invitation from the host before I could attend such a function. Shortly thereafter, I received a warm invitation from Commodore Hernandez, which I accepted.

I had met Hernandez earlier when I arrived in Puerto Rico. When Blanchard introduced me to Prime Minister Eugenia Charles, I was in awe meeting such a stately Black lady. We had a delicious meal and an interesting, nonpolitical conversation afterwards. As the Commodore escorted Prime Minister Charles around, Blanchard and I chatted for a while. I reminded Blanchard of the first time I'd ever eaten a cucumber sandwich, which was at a hotel in Dominica. When departing, I thanked Commodore Hernandez for the dinner, bade farewell with PM Charles and advised her that I would visit her beautiful country again.

A few days later, the United States invaded Grenada. I saw PM

Charles on television, participating in a press conference with President Ronald Reagan about the invasion. Prior to the invasion, I had never really cared for Reagan as an actor or president. I gained a lot of respect for him for his decisive actions in Grenada, Libya, and Iran during the Hostage Crisis; not the Iran Contra incident, and his conversation with Gorbachev regarding tearing down the Berlin Wall.

I later had a dislike for him regarding his aid to Iran, a purported enemy. In the Iran Contra incident, despite an embargo, in 1985 President Reagan secretly authorized the sale of weapons to Iran in their war with Iraq. Iraq at that time was a closer American ally. He used Israel as a broker and transshipment point. I telephoned the American Embassy in Bridgetown, Barbados regarding possible assistance to Grenada after the invasion. I was taught a new synonym for invasion; I was told that the U.S. had made an incursion into Grenada, not an invasion.

About three weeks later, I made a liaison visit to Grenada and was shown several mass graves where the Cuban and Russian troops were billeted. My escort told how harsh and disrespectful the Russians and Cubans had been to the Grenadians, how they had mistreated and slapped them around.

My escort related that when the Cubans and Russians turned on then Prime Minister Bishop, they gathered several crowds of people, including women and children at the rear of the police station and shot them. They fell off the cliff into the bay. He related that he had been placed on the wall with a group and was in the process of being shot when one of the soldiers, a friend, recognized him and allowed him to leave. Immediately after he ran from behind the police station, he heard people being shot, crying and falling off the cliff.

According to the escort, the smell of death filled the air for several days thereafter. The Grenadans then realized that their fate was in the hands of their captors, intruders who had initially duped them under the guise of providing aid. While relating the incident, the escort trembled and at one point cried briefly.

On the second night in Grenada, while having dinner I met an unusual man. A White male approached me and asked to join me for dinner. He introduced himself as Carl and asked what brought me to "this neck of the woods." I purposely lied to Carl telling him my name was Wilburn and that I was with the U.S. Department of Agriculture (USDA), Foreign Reforestation Program. Carl remarked, "That is strange, I am also with the USDA, but with the Aphis Section. I knew then the identity of Carl's employer.

Carl chatted idly about the incursion and related how unsure he was for the need of an invasion. At one point he opined that the CIA and Department of Defense had concocted an activity that had threefold benefit: (1) one could test its intelligence, (2) define its weakness to obtain additional funding, and (3) could assess their operations in a real environment interacting with the military. According to Carl, the military could utilize the incursion as on-the-job training for additional funding.

Carl then shifted the conversation to the medical school in Grenada. He then explained how all the "White quality students who had been denied entrance to medical schools in the United States, due to quotas and limits set by Affirmative Action; and in order to thwart Affirmative Action efforts, they had to establish a medical school "to accommodate those qualified students." According to Carl, all of the students were White and mostly Jewish. Carl went into a long diatribe about the Jews causing the incursion and that they were in control of everything. Carl believed that the incursion was initiated, by some rich Jewish politician, to protect the students affected by the Cubans and Russians in Grenada.

I have been known to be a talker but I could not get a word in edgewise with Carl. He only paused to inhale and he immediately started talking rapidly and gesticulated with his hands as though acting or role-playing. After quickly finishing my meal, I told Carl to excuse me and attempted to leave. He grabbed my arm and stated. "Look Wilbur or John whatever your name is, it is John isn't it? Anyway if you ever want a real job, call me." Carl then handed me a business card, from Evergreen International, with several telephone numbers in the Miami area and two 800 numbers.

I was then convinced of Carl's identity, especially his conversational mode to elicit information. I did not bite on his bait alluding to racial differences involving Affirmative Action or his comments about the Jews. Although he mentioned Affirmative Action several times, at no time did he mention it benefiting Blacks, nor did he use or refer to Blacks in his conversation.

On the next day, the escort took us on a tour of the island. I was entertained by its beauty, the thick heavy foliage green canopy forests, the numerous small mountains, foothills each crested with green trees, a deep green that appeared unaffected by the sun.

At Gand Anse Beach, I saw beautiful women, mostly tourists of European descent, basting gingerly on the white salt-like sandy beach. Local vendors sold a variety of items along the shore. I walked barefoot on the sandy beach and felt the warmth of the sand on my feet; it was very soothing and relaxing. I saw tides come in; forming small white frothy pools and go back out to sea as clear water.

I was approached by a vendor carrying a liquid in plastic bottles wrapped around his neck, shoulders and arms like a bandoleer. He related they contained a tea made from a root called bois ban de, only grown in Grenada. The vendor related that it was the only true aphrodisiac in the world.

We drove to St. Mark's Bay, Victorian Pearl's Beach, and back to Greenville, St. David's and Westerbil. One of the most beautiful things I experienced in Grenada was the friendliness of the native people. They smiled frequently and were very proud people. Almost all Grenadans I met had small stories to tell.

I had a long conversation with my escort before leaving. He told me that I was rich and related richness to owning a home, clothing, a refrigerator with food, color television and a car; the ability to drive anywhere I desired, see different movies and eat various types of food. The escort related that spices are the major source of income in Grenada. I learned that Grenada produces 20 percent of the world's nutmeg.

I had never assessed richness like he imagined and then decided to really assess why I love America. Although we have murders in most of our cities, we do not have the mass murder that he had experienced. We do not have a government easily subjected to dictatorial rule. We are able to redress a grievance in a court system. Perhaps, most importantly we are a self-sustaining country. We have our own military, own currency, own strong government that is fail-safe from coups, military juntas, egotists, conquering countries and hostile forces.

All U.S. soldiers in Grenada were being treated as heroes, as welcomed liberators. I met the commander, a tall Black U.S. colonel, who strutted proudly about the garrison and in the city. I met the interim Chief of Police who was from Bridgetown, Barbados. Even the handful of representatives forces from the Eastern Caribbean countries were welcomed, proud and had been part of history in the retaking of Grenada. It made them and their mother island country aware, of just how vulnerable they are to hostile forces.

Our escort was very impressed with the U.S. intelligence capabilities. He related that the U.S. had filmed the massacre behind the police station via satellite. According to the escort, he personally viewed the film and saw several children killed and some who, upon seeing their parents gunned, down jumped to their death.

Although we had rescued the Grenadians from communist influence, assisting them in establishing a government should not reflect puppetry on our part; but should be considered as helping a friend in need.

I learned from PM Charles that in crucial times when friendly countries are invaded, help must be sought from larger friendly nations. I have tremendous admiration for her introspection and prediction in Grenada. I admire her most, for all the eastern Caribbean island leaders; being the only one who immediately stepped up to the plate and asked for assistance.

I admire PM Charles for being the first Black Prime Minister in the Caribbean, possibly the first in the world. I have the utmost respect and admiration for her ability to navigate in troubled waters and to avoid pitfalls that some of her colleagues fell into without much thought. Perhaps mostly, I admire her for the lead she took in bringing her island country into the world view, how she sought infrastructure and growth for her country, how she unselfishly worked hard for such little pay, but for the cause of her country.

XVII

ONE DAY THE DCM in Haiti telephoned and advised that a coup d'etat was taking place in Haiti. He requested that DEA San Juan limit all agency personnel travel to that location until further notice. The specific information that he provided, led me to strongly believe that he was orchestrating the coup.

Two days later the DCM called again and advised that the Haitians were releasing four Americans who had been arrested there on two separate occasions, with a ton of cocaine. We had on the first occasion attempted to take custody of the Americans but they were somehow unexpectedly released. The DCM related that the Minister of Justice had granted pardons and amnesty to all inmates in custody in Haiti but he had the foursome kept in custody for expulsion to the United States. With the Baltimore DEA Office, we completed the expulsion and flew them via a chartered airplane from Port-au-Prince non-stop to Guantanamo, U. S. base in Cuba.

A few days later, the DCM called and advised that Colonel Albert Pierre, who had escaped the rioters and was in hiding in the confines of a South American embassy, wanted to talk to DEA, specifically he wanted to talk to me. The DCM related that Baby Doc had been placed on a plane to Paris, but somehow had escaped from the plane before it took off, went back into the Presidential Palace and announced on the radio that he was, as in control as a monkey's tail. I was convinced that the DCM was orchestrating the coupe when he advised, "He is leaving Haiti whether he likes it or not, one way or the other."

Agent Walter Brown and I took an Air France flight to Port-au-Prince and upon arrival saw large crowds roving the streets around the airport and at the airport. As we walked outside to the rental car, a crowd of Black males attacked a Black muscular man. They beat and kicked him to death, then ripped off his clothing, doused him with kerosene and burned his body.

As we were departing the airport toward the embassy, we saw two men, each burning inside of a stack of old tires. Rioters ran the streets yelling, screaming and jubilating. The smell of burning human flesh and rubber filled my lungs with an odor I can never forget. While meandering out of the paths of rioters, we passed a BMW dealership previously owned by Michele Bennett's (wife of Baby Doc) father that was demolished. There were many wrecked, destroyed, overturned and burning BMWs about the area. North of the Iron Market, I saw several men freshly placed inside of burning tires and heard them scream until silenced by their death. In a short distance a large mob of rioters trudged almost rhythmically up the street in front of us several carrying what appeared to be placards. As they came closer to our location and we turned down the street in front of them, I saw that they were not placards but two human heads on sticks. We drove on toward the embassy as rioters flitted across in front of our car; throwing stones and sticks at certain passing cars.

As we parked on the street in front of the embassy, a Haitian man carrying a plastic pail of water and dirty rags walked up and started washing the rental car without even speaking. We joined the DCM and went over to the South American country embassy where we met former Colonel Albert Pierre. Colonel Pierre was calling in his chips by relating how he had cooperated with DEA during his tenure and cited several instances that I confirmed. He then requested to be transferred to the Miami area. As I was about to respond, the DCM interrupted and advised that he would handle the matter. He then related that he had moved Colonel Pierre's family safely to Miami but was certain that Colonel Pierre would be immediately recognized and would likely be killed in Miami. The colonel looked curiously at me. I agreed that he was an easily recognizable person and that the DCM was accurate in his assessment. I then sat and listened to the entire conversations of the DCM, other country embassy officials and Colonel Pierre. It was apparent Colonel Pierre was an operative for the agency, within the U.S. Embassy, as well as the other country. He was now calling in his chips; neither country was paying as he had expected. The colonel had been placed in a position, wherein; he now realized that he had been utilized in a way that made him the number one enemy of his own fellow countrymen. He had been made a puppet and now must move in accordance to the directions of his puppeteers.

The colonel was now a man without a country, a man with a death wish price on his head that he himself had placed there; by being the wild animal his handlers directed him to be. At the behest of his handlers, the colonel had tortured and killed thousands of innocent men, women and children, in part, because he had been elevated into a position to do so. The very sad part about it all, the colonel had been licensed to kill, had been given the green light to kill at his discretion, as long as the victims were of his own race; not white or passé blanc. A DEA agent advised he had seen Quarter Bouquet, where Colonel Pierre had tortured and killed the thousands of Haitians.

He described it as similar to the WW II death camps, with an eerie look and deadly smell. I did not want to view it; for having realized what the colonel had done irritated me beyond words. I surmised that his handlers realized that he had killed enough, that at some point his killing had to stop.

It was very disappointing that I had associated and worked with this little monster, devil, killer, torturer; who now at the end of his career, is powerless like a baby in his own country seeking safety from strangers and safety from his own fellow countrymen.

While sitting across from him I had to suppress laughter upon learning that he had eluded the rioters by dressing as a female; this most feared, most powerful, most influential, now existing as most nothing person. I sat and watched his handlers talk condescendingly to him, offering him nothing for his prior services and discouraging him from thinking about ever being reunited with his family again. I could not imagine what he must think and feel, especially now that his oppressed citizens have the gun. I immediately thought of an expression I had heard my mother say several times, "Hunting ceases to be fun when the rabbit has the gun."

Little did the colonel know or realize that his handlers knew beforehand how his fate would evolve, how he would be separated from country, job, home, family, and friends and be reduced to nothingness. They (the Coup managers) had already made plans for General Namphy to become the interim ruler of Haiti.

I learned that Colonel Pierre had been a holdover from Papa Doc's regime. Papa Doc had used him like a dog. It was reported that he rode with him and if Papa Doc saw someone he disliked, he would sic the colonel on him or her. The colonel, a boy at the time, would beat men for Papa Doc. The men were afraid to talk or fight back in fear of Papa Doc's revenge.

I learned a very interesting historical lesson from Haiti. That despite being the second republic in the Western Hemisphere, and since first singing and chanting "Gonaives, Gonaives, Gonaives," Haiti historically has been the victim of numerous interventions, agent provocateurs, puppet mastering countries and today actually exists in a climate of slavery. Seeing people scared to speak is frightening in itself. Seeing the people suspecting that they are being watched and not knowing the identity of the watcher often causes suspicion within families and reflects a sad way of life that does not occur in America.

I was more than certain that America had put the coup d'etat in action.

I started losing the little respect I had hesitantly garnered for President Reagan, knowing that this orchestrated violence could not have been set in motion without his stamp of approval.

It was not surprising that they had selected General Namphy as the interim ruler of Haiti. It was not surprising that the Haitian military and police reacted as directed by the coup master planners, that they immediately became dysfunctional and submissive.

I learned there are countries with the wherewithal, that prey on developing countries they frequently called Third World. The United States is not the only country involved in puppetry. There are eight major countries involved on almost a larger scale as the United States. The master and originator is the British Empire, now called Great Britain.

A most important lesson I learned from my Haiti experience was finally recognizing how expendable humans are to their own kind and to others who are different. There are certain people who have the ability to torture and kill without remorse. There are governments that willingly propagate such activities under the guise of national interest.

Haiti, our neighbor and friend in the Western Hemisphere, is the poorest nation in the west and could possibly be the poorest in the world. Although Haiti has never been hostile to the United States, we as a friend and neighbor have done little to nothing to assist in its further development.

Up to this point in my life I had seen a lot, riches, beautiful mansions, valuable paintings, expensive cars, yachts, boats, planes, jewelry, Rolex watches, various precious stones and attractive and alluring women. There is nothing in the world that could make me into what I found Colonel Pierre to be. Hereafter, I vowed to be more cautious and less trusting of people like him. Albeit, he was used, discarded and stripped of everything, he emerged ahead of the game, because he came out alive, despite all the people he had tortured and killed.

One week Senator Strom Thurmond visited Puerto Rico on a boondoggle and was hosted by then U.S. Attorney Danny Lopez-Romo. I met with them briefly and sensed a racial coldness about the senator that was inexplicable. I immediately recalled an old television clip of Senator Thurmond spewing the word Niggers in his speech. Even then his mouth was fixed like he was about to say "Niggas". When I looked in the face of Senator Thurmond, all I could see and sense were intense racial hatred emitting from him. The few words he spoke in my presence seemed as though he had pain in doing so. To me, his whole aura depicted what I had seen in the past, in extremely racially biased persons. I surmised that seeing him in person and realizing his racial history, rather outspoken dislikes for Blacks was the root of my angst. I made an intense and successful effort avoiding him throughout his visit.

Shortly after Senator Thurmond's visit, the Task Force office developed information that a prominent defense attorney was introducing cocaine into the Rio Piedras Prison. A thorough investigation was conducted and a plan was devised to arrest the attorney in the process of delivering cocaine to an inmate at the prison. The attorney was subsequently arrested along with another subject in the process of delivering the cocaine to an inmate inside of the prison.

At the time of arrest, the U.S. Attorney for the District of Puerto Rico, an apparent friend of the crooked attorney, was on vacation in Spain. Upon his return, he immediately tried to accuse me of misusing one of his Junior Assistant U.S. Attorneys. He then tried to belittle me, and my position, as office head by insisting that I appear before the U.S. Magistrate when the arrested attorney appeared. I found it most unusual that a person in his position would stoop to such a low level of professionalism, and in doing so; try to down play the seriousness of the offense. In my conversation with the U.S. Magistrate prior to the arrest, he advised that he was also a friend of the attorney, however, he did not waiver in the issuance of a provisional warrant.

I learned that in certain circles, there are occupants of fiduciary positions who readily bend and waiver to curry favors for friends, despite the seriousness of their involvement in criminal or amoral activities. There are others who take their positions and duties very seriously and at decision-making times will fulfill their obligations and duties in a fair and just manner— they believe in fairness and justice for all.

On several occasions, I traveled to the beautiful island of St. Maarten/ St. Martin, an approximately 23 square mile island equally divided between France and the Netherlands: one half French-ruled and the other half Dutch-ruled. It was ironic seeing the descendants of African slaves speaking Dutch, French and Papimiento, a Dutch Creole language. I enjoyed working with both the Dutch police and the French gendarmes. I got to know St. Maarten's legendary police detective Jack Monsanto, a highly professional and respected man. I had angst about visiting with the French on the other half of the island because they always brought out the whiskey tray to celebrate, regardless whether it was early morning, afternoon, evening or night. Today I still have a stereotype of the French, that is, I believe they have the strongest livers of all nationalities; they are big-time imbibers with strong penchants for brown water (alcoholic beverages).

While in charge of the San Juan DEA District Office, I received an unusual request from Senator Richard Lugar's Office in Washington, D.C. A judge from the Midwest was with his wife, mother and friends vacationing on Saint Eustatius, a Dutch Caribbean Island. After, an argument with his wife, he decided to go climb the Quill, a dormant volcano, by himself. The judge left the hotel by taxi and when he did not return in two days, his family became alarmed that something untoward had happened to him.

I contacted Senator Lugar's office and was put in contact with the judge's family. They had contacted everybody they could and had reached a dead end. The family was desperate to have a major search of the volcano area made, as soon as possible.

After thoroughly coordinating with the appropriate authorities and receiving $10,000 from the judge's family, I assigned two DEA agents and 15 Puerto Rico Police Swat Officers, in two rented airplanes to Saint Eustatius, where they searched the entire volcanic mountain and rain forest crater, but did not find the judge. During the search, they encountered a family friend in the area.

About a month later, I received a telephone call from a man who identified himself as a friend of the missing judge's family. He related that he had an unusual request, for my assistance in further search for the judge. He wanted to travel to Haiti and consult with a voodoo doctor (VD) to determine if he could shed some light on locating the missing judge. Initially I thought the call was a prank, especially after surmising that the caller was a White male. The caller advised that we could use a VD in Puerto Rico if one was available. He was flying into San Juan that Friday and gave me his flight information.

I telephoned a friend and told her what had happened. She gave me a telephone number to a voodoo doctor in Carolina. I telephone the VD and told him about the pending client. The VD related that he could "enter into the environment where the judge could be reached whether live or dead." He needed a personal item of the judge in the session. I telephoned the family friend and advised what was required.

That Friday I met with the family friend upon his arrival at Munoz Marin International Airport. I spent about an hour chatting with him in a restaurant inside of the airport to discern if he was sane. The friend of the family strongly indicated that he was not representing the family. We drove over to the VD's house, located behind Basic Supermercado. As we entered the house, I saw two goat heads, one brown and black and the other white with a black spot on the tiled floor. There were several glasses filled with water turned upside down in saucers, feathers were attached to the saucers with what appeared to be dried blood. There were lit blue candles in the room. The VD, a tall, robust, effeminate black male quoted prices and related that his services would cost several hundred dollars. I thought I was hallucinating when the VD told the friend of the family, if he was able to reach him alive that he would try to get a telephone number or address.

When he asked for the personal item belonging to the judge, the family friend gave him a shirt. The VD took the shirt, felt it and rolled his eyes back into his head almost completely concealing his pupils and closed his eyes. He trembled then jerked his body forward, opened his eyes and asked, "Is this some kind of joke?" I was taken aback by his question and noticed that the friend of the family seemed somewhat pleased and asked, "What do you mean?" The VD advised, "This is not the personal item of the missing person. I feel strong deception here." The friend of the family left the house and retuned and handed the VD a blue dress shirt. The VD then told me to leave the room. I walked into the kitchen and stayed near the door.

I heard the VD go into a sort of ritual, gasping for breath and calling the judge, by his first name, to step forward, pled then commanded him to step forward. He then appeared to talk to the judge. He never repeated the judge's purported answers and ranted on in a gibberish tone for several minutes, uttering nonsensical phrases. I heard the friend of the family tell the VD to tell the judge that he was completely forgiven by his wife. Ask him to come home or call a friend. I did not hear the VD make the requests. A short time later, the VD calmed down and chanted unintelligible words as though talking in tongues. When the friend of the family and the VD came out of the room, the VD was wringing wet from perspiration. The friend of the family had not perspired. After sitting down and drinking water, the VD's skin seemingly turned darker, pale and ashy. The VD then related that he had seen the judge in a whorehouse in Trinidad, sitting half-dressed between two robust light complexion females of Trinidadian descent. He further advised that the judge had become extremely dejected and disappointed with his marital life and career and had gone to Trinidad for a new life. According to the VD, the judge had no intentions of ever returning to the states; he has gone underground for the rest of his life. He then told the friend of the family that the judge only came forward on the agreement that there would be no friends, relatives or law enforcement personnel involved. The VD added that had the friend of the family made inquiries of the judge, he would have departed for good. The VD also added that he did not seek an address or telephone number from the judge because he feared the judge would abruptly leave the session.

The friend of the family paid the VD $300 and on the following day he left San Juan for Port-Au-Spain, Trinidad. For a long time, I could not believe that I had gotten involved in such witchcraft. I learned that with money, one is able to pursue almost any venture, including finding answers, whether they are real or unreal. I also learned that one tends to believe what one wants to believe, whether the information is true or false. While I do not believe in voodoo, I have seen some of the effects it has had on those who believe in it.

I never saw Colonel Pierre after the revolution (coup d'etat), which apparently was his coup de grace. I have seen Colonel Acedius Saint Louis on several subsequent occasions, about 10 years later in the United States; one was at the International Chiefs of Police National convention in Detroit, Michigan and at The National Organization of Black Law Enforcement Executive (NOBLE) National Conference in New Orleans, Louisiana. For some reason, I often saw Colonel Saint Louis as a very proud professional law enforcement executive, with a sense of care, concern and compassion for others and his profession. He did not have that cold, eerie look of anger, authority, revenge, grudge and lack of remorse on his face, as Colonel Pierre. I ponder, even today, if he was aware of the heinous and treacherous crimes and acts that had been committed by Colonel Pierre. I also wonder if he was aware that Colonel Pierre had been reduced to a level of ruin, separated from his family, having to seek protection in his own country from strangers, and sent into exile by non-countrymen.

While in Puerto Rico, I obtained custody of my two daughters. One year we flew back to Los Angeles for the Christmas holidays. The day after our arrival, my daughters had eye infections in both eyes. I telephoned Dr. Woods office and was given an appointment for that afternoon. The male receptionist asked my name and I gave him my name and the names of my daughters. Shortly upon entering the waiting room of Dr. Woods' office and speaking to waiting patients, a male voice stated, "Big John, I see you, Ila and Tinessa have arrived." I walked up to the receptionist and immediately detected that he was blind. He laughed when I asked him how he knew who I was and explained that he had recognized me by my voice. After hearing my voice on the telephone, the receptionist estimated my height at 6' 2" and my weight at about 225 pounds. He was correct on the weight and only off two inches in the height.

When Dr. Woods looked at my daughters, the first question he asked was if they were wearing new eye make-up. He looked at their eyes and advised that the make-up had caused the infection. I told Dr. Woods that I had been transferred to Puerto Rico and invited him to visit us sometimes in Puerto Rico. Having seen my daughters before, Dr. Woods commented on how pretty they had grown up to become and told me to continue taking good care of them.

I recall that over time, Dr. Woods and I had had many conversations about various things. Perhaps in one of those conversations, I apparently told him about my encounter with Reverend Farrell.

About two weeks after we arrived back in Puerto Rico, I received a letter from Dr. Woods encouraging that I find God again and to encourage my daughters to also find God. He also lauded me for quitting smoking and drinking.

I learned that Dr. Woods had experienced discrimination, disparate treatment and disappointments from White America. I laud him in continuing to move forward despite those pitfalls. I admire him mostly because he was a frugal man like my uncle, that flashy cars, jewelry, clothing, buildings, fancy foods and worldly things seemingly had little meaning in his life. I admire him equally for hiring a blind man and people from the community where he practiced.

Dr. Woods was a paradigm of a minority with a strong will to succeed, despite all racial obstacles. After obtaining his goal, he assisted others in pursuit of theirs. One of Dr. Woods' callings/gifts involves encouraging people to seek God. He has a gift to heal and a strong gift evangelizing for God. Hearing a doctor tell me to seek God was a blessing in itself. I will always remember Dr. Woods for the sage advice he provided.

I further admire him for his love for people, including aliens/foreigners, and especially, for learning their language in order to serve them better.

Prior to being assigned to Puerto Rico, I had no concept of the knowledge of its Commonwealth status, and like many uninformed Americans believed that there was an U.S. Embassy in Puerto Rico. I had little knowledge of the U.S. Virgin Islands as well, however, I did recall that before Black American females, because of their race, were allowed to participate in Miss America and Miss Universe pageants, that there were Black females from U.S. Territories participating in them.

I made liaison visits to Anguilla and met with Chief Joseph Payne and his Deputy Chief Richardson. Subsequent to the visit, DEA agents from my office assisted the Anguillan police in the seizure of over 800 kilograms of cocaine that was flown from Colombia to Scrub Island, Anguilla. After the seizure, I had the cocaine shipped to the DEA Laboratory in Miami.

A few months later, a DEA agent was indicted involving that seizure. Several months later the British Governor of Anguilla requested that the cocaine be turned over to the British government under some assertion that it had medicinal value.

It was difficult explaining that the street value of the cocaine was an estimate, as it related to the underground criminal culture. Even, after being told that the cocaine had been made in a jungle, non-sterile environment and likely contained many impurities, the governor would not relent. It was apparent that his duty in the British island was to garner things of value for the United Kingdom.

I became aware that even today, Great Britain owns land, even Crown property almost all over the world, especially in previously ruled areas.

XVIII

SHORTLY UPON MY arrival in Puerto Rico, I met then Governor Carlos Romero-Barcelo at a meeting of heads of federal and local agencies. The meeting was held at La Fortaleza, the governor's mansion. I wore a navy blue suit and a white and navy necktie. Of all the agency executives present, Governor Romero paid special attention to me and mentioned my name on several occasion. Shortly after leaving the meeting, the head of U.S. Customs asked me how long had I known the governor and remarked that the gist of the governor's conversation gave the impression that we were old friends.

After I arrived back at the office, my secretary explained why the governor was so friendly toward me. I, unbeknownst, had worn his party colors, blue and white. I had a good work relationship with the governor, other federal and local agency heads.

I met a few Puerto Ricans who harbored a strong dislike for America. They view the relationship as a type of colonial rule. There were terrorist groups, like Los Macheteros, and others that espoused strong hatred and dislike for America. One fired a light, anti-tank missile at the communications area of the FBI headquarters. Prior to my arrival, one group had attacked a U.S. Naval facility at Sabana Seca. Two or more murders were committed daily in the greater San Juan area.

There were two major outlaws, one called "Paco, El Carnicero" who reportedly had butchered two males, by cutting their bodies into 69 different segments and wrapping them in plastic bags; I saw the photographs.

As the DEA office head, one of my primary responsibilities involved the safety of DEA personnel and families, including Puerto Rican police officers assigned to the task force. The office had an area of responsibility covering: two U.S. Districts (District of Puerto Rico and District of the U.S. Virgin Islands), Haiti, the Dominican Republic, the British Virgin Islands, St. Kitts/Nevis, Antigua/Barbuda, Montserrate, Anguilla, St. Maarten/St. Martin, St. Barthelemy, Martinique, Guadalupe, Barbados, Dominica, St. Lucia, St Vincent, Grenada, Saba and St. Eustatius.

It is unfortunate, that I had a very prejudiced WASP for my immediate supervisor. Since he has passed on, I will refer to him as a Feckless Manager (FM) and not elaborate too much on what I had to undergo, while working under his supervision. Perhaps, most bothersome was that he was ignorant, sometimes too ignorant to suppress his racial biases toward me and other non-WASPs. On every occasion he found an opportunity, he tried to berate me, but not in my presence.

The FM was angered beyond comprehension when we were at the embassy in Panama going into the Skiff for a briefing. He was not allowed entry into the Skiff because of a lack of sufficient security clearance. His ego was totally deflated when I was admitted and he was not. FM turned red and asked loudly, rudely and profanely, "How can this motherfucker be allowed inside and I can't and he works for me?" His question fell on deaf ears.

Upon our return arrival at Miami International Airport, FM, not knowing I was standing behind him at the luggage carousel, blurted out to the FBI agent standing next to him, "Can you believe this Black Nigger motherfucker makes over $100,000 a year," referring to the Black skycap that was removing luggage from the base of the carousel.

After realizing I had heard his racially derogatory remark, FM all of a sudden wanted to help me clear U.S. Customs, as though I was an alien without a passport and needed assistance. I had a White friend in the Miami office, purported to be one of FM's boys, and advised me that, often in certain circles, FM referred to me as the "Nigger in Charge" of my Puerto Rico office.

FM was one of the most biased White persons I had ever met. Although he tried to mask it, often he would display it, especially after consuming a few beverages. It was very difficult being supervised by an overt racist who lacked the finesse to mask his biasness.

The FM tried to undermine me on numerous occasions and when caught in the act he merely lied, denied and lied again. It bordered on being criminal, having a government employee, in the Senior Executive Service, with such bias and malevolence toward a subordinate employee or civilian based strictly on race.

I learned from the FM biases that there is nothing one can do to change a person's dislike for another person; whether it is based on race, creed, national origin, sex, financial status, size, shape or political affiliations. Individuals like the FM will forever exist and do those inhumane, silly, biased and unfair things they desire without remorse of afterthought or that the same could happen to them. They could never believe that "the rabbit could have the gun." I learned not to hate people, despite what they did, tried, will try do to me. I was able to reach back and grasp wisdom from my mother by "fighting evil with kindness. Instead of using violence, use high mindedness to overcome anger and evil intentions."

I mentioned the FM, not to vent any hidden or deep-seated anger, but because Blacks often tend to accept disparate treatment in work and non-work situations as a way of life. In doing so, to the twisted perpetrators it provides psychological support that this is what is expected. I also mentioned the FM because I am aware what many Blacks encounter in the workplace, whether from a worker bee, to a top management, or executive position. I further mention him because most Blacks today are naïve and continue to think that they are playing on a level field. I harbor no dislike for the FM and pray that he did cross over into heaven; despite his shortcomings.

Living in Puerto Rico for four years increased my love for America, for the good life, the foods, the beauty, climate and perhaps most importantly, the friendliness of the Puerto Rican people. Although a commonwealth, there are equally strong political factions favoring status quo or statehood; it is a hidden American paradise.

How could I not love America having a territory like Puerto Rico? I enjoyed body surfing on the beaches, the various towns— each with a history of it own, the villages, sunsets, dances, beaches, the kiosks on the balenarios, virgin pina coladas, conch salad, octopus salad, pollo, cold coconut juice, the sweet green oranges, roasted chicken from Bebo's, canapers, fried platanos, amarillas, bread fruit, Guanabana, mangoes, arroz con gandules, arroz con pollo, the beautiful flowers, the beautiful bird of paradise, the yellow, red, orange, lavender and purple majestic bougainvillea, banana trees, ferns, the magnificent flamboyant tree, and the exotic mari vivir plant that moves when touched.

I enjoyed watching the wind surfers at Isla Verde, fishing from Dos Hermanos bridge, the bridge to Loiza, Fajardo, Catano, Aricebo & Cayo Icacos; buying native food from kiosks at Loquillo Beach, dancing the merengue, salsa, cha-cha-cha, and samba at Loiza and Loiza Aldea; listening to the music of Willie Colon, Ruben Blades, Johnny Ventura, Celia Cruz, Menudo, Iris Chacon, Lourdes Chacon, Charatin; watching old timers play dominos and checkers in the plazas and talking about days long passed.

I enjoyed numerous visits to El Yunque (the tropical rain forest), the little towns and villages of Jayuya, Adjuntas, Utuado, San German, la Parguera, Boqueron, Mayaguez, Maricabo, Anasco, Aguadilla, Santurce, Quebradillas, Camuy, Arecibo, Manati, Vega Baja, Trujillo Alto, Bayamon, Catano, Hato Rey, Carolina, Isla Verde, Caguas and the hand drawn ferry across the river into Loiza Aldea.

It was beautiful seeing the old timers in the various little towns sitting at a bodega, drinking a Cuba Libra (rum & coke with a lime twist) and dreaming of times from their pasts; listening to most of them laying claim to having served in the 65th Infantry, a heroic unit in WW II. They beamed with pride for having a major street named after their military unit. From the Puerto Rican inhabitants, I learned a strong sense for family, fellowshipping with family, maintaining contact with family members, including distant relatives. Despite a prevailing near perfect climate that is conducive to outdoor living, I found far fewer homeless people in Puerto Rico, than in eastern and northern cold wintry cities, which is attributable to the strong family ties that exist there.

I learned that most Puerto Ricans are proud of their Spanish and African heritage. Despite the prevailing hot weather, during most of the year, there is no siesta in Puerto Rico.

As my tenure came to a close, I somewhat dreaded leaving Puerto Rico, especially the friends I had made. Some of the sayings of old sages will be forever remembered, especially the moral meanings in them. One in particular, relates that a bird in the hand is worth more than a hundred flying.

XIX

THE MOVE FROM Puerto Rico, in the summer of 1986, to the Washington D. C. area was smooth and without much fanfare. Upon arriving back, I sensed a different America; as if I had been in a foreign country for a long period of time. I saw a flipping of the script in many areas.

I saw Black teens and young Black adults wearing their caps reversed, pants sagging, almost falling down around their ankles as they walked in a kind of shuffling motion. I heard words spoken that I did not know were in the English language, a kind of jargon completely alien to me, phrases and new idiomatic expressions that were difficult for me to discern. I heard Blacks referring to one another as "nigger" in one sense of endearment, in another sense to emphasize strength, power, hipness and camaraderie, to denigrate and to profoundly emphasize a point. I saw White teens and young White adults emulating Blacks in their dress, walk, talk, and action; often referred to as "wiggers" by some Whites.

Both groups drove cars with extremely loud woofers and tweeters and played music unbearably loud. I heard a new genre of music spouted by rappers screaming profanity and rhymes involving: bitches, whores, guns, dope and lawlessness. I noticed a strong trend among the youth, both Black and White, of admiring gangsters, criminal activities and lawlessness. I saw the emergence of violent street gangs in the Black,

194

White, Latino, and Asian communities. Some academicians opined that the basic cause for the emergence of gangs stemmed from a need for family, to belong, security and love.

I noted that the Federal Communication Commission gave sway to the recording industry and started allowing the most blatant profanity, lewd words and phrases to be broadcasted via our national airwaves, on radio and television.

I saw the proliferation of cocaine, specifically crack cocaine in the Black community, gradually spreading into other communities; open drug markets form on city streets and outside of crack houses female crack addicts clucking (begging to perform certain sexual acts for small amounts of money) in order to buy crack.

I saw White teens and young White adults in predominantly Black neighborhoods "copping" dope from street venders. As they departed the dope area, others came in and made their dope buys and drove back to the suburbs. I saw White punk rockers at the peak of the Punk Rock Mania coming down to some semblance of reality, but strongly leaning to join whatever was "in", despite how dangerous and outrageous it seemed to be. Some started inhaling gasoline fumes, secretly using heroin, speed, powder cocaine, and some marijuana with a content almost equal to hashish.

They started growing marijuana clandestinely on government lands in the U.S. parks and forests. They moved to indoor cultivating, eventually graduating to indoor hydroponic marijuana cultivation. They followed a Dutch master marijuana cultivator and developed a high THC content marijuana indoors, by isolating the female plant from the male plant.

They also used speed and other drugs. Some experimented with certain drugs to facilitate rape. Speed labs were set up in various places like hotel rooms, abandoned farm buildings, vacant inner city buildings, apartments, mobile homes, garages and other unsuspecting places. A large number were only detected by law enforcement after an explosion or fire.

Sixteen years later, the D.C. taxi drivers had not changed. They were still mostly foreigners and continued to hesitate to pick up Black fares. They bypassed Blacks whether dressed formally, casually or like a stereotypical robber.

I saw the murder rate increase in Washington, D.C. to such a level, that the media coined it Dodge City. Violent crime increased all over the

United States because of the Crack Phenomenon. There was a growing trend among young Black Americans to get rich and to get rich quickly, without putting forth much effort. Some pursued the drug business and others retired from the criminal life and while incarcerated decided to be rappers, rapping for a living. Some of the retired criminals only retired for short periods before re-entering the criminal world. While espousing violence, others apparently could not digress from old habits. The more bizarre and vulgar the song they produced, seemingly, the more successful the rapper became. Once famous, the movie industry grabbed some of the rappers and turned them into actors.

Education had become secondary and tertiary, with a desire to become rich quickly, being foremost in the minds of many. Most American universities, seemingly, started stressing athletics over academics. The more popular sports like baseball, football, basketball, boxing, soccer and any sport that lured students to the campus and provided revenue was emphasized.

I noted a drastic change in the lifestyle of academicians compared to the athletes. In the universities, Alumni Associations and Foundations (AAF) were formed and elevated to positions that now allow them to pay athletic coaches extremely high salaries, oftentimes, higher than chancellors, deans and presidents. In some cases coaches are paid two and three times more per year. I surmised that most of these coaches merely have bachelor degrees, a few with master's; as opposed to the requirement that deans, chancellors and presidents have doctorate degrees.

The AAF, in furnishing large amounts of monies to the universities, started, either making, causing or influencing major decisions for many universities and is now directly involved in compensation, the hiring and firing of coaches. Under this arrangement, some universities have easily and readily drifted from ensuring that students acquire a good education to ensuring that their school has a winning basketball or football team.

Coaches are, easily and often, fired for having losing teams. As one is fired, another coach plays musical chairs for his position, albeit for a short term. The firing is often laid at the feet of the chancellor or president of the institution, but in reality the AAF fires them.

A large percentage of athletes were being lured into displaying their athletic prowess over meeting academic requirements, thereby placing their mental ability to excel on hold. They are being encouraged to pursue certain majors and enroll in classes that require little mental assertion and very little effort. This process has resulted in producing a significant number of illiterate professional athletes. A former all-pro defensive lineman for the Washington Redskins immediately comes to mind. Out of this arrangement emerged the exorbitant cost of tickets for athletic events on the college and professional levels. Then came the commercialization of sports on both levels. During this same period, the use of certain drugs proliferated in many athletic areas. Legitimate pharmaceutical companies started experimenting with body enhancement drugs and graduated to steroids. Initially, steroids were used to treat injuries, strengthen muscles, tendons, cartilage and other body tissues.

Out of this great push for athletic prowess, Americans developed a habit we had often accused the Russians of doing, injecting their athletes with performance-enhancing drugs. Personal trainer positions emerged, further increasing the use of performance-enhancing drugs. It is amazing that, neither the pharmaceutical companies, nor the universities expended much effort on a drug, outside element or vitamin supplement to enhance one's mental ability.

The AAF plays a major role in this process. In some instances the AAF assists in finding ways to lure talented athletes to certain college campuses by providing certain perks to them and their families, under the table. To some, the athletes in these types of arrangements are big jokes. I strongly believe that they continue to have a major influence in causing some of the criminal behavior we currently see, involving certain athletes, especially the drug and chemical abusers.

Athletes involved in these processes; often, in retrospect view universities as crooked institutions wrought with wrongdoings, jokes, scammers, immoral; teaching coaches and athletes how to circumvent policy, guidelines, procedures and even the law.

It seemed that many Black athletes were being caught up in this trend. Many were recruited out of high school based on their athletic abilities with no intentions of them ever successfully completing college. Some parents received clandestine support and went along with the program, not caring whether the son received an education or not.

During this same period, Americans, with help from the media, in large numbers started admiring gangsters and criminal underworld characters, and those who broke the law and went unscathed. Mafia Don

John Gotti was profiled on numerous occasions and coined "The Teflon Don," indicating no criminal cases were provable against him. During this same time, Black rappers emerged spouting criminal activity and adopting criminal names. The mass media started glamorizing gangsters, advertently or inadvertently, depicting them beating the system, evading authorities and living the good life filled with: wine, beautiful women, pretty cars, luxurious homes and plenty of money.

Gangster rap started, eventually evolving into gangsta; they coined numerous words and phrases. Many of the West Coast rappers emerged out of Compton, California, where I started my law enforcement career. A significant number were small time hoodlums, street level drug dealers and petty criminals. They took profanity to a different level and redefined nigger to nigga, niggah and nig. They changed the word motherfucker to mothafucka and made it more derogatory by calling subjects "bitch ass motha fuckas".

The viler the lyrics and the more denigrating they were of Black females; resulted in increased and rapid sales of Compact Discs (CDs). Most of these rappers emerged from splintered, matriarchal-led families. Some had little or no knowledge of their father's identity.

Some were victims of "the crazy check syndrome (CCS)". This syndrome came about as a result of teachers, principals, school administrators and clinicians observing many Black children that were hyper, mostly from their food intake, and trying to rectify the problem by erroneously diagnosing that the student suffered from Attention Deficit Hyperactivity Disorder (ADHD). To purportedly correct this disorder, the student is administered a behavior modifying drug like Ritalin. Ritalin is purported to be a mild stimulant to the central nervous system.

Some studies reportedly have opined that a child on Ritalin is least likely to develop drug addictive habits. Some of the side affects of this drug are: dizziness, drowsiness, blurred vision, impaired concentration and growth suppression. I doubt if the schools in America, certainly knowing their cafeteria menus are deficient, have taken any steps to improve the diets to avoid or prevent ADHD in students. I believe it is widely known that the meals served in most school cafeterias are nutrient-poor: full of fats, sugars, dyes and chemicals that were long proven to have debilitating affects on frequent consumers. I surmise that the prevalence of diabetes, so widespread in our young children, in part, can be traced back to the poor food, mostly fast foods and junk foods that are served in our school cafeterias.

Once diagnosed or labeled ADHD, the child/family, depending on total family income becomes eligible to receive Supplemental Security Income (SSI). In the Black communities I saw Black men relinquish their responsibility of fatherhood; merely becoming sperm donors. There was an increase in young teenage girls, babies in reality, having babies. Their children grew up emulating their parent(s) by also having babies at an early age. As a consequence, they became mired in low-income jobs or unable to find a job.

A large number of low-income single parents have had their children declared or misdiagnosed ADHD, in order to receive additional income, SSI. In the public schools SSI recipients were called "crazy checkers" and jokes were often blurted out in school about them receiving a crazy check.

I found that the FCC completely failed in one of its critical responsibilities and has allowed the airwaves to be flooded with this blatant, deliberate increased and widespread vulgarity. Black families and Black institutions also failed in curtailing this flood of profanity, denigration of Black women and Blacks per se and ceded to commercialism.

Contemporaneous to this time, I saw a rapid increase in violence in many games, toys and video games; where children were allowed to simulate killing others, irregardless whether good guy or bad guy; simulate destroying property, defying authorities and walking away as victors. I read newspaper accounts of children: committing the most bizarre crimes, involved in mass murders, kidnapping, drive-by shootings, carrying, possessing and having access to a variety of firearms.

I saw an emergence of juveniles committing major crimes and saw the scale of their ages drop below the teenage level. Along with this, arose a tendency of the courts to charge juveniles as adults. The age to try a juvenile in some states dropped to almost the preteen age. The courts weighed heavily on the severity of the crime and viewed the mindset of the perpetrator, devoid of sufficient information regarding the causes.

In Washington, D.C. during my first winter, I saw many crowds of homeless people, mostly Blacks, walking the streets; some were women with under school age children. I was advised that the women with children were housed in a homeless shelter during the night but had to vacate the shelter doing the day; they could not return until 4:00 PM.

At D.C. General Hospital, I saw about twenty Black "crack babies" in playpens that resembled cages and animal pens. I learned that they were abandoned babies of crack-addicted mothers. I watched them play and noted that they had different behaviors than what I had seen in babies ranging from one to four years of age. Some were extremely aggressive and others were very withdrawn. A few were crybabies. I saw three Candy Stripers holding each baby for 10-minute periods. I learned that holding and cuddling a baby are necessary to promote their growth; that it took the hospital employees a long time to discern that this was why abandoned babies were not developing normally.

In the Washington, D.C. area I saw, for the first time, several Black grandmothers 29 and 30 years old; a perpetuation of babies having babies by young fathers barely into puberty. I saw a mindset of people with a strong penchant for lawlessness; formally educated workers with high paying U.S. Government jobs and poorly educated workers eking out a living, some working two jobs to make ends meet.

One of the best public transportation systems in the United States, I surmise, is the D.C. Metro system. It is clean, proficient, devoid of the crime usually associated with a mass transportation system, and is effectively operated.

The crime in D.C. was high with robberies, shooting and major crimes occurring throughout the city; but mostly in the residential areas, especially in the densely populated Black areas. On occasion, law enforcement personnel were reportedly robbed. Although being assigned to the DEA headquarters, most agents always went to and fro armed; some even wore their weapons inside of their office. One winter evening after work, I decided to join two coworkers for refreshments (coffee, water and soft drinks for me because I had broken the brown water habit i.e. drinking alcoholic beverages) at Mingles, a bar in a basement, diagonally across the street from the DEA headquarters at 14th and I Streets.

While sitting and chatting about the job and various other subjects, I noticed a large Black man staring at me on numerous occasions. On a couple occasions he seemed to increase his focus on me. On one occasion, he got up and walked past our location and returned to his table. After about an hour, we got up to leave. I noted this Black male also got up and started to leave. As we walked up to the street level, he followed us. The Black male then said, "Hey mister, you in the black coat; wait a minute!" I turned and faced the Black male; my right hand in my pants pocket with a 6.25 caliber, eight shot, automatic pistol aimed secretly at his torso. After I flipped the safety off, I responded, "Yes, what do you want?" He asked, "Are you John Sutton from Compton by any chance?" To which I replied, "Yes I am, do I know you?" The Black male then smiled and extended his hand to shake mine and related, "You might not remember, but you arrested me when I was a teenager driving a stolen 1964 Chevrolet." The Black male told me his name, showed identification of his employment with Xerox in Virginia. He even showed a pay stub, as an indication that he was very proud of his job, wages and lifestyle in the area. As my colleagues and I listened, the Black male related that I had made a major difference in his life. He related that after I arrested him, that I had lectured him about his ability to do something legal for a living and how I had described the unpleasantness of prison life. According to the Black male, no other male had ever talked to him in a fatherly way, until his arrest. He made a decision then, to change his life as he had promised me when I was placing him in the juvenile detention section of the jail.

With my ego inflated, I rode the metro home realizing that I had made a difference in someone's life. I recalled the difference the LASO deputy made 30 years ago in my life, in the incident at Mona Park with Leotis et al. I was in awe and found it difficult to believe that I was made aware of this incident almost 3,000 miles away from where it occurred and almost 20 years later. I felt very proud that my days as a Compton police officer were not in vain; very proud that I had somehow made a difference in someone's life that was not a relative.

During my first year at DEA headquarters, I was the Deputy Chief of the Cocaine Investigation Section. During that period, we initiated a major cocaine suppression effort by inserting U.S. troops and Black Hawk helicopters in Bolivia to assist the Bolivian authorities in locating and destroying clandestine cocaine labs in the heavily canopied jungles of Bolivia.

I traveled to La Paz, Bolivia during the onset of the operation and was assigned a hotel room on the 22nd floor. Immediately, I felt light headed, a shortness of breath and could hear my heartbeat in my chest. I went to bed to rest, thinking that the feeling would pass. While in bed, I noted my heart beat faster and the sound seemed louder. I surmised that I was reacting to the high altitude of the city and called the desk to inquire and advise how I was feeling. The receptionist advised that I was reacting to the high altitude and suggested that I go to the restaurant on the top level and drink a cup of tea.

I went to the restaurant and ordered a large cup of mate de coca tea. Immediately after consuming the tea, I felt better, relaxed, as though my heart had stopped beating rapidly and felt at ease. I drank another cup, returned to my room and fell asleep. On the following day, I was apprised that I had consumed a tea made from the coca plant and likely had ingested a small quantity of cocaine.

In the downtown section of La Paz I saw Bolivian Indian females "Pajaritas" wearing derby hats, shawls and plaid skirts sitting all over the city selling items. They closely resembled the American western Indians in complexion and mannerism.

That afternoon we flew a helicopter to Santa Cruz. As we were arriving at the airport, I gazed out the window and saw two of the largest airplanes in the world; the U.S. C-5A and the C-141. After we landed, the C-5A appeared to be as long as a football field and taller than many of the buildings in Washington, D.C. The nose of the C-5A was raised almost perpendicular to the ground and the rear doors were open. The soldiers pulled six Black Hawk helicopters from inside of the fuselage and readjusted their rotors, performed maintenance, and then they were flown away to the base camp.

I saw several Bolivian soldiers and Mobile Rural Patrol Unit (UMOPAR) soldiers inspecting the C-5A; in awe of its size, capabilities, shape, form and appearance. One of the UMOPAR soldiers remarked in English, "If I was fighting and saw the enemy coming at me with a plane this big, I will just shit my pants and quit."

On the following day, I joined other DEA agents and UMOPAR troops headed to a clandestine lab in the jungle. En route, I noted the UMOPAR troops were not crisp soldiers or crime fighters like other foreign counterparts. They were armed with old U.S. M-1 rifles and they carried their ammunition, about eight rounds, loosely in their fatigue pockets. While walking down a beaten path we passed two locations that appeared to have been a kind of squatters' camp. Shortly after leaving the second location, a chicken ran across the path between us. One of the UMOPAR soldiers ran after the chicken. A few minutes later, he joined us with the chicken strapped to his web belt, flipping from side to side as he walked. It was an amusing site.

From this little trip, I learned how powerful the United States military forces are and got an idea of the advance equipment available to them; that we are a world power with numerous assets that awe many foreigners around the world. I was fully aware how we were able to locate and target clandestine drug labs in the jungles of Bolivia without going there or devoid of "ground truthing". I am proud to be a citizen of a country with such technology.

When riding from La Paz Airport on dirt roads, I saw people walking, riding bicycles and in vehicles with opened windows that had no choice but to ingest the dust of passing cars. I became more appreciative of the things I have in America, with little to no thought about the things I did not have.

During this period I also traveled to Chile, Argentina, Peru, Ecuador, Colombia, Panama, Costa Rica, Brazil and Venezuela. None of these countries could compare to the amenities we enjoy in the United States. Almost all of the inhabitants I met in those countries expressed a desire to live in the United States. As Deputy Chief of the Cocaine Investigation Section, I traveled to the International Drug Enforcement Conference (IDEC) in Sao Paolo, Brazil. I thought New York, Los Angeles, Chicago, Philadelphia, Hong Kong, and Bangkok were large cities; until I saw Sao Paolo. It was so large I was afraid to venture on a walking tour. The IDEC conference was held in the Maksoud Hotel in the heart of Sao Paulo. I looked out the window of my 20th floor room and all I could see was city. I went into the hall and looked in both directions and saw the same, a large city that expanded beyond my ability to see. A few days later I went up to the Skyline Lounge for a panoramic view of the city. As far as I could see were buildings, houses and built up areas of a sprawling and massive city.

When I looked down on the busy streets, people afoot, on motorcycles and cars resembled a huge ant colony.

At the time the DEA Panama Country Attaché, was a former supervisor under me in San Juan when I was there. He advised that General Manuel Antonio Noriega was flying to Sao Paulo to attend the IDEC.

I witnessed his arrival at the hotel, noting that it resembled that of the president of the United States when traveling. Some of the most beautiful women from Panama were in General Noriega's entourage. He was a short little man with dents in his face. The nickname cara pina (pineapple face) was apparently due to his pockmarked face. General Noriega winked at me as he passed with five lovely young women following him. Although he appeared to be about 5'4" tall, he had an ego and the aura of a giant.

My opinion of his huge ego was strengthened when I saw his entrance to the Plenary Session. He was escorted up to the dais by a colonel and his slow walk was reminiscent of a king's arrival. I was told that he was a puppet dictator, installed by a former head of the CIA and former U.S. President.

During my tour in Puerto Rico, Noriega had been very cooperative assisting the U.S. in expulsion of wanted criminals from Panama back to the United States. He was, despite his stature, one of the meanest dictators I ever met. I learned that the smaller a person is in size has a correlation to his evilness. I surmised that there is some logic in Alfonse Bertillion's theory about criminals associated with their size and body description. I further learned that it is difficult to create a dictator and expect his behavior to suddenly change.

Although Noriega was eagerly assisting in expelling undesirables from Panama to the United States at our request, it was suspected that he was also seizing, rather taking, large sums of money from them in the process. In reality, we were naïve to think that we were getting something from him for nothing in return.

During my first visit to Lima, Peru, when leaving the hotel one morning to jog, I heard a loud thunderous blast and felt the vibrations of the buildings that were close to our location. An American embassy official who was with us remarked, "There should be another one in a few minutes. They usually explode in two's or three's." A few minutes later a louder blast occurred. The embassy official explained that the blasts were the acts of terrorists called Sindero Luminoso (The Shining Path) with a long violent history in Peru.

Later that day, I read a Peruvian newspaper cartoon involving two boys asking each other what they wanted for Christmas. One wanted a motorcycle and the other wanted a ton of dynamite.

Albeit we have drive-by shootings in many cities in the United States, we have not yet had the number of terrorist explosions that occur in other countries. I love America for the security we have, the freedom to go about without being accosted, or restricted by the government or vigilante groups espousing loyalty to a certain group.

On my first trip to Colombia, I arrived in Bogotá the day after Colonel Jaime Ramirez, the head of the Colombian Narcotic Unit, had been assassinated. There were police and soldiers all over the city, many on foot and some on horseback. Entering the U.S. Embassy compound was almost like crossing the Berlin Wall. The guard even looked under the car with a mirror and closely scrutinized us, despite knowing the DEA agent assigned to the embassy. Colombia is a very beautiful country with many natural resources and the means to be self-sustaining.

Although considered an economically stable country, Colombia is rife with terrorists, assassins, drug traffickers and violence. It has a population of about 38,000,000; almost equal to the population of Canada. During this period, Canada had slightly over 400 homicides, while Colombia had over 14,000. The assassins developed a pattern similar to that used, by the old western crooks, during our early cowboy days; they bushwhacked and rode by shooting. They used motorcycles and machine guns.

Although very beautiful in many places, Colombia has a fearful aura about it that makes one often think about and fear public assassinations. A presidential candidate and several police officers were killed during this period. Perhaps, the saddest part of Jaime Ramirez' assassination is that the assassin was tipped off regarding his travel plan by someone inside of the police department.

Colombia has several long-existing terrorist organizations that wreak havoc on the country with impunity. The Revolutionary Armed Forces of Colombia (FARC) is the deadliest. FARC has a long history of kidnapping, murder and blowing up buildings.

Living in America without the attendant violence of these groups is a godsend. Although we do have sporadic medium scale acts of violence, other than 9-11, nothing in America today, can compare to this type of long standing violence. I developed a stronger appreciation for our freedom, safety and ability to live in less fear than others in their homelands.

During this time, Rayford Edmonds III, a Black drug kingpin was running a large drug ring in the Washington, D.C. area that resulted in a large increase in murders in the District. Drive-by shootings escalated and happened frequently in the predominantly Black neighborhoods of the District. Many families started purchasing old-fashioned legged bathtubs for concealment and protection when gunshots rang out in their neighborhoods; for some, especially in Southeast, gunshots were frequent occurrences.

I saw Washington, D.C., our Capitol, as the cardiovascular system of America; where decisions are made and laws are passed that not only change America, but impact heavily on the entire world. It has some of the most beautiful federal buildings in the world; most of them appear majestic and authoritative. They have perfect landscapes and the lawns are always neatly manicured and well tended. A large number of private buildings are modern; some are mixed with or in close proximity to older well-built federal buildings. Seeing the beautiful spires, domes, gargoyles, bronze statues of various American heroes, parks, trees, names on trees, landscapes, the whiteness of the White House, the Supreme Court building and the huge granite stones of the Capitol and Department of Treasury buildings, the hustle and bustle of the cars in traffic entering the District across the 14th Street Bridge are sights to behold.

There are numerous elegant dining facilities in D.C. and the seafood is outstanding. Visiting the seafood markets on the Potomac was an enjoyable treat. One of the best meals I ever consumed was while visiting friends, who had a "Crab Pick," where three bushels of steamed blue-fin crabs were purchased and we sat around tables with old newspapers and ate crabs for seemingly hours.

One of the cruelest ploys I ever heard of in D.C., involved a habit practiced often, by some politicians: passing laws without funding, to make the law effective, in order to pacify constituents. Smalltime politicians found old-liners tough to deal with; while some were of the opinion that backstabbing was a way of life "along the Potomac." One DEA administrator frequently related that he had found that a friend in Washington, D.C., is one who stabs you from the front.

Being in D.C. for four years, I learned a lot regarding the functioning of various government agencies: how very few representatives leave Washington, D.C. poor, how the various corporations buy politicians, their influence, receive gifts, perks, things of value from lobbyists and other representatives for political favors; how certain politicians and political groups circumvent contribution ceilings/thresholds by attending $10,000 to $20,000 coffee clutches; how politicians so swayed by contributions openly promote laws they know are debilitating, not only to the public, but also to the nation as a whole.

I saw an erosion of previous HUD efforts to restructure, rebuild and strengthen our cities. I surmised that this would be the beginning of the decay of the core of many cities, specifically inner-city downtown areas.

I became perplexed at our continuous building and assistance in building inner city infrastructures in foreign countries; while allowing our own cities to rot and become slum-like. I lauded the intense efforts made that modernized Washington, D.C.; especially the efforts that reversed District inhabitants from fleeing to the suburbs.

Washington, D.C. has long been known as one of the few cities that reversed the trend of losing residents to the suburbs. With HUD assistance and strong building and improvement programs, most of the old large two and three storied brownstone homes were renovated; streets were repaired and beautified. This caused an implosion wherein many residents and new arrivals moved into the District. The old brownstone homes and buildings that previously sold for far less than $100,000; have skyrocketed in value over the years. The citizens who hastily relocated to the outer Beltway cannot afford the prices of their previous homes in the District; and now have to face the arduous task of daily commuting into the District.

In order to cope with the heavy flow of traffic, a High Occupancy Vehicle (HOV) lane was established, to facilitate the smooth flow of peak traffic, inbound and outbound during rush hours. In order to drive in the HOV lane, the car had to contain at least two occupants. Some enterprising commuter purchased inflatable mannequins as a second passenger. It was kind of freaky seeing a driver and mannequin pass you on the interstate.

Carpools and vanpools were started, some transporting as many as 12 passengers that paid a monthly commuting fee. A new thing started called "slugging," a definition for hitching a ride. There were certain points in the city where commuters would meet and join an outbound driver (slug) to enable the driver to utilize the HOV lane.

My DEA position in Puerto Rico required that I hobnob with the governor, mayors, heads of Caribbean Island countries etc. The only time I involved my two older daughters in meeting such officials was on a trip to St. Kitts. On that occasion, the prime minister of St. Kitts, accompanied by U.S. Consulate General, Brian Salter came to the hotel restaurant where we were dining. They were thrilled meeting a Black official of such status.

Shortly after our move to the Washington, D.C. area, we attended a picnic at a park in the District. About 30 minutes after our arrival, D.C. Mayor Marion Barry arrived and casually walked around meeting and chatting with people. My daughters were with a small group at a hotdog stand when the mayor walked up, introduced himself to the group, got a hot dog and chatted with them. I noted that my daughters were awed by his presence and were thrilled having been in the presence of the Black mayor of Washington, D.C. While at the picnic, I was apprised by several old timers that Mayor Barry was very involved in ensuring that Black and White business owners who lived in the District received a fair amount of the government contracts that were being awarded. Reportedly, prior to his term, the contracts historically had been awarded to contractors residing outside of the District.

After the picnic, on several occasions, I overheard my daughters on the telephone telling their relatives in California they had met Mayor Barry and what a nice man he is, how he visits local schools touting "say no to drugs". In early 1990, my daughters and I were watching the evening news when it was reported that Mayor Barry had been arrested, by the FBI in a federal drug sting.

I was very disappointed with the mayor, especially watching his arrest by the FBI, and instead of asserting his innocence, merely stating, "I knew I shouldn't have brought my black ass up in here." It was very disappointing seeing a high government official involved in the very same thing he publicly espoused against, especially teenagers and students. As a parent, it was difficult convincing my daughters and their friends that the mayor's arrest was an aberration.

Around this time, I read several newspaper articles regarding ministers and priests being caught in various unethical situations. One, involved a priest accused of molesting an alter boy over a significant period of time. After reading the article, I shredded it to protect my daughters from it. The mayor's arrest had been almost too much for them to fathom.

XX

BEING TRANSFERRED FROM Washington, D.C. to St Louis, Missouri was analogous to being paroled; a welcomed event. Shortly upon my arrival in St. Louis, I was asked to serve as a member of Governor John Ashcroft's Crime Commission, headed by the Missouri attorney general. After conferring with several long-time residents of Missouri, I was apprised that Governor Ashcroft, in his position as state attorney general and as governor, had displayed and continues to display a strong dislike for Blacks as a whole. He reportedly had fought school desegregation efforts with such fervor; it led some to believe he was trying to reverse Brown V. The Board of Education.

There were many bad reports about Governor Ashcroft: reports of him using Black prisoners as servers in the governor's mansion and reports that he was a member of various racially elite organizations. One described him as a "Jesus Freak" and related that during his two inaugural balls, instead of having the customary first dance with his wife, on both occasions he played the piano.

One of the most alarming reports about Governor Ashcroft was that he was a strong believer that women should obey men; that they are secondary citizens whose functions are basically that of wife and homemaker. He was described as a monogamous man who would not accept a sexual gift from a lady; that he was true to his wife, law abiding and a frequent prayer.

Certain Missourians were of the belief that there was no lottery or gambling casinos in Missouri because of Governor Ashcroft. Blue Laws existed that prohibited the sale or purchase of alcoholic beverages on Sundays, reportedly all because of Governor Ashcroft.

The partying crowd made frequent trips across the river to Illinois to purchase liquor on Sundays. They traveled daily across the river to purchase lottery tickets and to gamble on the riverboat casinos in E. St. Louis and Alton, Illinois.

I felt a moral obligation and duty to serve on the governor's Crime Commission, headed by the Missouri attorney general. When I first met Governor Ashcroft, he appeared very professional, friendly, polite and with a desire to effectively deal with crime.

The attorney general, on the other hand, was different. He appeared to be comfortable looking and talking to you eye to eye, although he had an aura of suspicion about him that was difficult to explain. I joined the Crime Commission and provided my full support.

I joined several Metropolitan Enforcement Groups (MEG) in the St. Louis area: the Missouri Sheriff's Association, Missouri Police Officer's Association and the International Association of Chief's of Police. I had joined the National Organization of Black Law Enforcement Executives (NOBLE) when I was stationed in Detroit. All of these organizations were highly professional entities with strong desires to make a difference and to be successful.

I was invited to be a keynote luncheon speaker at the Missouri Sheriff's Annual Training Conference in Branson, Missouri. I had previously met a lot of Missouri sheriffs at meetings in Jefferson City. I found Branson, Missouri to be an inland secret paradise; a mecca for country and western singers.

On the day of my speech, I rehearsed it to the point of knowing it verbatim. I remembered a lot of statistical data, some with as many as seven and eight digits, like the populations of Missouri, Colombia, and Canada, in addition to the total marijuana seized in DEA's Domestic Marijuana Eradication Program. The latter was easy to remember because I had just transferred from DEA headquarters where I was Chief of the Cannabis Investigation section.

I gave what I thought was an outstanding presentation for 25 minutes leaving five minutes for questions. After my speech and as I was walking back to my table, I was accosted by three sheriffs who commended me on the contents of my speech and told me that I had "pissed us off unmercifully talking about how good the State Police is." I thought they were going to attack me and was unaware that they had such disdain for the Missouri State Police. I walked back onto the stage and the emcee related that I wanted to say something. When I told the sheriffs that I apologize for mentioning their dear friends, the State Police, and how professional they were, they broke out in loud applause.

I learned from the speech that there are purportedly professional people who dislike other professionals, merely based on the color of their uniforms; that there exist real and unreal reasons between organizations that cause them to dislike or avoid encounters with each other. Despite differences, in cases of emergencies or needs, they readily set those differences aside and get on with the job that needs to be done. It was apparent that the level of training and ability to interact on interagency projects had caused some of the dissension. The State Police were the most educated; while some of the sheriffs and elected officials, were not required to have as much training or education. In some law enforcement circles certain sheriffs' were identified as lacking the ability to read or write.

I saw Charlie Pride and Jerry Clower, the mouth of the South from Yazoo City; perform in Branson. Jerry was funnier than his tapes and kept the crowd in stitches.

At the time of my arrival in St. Louis, there was no major football or basketball team in the city. I decided to do something that I had never done or thought of doing in my life, deer hunt. I purchased a Remington 30-06 caliber rifle, bright orange cap and jacket, hunting license, a scope, ammunition, hunting gear and practice targets. When in the sporting goods store, the salesman asked a few questions that I could not answer. He then told me that I would have to dress the deer in the field and asked if I wanted to take care of that while getting other gear. When I agreed, he called another salesman over and related that I wanted to dress the deer. The other salesman, realizing I was a novice hunter, asked, "Do you want to buy a sweater or jacket for your deer?" After pausing for several minutes, the other salesman stated, "I would recommend a sweater for a first time hunter." I told them that I was not sure and made a telephone call to SA Paul Robinson, who was taking me on my first hunting trip, for advice.

When I asked Paul about what I should buy to dress the dear, he told me a sharp knife, that he had all the other required equipment. When I asked about a sweater for the deer, Paul laughed uncontrollably and related that he had participated in the joke. I learned that dressing a deer is the act of removing all of its innards: including lungs, liver, heart, intestines, basically everything inside of its body from neck to rectum. I later fired about 50 rounds with the rifle and calibrated it.

The day before the opening of hunting season, I drove to Brookfield, Missouri, where I joined Paul and his son Warren. We went over to Smith Street, where I was introduced to Charles Eugene "Gene" Crafton, the owner of 59 acres of woods where we were to hunt. Gene was a middle-aged White male, with lower body paralysis, who moved about in a wheelchair. Gene was delighted to meet me and immediately gave me the first summer deer sausage I had ever eaten. He was very hospitable and I felt very relaxed and at ease in his home. I was cognizant that there were no Black families in the town of Brookfield and that the economy in that area centered on agriculture and animal husbandry.

Gene's adult daughter Alice was also a hunter. I discerned that hunting deer, birds, ducks, squirrels and rabbits were regular pastimes in that part of the state. In preparation for the hunt, I was told not to use soap when I showered or toothpaste or mouthwash before going into the woods to hunt because deer have a very strong sense of smell. I was further advised that we should walk into the woods and take a position 30 minutes before sunrise. Gene, being in a wheelchair, was allowed to hunt on the roadside of the field from his car.

The following day, we drove in tandem to the woods, where we entered the woods with Gene's daughter and her friend. After three hours in the woods, Alice spotted a deer walking slowly and somewhat camouflaged in the woods across the railroad tracks to our front. She shot and the sound reverberated in my ears. The deer took off running in the woods. She stated, "I got him; I heard the bullet tear into his flesh." I surmised Alice was merely trying to impress a new hunter. As we walked toward where the deer was last seen, she stated, "I think I hit him just above his front legs around his neck."

We found the deer about 50 yards away, down and near death. Alice retrieved a pistol and immediately shot the deer in the head stating, "That will take you out of your misery. There is no need to suffer more." The deer was a 6-point buck and was hit in the area Alice had mentioned. I assisted in cutting a slit in the lower part of its legs, stuck a strong stick between the bone and tendon in each leg. We tied a rope on the stick, tossed it over a tree limb and hoisted the deer up about two feet off the ground.

I watched Alice cut a slit just below the deer's lower ventral neck area, placing two fingers inside the hole; she slit the fur and cut it apart down to the rectum. She then put a sharp serrate knife in the upper part of the deer's torso/rib area and cut the cartilage in the breastbone of its chest. Next, she cut the deer to its rectum and removed the intestines, stomach, lungs, heart etc. She placed the heart in a plastic zipper lock bag and handed it to me, advising that it was delicious. Alice then removed the liver, placed it in a plastic bag and handed it to me advising it was also very delicious and nutritious.

Two additional deer were killed that day. We left the woods around sunset. Later, during dinner at Gene's home he recalled his days as a pilot during WWII airlifting prisoners out of Belgium at the end of the war; how his airplane became overloaded with prisoners rushing onboard his initial flight because they didn't want to chance waiting for the next airlift.

The next day we went back into the woods, without Alice and her friend, before sunrise. I took a position north of Gene's car and entered the woods where his property bordered a fenced pasture. I walked gingerly and quietly into the woods toward the railroad. A couple of hours passed before I came out of the woods and joined Gene at his car. We had been talking for a while, when Gene pointed to a small, brown object on the ground and asked me if it was a deer dropping. I did not know. He asked me to pick it up and bring it to him; which I did. He put the object in his mouth, chewed and swallowed it; stating definitively that it was buck's dropping. He then had me bring him another one off the ground and he put it in his mouth and smilingly said, "Now that's a doe John, that one is surely a doe." Needless to say, as someone who has seen and experienced a lot, I was so taken aback by Gene's actions; I immediately went back into the woods. I saw Paul and Big Ed, at the inside edge of the woods, laughing so hard that both were red in the face. It was then, I realized that I had been the brunt of a hunter's joke. They had taken milk duds, dipped them in honey and rolled them in cocoa to make them resemble deer droppings. According to Gene, after he had eaten the second milk dud, he thought I had turned white. I killed my first deer the following day and was taught how to field dress it. After the last hunting day, we had dinner at Gene's house.

When departing, I thought I saw Gene's eyes become watery. Paul later told me that Gene did cry when we left and made him promise to bring me back anytime. I knew I had met a friend for life. I learned that despite one's impairment, there are many things in life to continue to enjoy. Stealthily walking through the woods, while deer hunting, listening to the sounds of nature's various animals and birds, and seeing the variety of fallen leaves is a joyous experience.

On my next hunt, I felt like a millionaire on an African Safari. I now knew the ropes and other hunters were unable to pull a fast one on me. While hunting on the property adjacent to Gene's land, the owner, whom I had not yet met, drove up in a truck. I came out of the woods and joined him. He asked if I was having any luck and related that he had not seen me around that area before. I told him that I was a new hunter and had shot at something that had moved and it fell. I also told him I was going back to get the other hunters to help me. I watched his face turn red with suppressed anger. The owner then asked the color of the animal and I told him brown with a white spot about its belly, although I had not approached it yet. The owner then peeled rubber and drove down the road where Gene was sitting in his car. I walked down to their location and found them both red-faced from laughter. The owner admitted that I had pulled one over on him. He owned dairy cows on 100 acres north of Gene's acreage. He then related that earlier that year, someone entered his land, killed a cow and butchered it on the spot, leaving the remnants in the field. He surmised it was a professional meat cutter and related that rustling a cow or bull was known to occur in the area about once or twice a year. I found hunters to be very friendly, earthly, cooperative, innovative and interesting people. I learned different hunting tips and how to enjoy venison prepared in various ways. The summer sausage, some with jalapeno pepper, some with pepper and cheese; and other variations.

One of the most interesting tips I learned involved how to lure bucks, male deer, to your shooting location; this entailed spreading a concoction mixed with urine from a doe in heat. It has the most awful smell, but is a major attractant for bucks. I think this type of lure is unfair to the buck, especially luring him to a location to become sexually involved, where he is instead, shot and killed. One hunter advised me that when a buck full of adrenalin and testosterone, is killed the venison is very tender and does not have a wildlife taste. Some hunters, not using the urine, marinate bucks in milk before butchering for consumption. I learned from hunters that in early history, deer and other animals for consumption were killed during the winter or late fall when it is cold, to prevent the meat from spoiling or putrefying. A lot of brine, salt, and smoke was utilized in early times to preserve the meats. I further learned that settlers stored wrapped foods (meats and cheese) in pits and caves in the ground located close to rivers, streams, ponds and lakes where it was cold. I further learned that smokehouses were used before the invention of refrigeration.

Another hidden paradise, in Missouri, is the Lake of the Ozarks with its many resorts. It is a beautiful area of pristine mountains and foothills with plush green valleys, a beautiful lake, golf courses, fishing areas and a discount outlet mall. It is the home of one of the largest man-made lakes.

St. Louis was very different now, from what I recalled of years prior; when it was a flourishing metropolitan city of almost a million inhabitants with beautiful buildings, homes, restaurants, parks, golf courses and riverboat supper clubs that provided meals and entertainment such as: dancing and music.

Throughout the entire city, especially close to the downtown area, were abandoned buildings, some boarded and others with broken windows, doors, and garages ensconced in an overgrowth of weeds. There were patch vacant lots, where houses had been razed and never replaced, in numerous areas of the city. Many of the old brick buildings had decayed roofs, broken chimneys, windows and sashes. The inner city was starting to look like a part of the infamous Chicago slums with unoccupied, unkempt buildings and houses.

St. Louis was suffering the ills of a HUD administration's failure to help maintain and rebuild the infrastructure of the inner city. There were abandoned properties all over the city that should have been sold by the city to earn some revenue, as opposed to being an eyesore and city-owned hazard. Because of HUD's failures, lack of funding and lack of meaningful programs, St. Louis was becoming a city also abandoned and left to self-destruct.

A large percentage (over half) of its population moved from the city to the suburbs, establishing 92 small cities and municipalities within St. Louis County. Most of its Black population lived in North St. Louis. One of the most beautiful sites in St. Louis is Forest Park, which is touted to be one of the largest city parks in the world. It has three golf courses.

I participated in numerous community activities and was very active in NOBLE. Every year the St. Louis chapter of NOBLE had an "Oldie but Goodie" dance as one of its fundraising activities. During my first participation in this event, I was tasked to direct participants from the food purchasing area to a designated eating area within the dancehall. Several NOBLE officers from St. Louis Police Department were operating the food concession. I overheard a man at the counter order a "listener." I didn't have a clue what he wanted and did not want to be too inquisitive, so I watched a NOBLE officer place two pieces of sandwich bread on a piece of wax paper, reach into a pot and remove two pig ears, sprinkle them with Tabasco sauce and fold them into a sandwich. He handed it to the man and said, "That'll be $2.50." The man paid for the sandwich and a bottle of beer and walked over to the designated dining area. Ironically, I learned what a listener was by listening. A short time later, another man walked up to the food counter and ordered a "snout sandwich." I was aware that a snout was the projected nose of a pig. I watched the NOBLE officer repeat the same procedure, this time removing a large pig snout from another pot on the stove and making it into a sandwich; for which he also charged $2.50.

About an hour later, another man walked up to the counter and ordered a "wiggler", which I later learned was a sandwich made of pigtails. After seeing these three transactions, I lost my appetite for the Kansas City type barbecue.

Of all the cities I had visited, I had never seen one with as many tobacco users as in St. Louis. They had vast selections of cigarettes, chewing tobacco and snuff supplies in almost all of the stores, and more so in liquor stores and supermarkets. Two of the most productive agents and one of the first line supervisors in the St. Louis DEA office were tobacco chewers.

In 1992, when President Bush came to St. Louis on a campaign stop, I arranged, with Secret Service Special Agent in Charge (SAC)

Don Snyder, to have a photo opportunity with him. There was a new U.S. Attorney (USA) for the Eastern District of Missouri who seemed to ignore my telephone calls in regards to addressing certain issues. Unbeknownst to me, the USA had also requested a photo opportunity with President Bush.

After President Bush finished speaking at the fundraising coffee clutch, at a St. Louis airport hotel, Snyder had all participants for the photo opportunity line up close to the President's limousine. I was first in line, followed by a St. Louis County police captain, the USA, a female member of the Police Board and a colonel from the St. Louis City Police Department.

When President Bush came over, Snyder introduced me as the Special Agent in Charge of the DEA St. Louis Field Division. President Bush, spoke, shook my hand and posed for his photographer who took our photograph. President Bush advised that he was proud of the job we were doing in our fight against drug trafficking and encouraged me to keep up the good work. He then shook the Captain's hand and was photographed. After SAC Snyder introduced the USA, a presidential appointee, to President Bush, he spoke, shook his hand and immediately turned toward me and told the USA, "I want you to fully cooperate with DEA." I had a hard time convincing the USA that I had not talked about his cooperation, or lack thereof, with any official. Thereafter, he promptly returned all of my telephone calls.

Meeting the president of the United States and shaking his hand was the epitome of my law enforcement career. Never in my life did I ever conceive being close to the president and certainly never believed I would have the opportunity to shake his hand. Seeing the Secret Service Agents protecting him and how people admire his position projects an aura of world power; an aura of importance that is difficult to explain.

During that year, Governor Ashcroft left office after his second term. The Missouri attorney general followed his predecessor Ashcroft and ran for governor. He won the Republican primary nomination and faced Mel Carnahan, the Democrat candidate for governor. The former attorney general became embroiled in a criminal investigation, involving corruption regarding a fund that he had managed as attorney general. He lost the election to democrat Mel Carnahan. From my first meeting of Ashcroft, I could not imagine him being involved in any criminal activity. He had a spirit about him that indicated he was too straight-laced to break the law.

I surmised that incumbent President Bush would loose the election; in part, due to his appointment of a person like Clarence Thomas to the Supreme Court. I had previously watched part of his Confirmation Hearings on television. On one occasion Thomas' wife, a moderately attractive White female, accompanied him to the hearing. On that same day when I saw Senator Strom Thurman place his hands on Thomas' shoulder, I thought I was hallucinating. During the hearing, many Blacks were strongly against Clarence Thomas. Some called him a "Civil Rights Nobody" and some blatantly referred to him as a "White Folks' Nigger."

Unfortunately, later President Bush, the incumbent president, lost the election to a purported small-time southern state governor, William J. Clinton. When President Clinton was sworn into office in January of 1993, the whole country appeared to go in a different direction. 1993 was a very interesting year. America had a new and a democratic president. Shortly after being sworn into office, he started appointing numerous Blacks, minorities and females to political positions in his administration. For the first time in our history, America had a female attorney general and perhaps also the first female Secretary of State and a Black female Surgeon General. Most of the presidents before President Clinton, some when campaigning, gave the impression that they wanted their administration to reflect the make-up of America, but merely appointed a few Blacks as tokens.

During this same period, former governor, John Ashcroft was out of office and practicing law. I exchanged greetings with him when passing several times on the streets close to the County building in Clayton, Missouri. I saw him approximately 12 times and he was always wearing, either a blue, or a black suit and always with a white shirt.

I read an article in the newspaper and saw television reports of the former Missouri attorney general pleading to a felony charge. In one, it was reported that he was sentenced to two years in prison. I felt sorry for him and realized the look that I had seen on his face on first meeting, was a look of dishonesty or being involved in something that was causing him to be sorry. It is always very sad to see a law enforcement person break the law, especially when the position itself demands that the holder be an upstanding person, devoid of criminal activity or activities that could cause embarrassment to the law enforcement profession.

With over 25 years of law enforcement experience at this time, I was reassured that the cause of corruption in law enforcement stemmed mostly from three sources: money, women and intoxicants (liquor/drugs).

While in St. Louis I met a very special person that really had a major impact on me to give, not merely money or material things; but love, myself, my time, my assistance, my friendship, fellowship and most importantly my understanding and appreciation of others. During my first Thanksgiving, I was encouraged to cook a 22-pound turkey, deliver it to the New Life Evangelist Center (NLEC) and help serve the homeless and the needy.

A week before Thanksgiving, I was required to attend an orientation at the NLEC. We sat in a theater section of the center as the plans were being explained. When I first arrived I saw several workers that appeared to be having a polyester convention, based on the old clothing they were wearing. About half way into the meeting, a White man wearing old pants, shirt, and shoes sitting in the same row two seats to my left asked, "What do you think about some of us actually sitting down, eating and talking to our guest?" I noted that there was something about him that I could not immediately recall.

"That's a good idea Reverend Rice, that is a very good idea; what do you all think," someone asked the audience. I then recognized the, not so modernly dressed, middle-aged man as Reverend Larry Rice, the head of the NLEC.

I had seen Reverend Rice on television during cold wintry days giving blankets, heaters and articles of clothing to the homeless throughout the greater St. Louis area on numerous occasions. Even then he appeared more as a recipient than a giver. I immediately admired him for the work I had been apprised, that he had done and continued to for the homeless. I admired him more for, as a servant of God, not taking away most of the gifts, as so often is the case with many purported ministers of the cloth. Seeing him roll up his sleeves and serve others was awe inspiring; seeing him living the simple life was even more inspiring.

Prior to meeting Reverend Rice, I had been personally told by numerous people how he helps the needy. Several individuals told me how he had personally helped them, their families and others in times of need regarding food, money, clothing, utilities and even a place to stay. One man reported that his father is buried in a cemetery that Reverend Rice had purchased, in the county, to bury homeless people.

I was tremendously moved by what I personally saw Reverend Rice do and believe that he is certainly a true server of God. Words are insufficient to describe the difference his serving has made and is making in the St Louis area. I made a regular habit of preparing food to feed the hungry and homeless at the NELC. One Christmas while serving at the NELC, a man walked up and told me that he knew me from somewhere, but could not recall where. After I identified myself, we both recalled having met previously in Branson, Missouri, where I had made a speech at the Missouri Sheriff's Association Annual Training Conference. He was a sheriff from one of the outer counties. It was inspiring learning how much he admired Reverend Rice and the work that he was doing for the homeless, hungry and needy.

While working for housing of the homeless at my church, I met a young Black man (YBM) with a White girlfriend, two children and another one pending who was homeless. He and his common-law wife and family had become homeless, as a result of his gambling habits. The YBM related that when growing up in North St. Louis his father lost his job at the time he was supposed to purchase the home they were renting with an option to buy. His father had used all the saved money and was at the point of, either being put out of the house, or having to make a significant payment toward the purchase of the house. The YBM further related that someone from their church had related his father's plight, but seemingly no one came to assist. On the day the owner was due to arrive, the YBM related that he saw a White man walk up, place an envelope in the mailbox affixed to the front door and walk back to an old car and leave. He recognized that it was Reverend Larry Rice. Using the money sparingly, his father was able to purchase the residence. The YBM had nothing but high praise for Reverend Rice.

Of all the ministers I have met, next to my father, I believe Reverend Rice is a Godsend. He has aura of righteousness about him that is hard to explain.

If most ministers were as concerned about man, as Reverend Rice has proven to be, there would less violence, fear, hunger and need in the world. Perhaps, what sets him above many are his overt acts of unselfish-

220

ness, his understanding and treatment of the homeless, needy, unkempt, unloved, lonely and unattractive as what we are: Children of God.

Another interesting character I met in St. Louis was Mike Williams, a St. Louis County police officer assigned to the DEA Task Force. Mike was married and had children. Of all the young men in his age group, he was one of the few that gave a lot of his time coaching young boys in the North County Athletic Club (NCAC). Mike was the NCAC. He coached football, basketball and baseball in the NCAC and never once did he indicate that he was tired, disappointed or displeased with a single player. One of his most effective attributes is the respect his players have for him and how he was able to gain and sustain their respect. Another one is his frequent smiling and friendly face. I saw Mike do what coaches do: he molded boys into good men, helped them develop character, high self-esteem, good moral values, taught them a sense worth, the value of property, the value of team work and assisted them in excelling in their pursuits.

I saw Mike on many occasions transport fatherless sons to and from practice, spend his own money sharing with them; teaching them skills that they will keep for a lifetime, not just skills in an athletic environment, but skills involving competing, coping, working as a team, caring for others, not being selfish and how to believe in a power greater than man— God.

One of the most unusual things I saw Mike do was on a campout at a ranch in Washington County Missouri. I was helping Mike barbecue hamburger, hot dogs and pork steaks. In the process one of the pork steaks fell to the ground. I picked it up and started to toss it in the trashcan until stopped by Mike. Mike got the steak and told one of his football players that it had fallen on the ground and asked what we should do with it. One of the players advised, wash it off and put it back on the grill. He added, "We don't throw away meat in North County."

About five years ago, Mike told me that four of the young boys who were at the campout had been drafted into the NFL, two went in the first round. One of the draftees mentioned the campout and related that his goal was to have a ranch similar to the one he'd camped at as a youth; making it available for inner city youth who have never been camping and those without fathers or any male to take them places.

Because of Mike taking the time and coaching young men, about 20 of those young North County players have been drafted and are professional athletes. Mike is an outstanding and unheralded testimony; one of those heroes seldom recognized for all the hard work, dedication, coaching, teaching, training, mentoring, giving and being a surrogate father to many youths. As a result, they continue to grow becoming fine, prosperous young men; who then want to emulate Mike; they want to make a difference in their community.

So often, unheralded Black men, like Mike, give for years and sometimes are not even recognized by the recipients, community, parents, or others. They do not consider it giving, but as Christians, consider it sharing; sharing their time, knowledge, wisdom, guidance, food, transportation, money and love. I saw Mike's role as a surrogate father to fatherless boys and boys with fathers who were too busy to spend the necessary time with their sons; as a mentor to others and a paradigm of what fatherhood is about; what a community is about. I believe that Mike is not completely aware of the differences he made that influenced the positive development of many young men. When, senior President Bush was in office, he had a program to honor the likes of Mike; those who have had and are having a tremendous and positive impact on the community. He recognized them with a "Point of Light" award. Mike is certainly well deserving of this award.

I was a Baptist all of my life, and for some reason, had developed an aversion to seeing women in the role as head of a church. It had nothing to do with machismo, or maybe it was because I had never encountered them. I went to Ward Chapel AME Church, in Florissant, Missouri, one Sunday and was very moved by the pastor, Reverend Annie O. McDonald. She preached a very good sermon and stayed the course of her message and did not get into slight entertainment. She was a good pastor and had a good spirit about her. I learned that she was a single parent and had come to Missouri from Arkansas.

After attending Ward Chapel for about a year, I felt moved to join, to switch from Baptist to Methodist. Perhaps the strongest things that pulled me to the church were God, its medium size and the work they were doing in the community, the services it provided to members, guests and others.

I was very impressed with Pastor McDonald, for she was also a leader and servant of God. Material things did not seem too important to her, especially fancy cars, jewelry and fancy clothing. She was also a middle school principal, but truly a servant of God.

One of the profound things I learned from Reverend McDonald is that material things are merely earthly, temporary things. I also learned something that I had never thought of prior and that is: Life itself is not everlasting, only if everlasting is defined as when you cease to exist. We are merely temporary inhabitants of earth. As a consequence, we should live our life in a godly way; always putting him foremost and encouraging others to do likewise.

I was blessed to meet another pillar of the St. Louis community, Oval "O" Miller, Executive Director of Black Alcohol/Drug Service Information Center (BASIC), one of the most successful drug treatment (non-methadone) centers in the United States. BASIC was located a few blocks from the NLEC. I was invited to serve on the board and was later voted president of the board of directors.

St. Louis residents enjoy a more peaceful life, that is, in a large sense attributable to the effectiveness of BASIC. It utilizes a 12-step program and insists that all participants be candid and strive to help themselves and others. It was exhilarating hearing each participant on a weekly basis stand and state "My Name is _____, dope fiend. I have been clean and dry for two years, 11 months, two weeks and six days. I've kept all my expectations and I am a very important person."

During one session, a client related that he knew he had to get off crack cocaine because of the debilitating things it was making him do. The client related that as a young man he had done a lot of things, but never thought that he would do some of the things he was driven to do while under the influence of the need, desire, crave and want for crack.

According to the client, one night when he was broke and in dire need to smoke crack, he lured the dope man and his henchman to his house under the false pretense that he had money. The client begged the dope man to give him a couple rocks on credit. Instead of agreeing, the dope man teased him unmercifully. The dope man then told him the only way he would give him even one rock, he would have to rape his mother. The client added that he was so sick that he agreed and told the dope man that he would do it but not in the presence of the henchman.

The client started crying and related how he had gone into his mother's bedroom with the dope man following him. When he saw the henchman peeking into the room, he called it off and feigned telling his mother he was going out with a friend. The client advised that he knew it was time for him to quit using crack, quit doing drugs period.

There were many clients with similar stories, all relating that drugs had taken over their body, soul and mind; making the pusher the most important person in their life.

Oval, related that he had been an old heroin addict and had bummed around quite a bit. When he came to St. Louis, he had a strong desire to kick drug addiction completely. He met Reverend Edmund Griesedieck, aka "Father Ed", a White priest who had a lot of trust and faith in him. Oval related that he was also supported by Father Ed and James H. Mc-Donnell, Corporate Vice President of McDonnell Douglas. In 1983 with the support of Father Ed and John McDonnell he launched BASIC. Both had the insight, that although chemical dependency had no preferences, there was a degree of uniqueness required to successfully treat Blacks. According to Oval, Father Ed put $50,000 in his hand and told him to make it work.

Oval related that he was shocked that a White man would put $50.000 in the hands of a dope fiend and tell him to find a cure. Because of the trust Father Ed and James McDonnell had in him, he knew he would never relapse into drug use and would do all he could to help others overcome dope addiction and chemical dependency, especially heroin the mighty enslaver of man.

Oval is one of the hardest workers I have ever met. He is very enthused and thrives on helping others overcome chemical dependency/addiction. Oval has built BASIC up from grassroots to a highly successful drug treatment center that is gaining worldwide attention. I assisted him starting a BASIC program in New Orleans over 10 years ago.

Oval is one recovered dope fiend that I trust to the highest degree and since knowing him 18 years; I have never had a reason to distrust any of his actions. He further strengthened my resolve to help, to give, to encourage, to trust and to put forth efforts to help those who have fallen by the side, fallen into an abyss from which it is very difficult to emerge.

Oval is one of those individuals, not truly recognized for giving so much back to the community, exerting so much energy and having an unquestionably positive impact on the lives of so many; many who have been lost in a system that, either forgot them, or completely gave up on their ability to recover; most with habits and addictions where successful treatments are cost prohibitive.

I sat in numerous meetings with an organization that provided peanut size funding to BASIC. I watched them rake Oval over the coals with questions, requests, directions and asinine issues for justification of the funding. I thought government agencies were mired in paperwork and explanations until sitting in a few of those meetings. The number of man-hours expended, far exceeded the amount of the contribution the agency made to BASIC. I watched Oval go through myriads of questions and answers for the agency, never showing displeasure at their relentless questions.

I developed a strong admiration seeing Oval participate in those meetings and never letting them ruffle his feathers in triviality. He always remained calm, polite and responsive to their myriads of insignificant questions and suggestions. Sometimes, the theme seemed directed toward Oval's honesty and management ability; which did not affect his candor, poise, openness and acceptance of their meaningful and useful suggestions.

XXI

IN AUGUST OF 1992, Hurricane Andrew hit the Florida coast and caused approximately 25 billion dollars in damages, killed 40 people and left hundreds of thousands homeless. During the following winter, the Midwest experienced record levels of snow, followed by an inordinate number of thunderstorms in the early spring. April started with a lot of rain that continued pouring heavily on already saturated lands.

The Mississippi, Missouri and other rivers flooded and peaked during the summer. The Mississippi and Missouri rivers started flooding from Minnesota continuing through Arkansas. Seemingly, the swift streams/ flows it picked up in Arkansas spared parts of Tennessee, Mississippi and Louisiana. It was a very sad occasion seeing people lose all of their household possessions.

I had gone through Alton, Grafton, and several small towns en route to a Federal Executive Retreat at Pere Marquette on two prior occasions; and recalled how close in proximity some houses and buildings were to the Mississippi River. Afterward, I saw many buildings covered with floodwaters as high as the roof. I learned that once a house is flooded it leaves an unbearable odor, melts or rots the drywall, causes mildew in the insulation, destroys the electrical and plumbing/water systems, and sometimes becoming a home for snakes, otters and other creatures displaced by the flood.

The sadness on the faces of flood victims indicates an unimaginable hopelessness. Many vendors in the Midwest were direct opposites of vendors in Florida during hurricanes. In Florida, they have a tendency to increase the prices on needed items and on many occasions, opportunists loot and pillage.

The vendors in the Midwest dropped their prices on most essential items like water, toiletries, food, clothing and ice. Some made large contributions and actually paid their employees to assist victims in the flooded areas. The Red Cross, Civil Air Patrol and others came from many states to assist.

In the St. Louis area, people from high crime areas went to the flooded area, not to loot, but to assist and help. The flood was one of the most devastating to hit the Midwest and caused approximately 15 billion dollars worth of damage. Buildings, homes, crops and levees were destroyed. One man removed sandbags from a levee, to keep his wife on the other side of the river, so he could continue partying. As a result, the levee collapsed; he was criminally charged.

A part of U.S. Highway 40 was destroyed at the border of St. Louis County and St. Charles County. A waste treatment plant was flooded and released a significant amount of waste in the area. Several large liquid petroleum gas tanks broke from their moors and floated away toward the Mississippi river. I saw the television reports of the devastation the flood was causing in Missouri and bordering states.

The saddest expressions I believed I had ever seen, were the expressions of sorrow, dejection, abandonment, loneliness, worry and everything sad you can think of on the faces of the flood victims. There were many organizations, groups, churches, neighbors, friends and companies readily providing assistance, however, none could replace certain things, including sentimental things that the flood had destroyed forever.

I drove down Old Halls Ferry Road and saw houses under water up to the eaves, cars, lawnmowers, bikes, and many articles; some floating about. One of the saddest announcements on television related that most of the flood victims did not have flood insurance, and some who did, had been advised by insurers not to rebuild or build in a flood zone. Some of the residents had been prior flood victims in the same area. A significant number had built homes close to the river because the land was cheaper.

In July of 1993, the DEA celebrated its 20th anniversary. I traveled to the Washington, D.C. area for the event and met the first female United States Attorney General (AG), Janet Reno. I had a photographic opportunity with her, which I cherish and consider a very important moment in my life. She had a "down to earth" aura about her that reflected a very intelligent lady, with a desire to serve and to serve well. I chatted with her for about two minutes and never felt the least uncomfortable or that she wanted to talk to someone else, that is, I never got the impression that she was hurrying me along for the next greeter.

Many male criminal investigators have long had an aversion to ever working for a female. I never harbored that thought and felt good about working for AG Janet Reno. When meeting her, she maintained eye contact the whole time. She had an aura of honesty about her, so convincing that she could easily discern what all humans are likely to do, that is, make an honest mistake in judgment.

Shortly after our initial meeting, I was honored to attend a working lunch meeting with AG Reno in the U.S. Attorney's office in Kansas City, Missouri. I caught onto one of her phrases, "forming partnerships and partnering" with other law enforcement agencies and the community.

The next time I was in her presence was at the U.S. Attorney's Office in Omaha, Nebraska regarding the delivery of over $1,000,000 in forfeited funds to the Nebraska State Police. On each occasion, Reno was highly professional and always put her audience at ease with her "folksy" mannerism.

The last time I was in AG Reno's presence was one of the most embarrassing moments of my career. AG Reno came to St. Louis, to participate in one of our Partnership Crime Suppression Conferences. The conference was held at Southwest High School in south St. Louis.

I arrived at the conference site 30 minutes before the starting time and consumed a cup of coffee. I asked a custodian for directions to the men's restroom and was told that I was early and since there was hardly anyone else there; he advised me to use the ladies restroom which was close by stating that he would remain outside to warn any females that it was occupied. I was in the restroom for about five minutes and when washing my hands, I exuded gas loudly several time and remarked, "Wow what a relief." Immediately when exiting the restroom, I encountered AG Reno sitting in the anteroom of the restroom having makeup applied to her face by an assistant. She smiled and we exchanged greetings. The assistant also smiled. I could not determine if their smiles were with or without humorous thoughts. Although embarrassed, I had a belief that the AG understood that restrooms are places to relieve one's self. I was in her presence several times during the meeting, and noted, on each occasion she smiled.

I immediately admired her for her stance regarding the Waco incident involving the Alcohol, Tobacco and Firearms' (ATF) and David Koresh's, Branch Davidians. In certain law enforcement circles she was highly lauded and compared to certain males who would have "waffled up" under such pressure. She was decisive and stated, "The buck stops here." This was a way of saying; if you want to blame anybody, blame me. My prior belief that she could accept an honest mistake in judgment was reinforced. I had seen executives and agency heads in similar situations, on many occasions, succumb to pressure and resort to sacrificing their own men; in order to pacify or quell bad publicity.

I have a strong respect for AG Reno and believe that she will be historically recognized as one of the nation's best attorneys general.

Having met AG Reno, I learned to be more accountable for my responsibilities and not to vacillate when things go awry, but to support what I believe is right, regardless of pressure or outside influences. I learned that a person who makes a decision, that is later found to be the wrong decision, is respected more than a vacillator or indecisive person. I further learned that a person who must make a decision and does, and in so doing, makes an honest mistake in judgment should not be sacrificed or punished. Perhaps equally important is that humans make mistakes. In law enforcement, an officer is empowered to enforce the law, trained to be an expert and to make the right decisions. One of the most agonizing situations arises when an officer is expected to be something he can never be; perfect. The intense agony arises when an officer makes an honest mistake and is punished.

Since my early days of federal employment, I had often seen weak male agency heads cave in to political pressure and sacrifice good employees in order to defray publicity or pressure. A pattern had existed in governmental agencies of rewarding certain employees for getting rid of coworkers. There was little consideration given regarding the cost to train the employee or that he/she could be corrected. Termination was the cure. Often I saw innocent employees terminated for little to no reason;

some terminated merely on an accusation of wrongdoing. I believe AG Reno's stance at Waco and her unwillingness to yield to other pressures served as major influences for male agency heads to really stand up and take a stand on issues they believed were correct. She was a major influence in stimulating and encouraging male leaders to lead.

In the fall of 1993, a young White female, fourth grader, was abducted in St. Louis County. She was found about a week later, dead and tied to a tree in the Busch Preserve area. She had been sexually assaulted and reportedly had died from cold weather exposure.

About a week after she was found, another young White female, 10 years old, was abducted. Contemporaneously, in the St. Louis area, a subject was arrested for attempted child abduction.

A day or so after the first abduction, I received a telephone call around 5:00 in the morning, advising that one of our helicopters had crashed in Jefferson County, Missouri. The pilot, SA Hawthorne Lee, had been seriously injured and his observer, Task Force Agent Stephen Strehl, had been killed in the crash. SA Lee was in the intensive care-emergency room at St. Louis University Hospital.

After apprising Strehl's chief of police, Clarence Harmon, of his demise, and arranging for SA Lee's wife, Audrie, to be transported to the University hospital, I joined other DEA agents involved in the incident at the hospital. I met with the chief surgeon and was advised that SA Lee had sustained major brain injuries and was dying. The surgeon related that he would likely die within the next six hours.

When SA Lee's wife arrived, I advised her that he was in serious condition, but did not give her the surgeon's prognosis. It was discerned that, neither Hawthorne, nor his wife was religious. SA Linda Deniece Winn, who was very religious, joined us at the hospital later and we went into the intensive care unit and prayed. A short time later the chief surgeon came in and checked Lee's vital signs, and related that there was nothing more that he could do. SA Winn stated, "Well we will now have to take this to the chief surgeon." The chief surgeon started to remark, "I am the chief..." and surmised Winn was referring to our heavenly surgeon. He remarked, "Go ahead, take all the time you need; let me know if I can help okay."

SA Winn led us in prayer for what seemed like an hour and she never seemed tired. It was interesting hearing his wife participate in what she described as her first prayer. Although Lee remained unconscious; his vital signs did not worsen. After about five days, he became somewhat conscious but confused. It was then we began to realize, that God was heeding our prayers.

I visited Officer Strehl's wife and three sons. Stephen Jr. had been told that his father was deceased, but it apparently had not registered that he would never see his father again. Officer Strehl's funeral was well attended and very sad. I advised his wife of certain Department of Justice entitlements. It was sad seeing her become a widow so young in her life.

The National Transportation Safety Board (NTSB) came out and investigated the crash. As result of not finding mechanical failure, the NTSB was leaning toward assuming pilot error as the accident cause.

After traumatic incidents, contract Clinicians are contacted to provide counseling to the agents and families. About this time, the second abducted little girl's body had been found, wrapped in a blanket and, dumped in a Black neighborhood in St. Louis. One of the Clinicians, utilized by our office, was contacted. He started a conversation about the recent child abductions. The Clinician profiled the suspect as: a White male of low intellect, drives a white pickup truck and working a dead-end, menial job. He added that the last body was intentionally dropped in a Black neighborhood to confuse the police. The Clinician was wrong on the last body. A Black male was later arrested, subsequently convicted and sentenced to death. There has been no arrest involving the abduction and death of the first girl.

SA Hawthorne Lee was the first Black person I'd ever met named Hawthorne. Ironically, he had a best friend, a DEA special agent named Hope Hawthorne that was stationed in the Detroit office. SA Hope came to St. Louis and prayed for his friend. After SA Lee became more conscious, his daughters came to visit. He had a dent in the left temporal region of his face that initially frightened them.

While recuperating, Lee was advised what had transpired. He started feeling guilty for possibly, causing the accidental death of a brother law enforcement officer. As a pilot, he was aware that the NTSB listed mechanical error, pilot error, weather and external objects as the major causes of aircraft accidents.

SA Lee eventually recovered with a degree of brain damage that rendered him incapable of performing the duties of a special agent. It was very difficult for him to accept that he could no longer fly an aircraft and more difficult to accept that he could no longer perform as a special agent. It was very difficult convincing him that he had to retire.

I learned that the job to some people is their life's cardiovascular system, their raison d'etre. Lee had a lovely wife and two beautiful daughters that apparently were tertiary priorities in his life. He had placed the job, primary, and flying secondary in his life.

It would be very difficult for him to survive without those important things in his life. God or a supreme being had never been a part of his childhood or adult life. I learned that he grew up in Detroit in a matriarchal-headed family with no real bonding with his father. His mother had deceased. Lee had a brother and a sister in the Detroit area, and an uncle whom he had maintained regular contact.

Although I had been a Christian for a long time, in the end I credit SA Linda Winn's prayer that proved the St. Louis University's chief surgeon wrong regarding Lee's prognosis. It was also the prayers of Lee's colleagues and his close friend Hope Hawthorne that kept him on this side for a while longer.

Since, neither SA Lee, nor his wife was a believer, I doubted that their marriage would survive. Lee's mental capacity had been diminished to a level where, at times, he could not remember being married. My main doubt about their marriage focused mostly on the fact that neither believed in the creator of marriage. I suspected that they would continue to be non-believers. I found that most atheists and agnostics have a tendency to be drawn closer to God or a supreme being after having a close encounter with death, and conversely, strong believers turn away from God when they believe they've been forsaken by him; often after the loss of a child. I surmised it would be difficult for her to cope with his attitude and to realize and accept that his mental abilities would no longer be the same, but very different.

I dreaded the thought that she would ever leave or divorce Hawthorne (SA Lee), but I was realistic that many contemporary wives have become fair weather wives; they are seldom in for the long haul, choosing to break camp at the slightest discomfort or disagreement, and oftentimes, merely on suspicion of infidelity. Non-believers are the most prone to dissolve a marriage, sometimes on the belief that they are being cheated or short-changed in some way. Hawthorne direly needed his wife, family and close friends. I never inquired about the possible impairment of his sex life, which could further complicate his marital status.

While Hawthorne was undergoing therapy, the acting DEA Administrator (ADA) flew from Washington, D. C. to visit him. He promised to assist Lee in any way he could, to help him recover. I took him to visit Officer Strehl's widow and sons. While visiting her, the ADA told Strehl's widow to sue the DEA and SA Lee. He repeated it twice and reinforced it by stating that is what he would do. I sensed that the ADA had taken the accidental death to a racial level. After his visit, there was a clandestine inquiry made to discern if Lee had consumed any alcoholic beverages prior to coming on-duty on the day of the accident. There were surreptitious inquiries made about his marital life; nothing significant was found.

Per SA Lee's and his wife's request to be moved to Washington, D.C., I requested on four occasions that the ADA relocate Lee from the St. Louis area to the Washington, D.C. area. He denied each request and related that he did not want to set a precedent, a purported reason for the denials. He even denied ever telling Lee that he would help him in any way he could, to assist him in recovering. I had known the ADA for a significant period and knew him to be a major vacillator. When he and I were both desk chiefs, at DEA headquarters, the ADA had related to me how overwhelmed he was by the desk chief position. He was being considered for the Deputy Administrator position, of which he had greater angst. I surmised his denial was of another persuasion. SA Lee and his wife were perplexed at the ADA's refusal to assist, especially after he had verbally advised he would. The ADA finally relented after I forwarded the get-well card he had sent SA Lee offering his help. In early 1994, SA Lee and his family were finally relocated to the Washington, D.C. area, where his wife had relatives to assist them in his rehabilitation.

Dealing with the death of a brother law enforcement officer has always been very difficult and sad. It becomes agonizing when trying to really assist the injured or deceased and having to seek support from a non-decision maker, a vacillator or an individual very insecure in his position. I surmised that the ADA had other ulterior reasons for hesitating to transfer SA Lee.

In losing part of his brain, SA Lee suffered from a significant degree of memory loss. At times, it was difficult for him to recall being married to his wife and having children. I believe he eventually accepted his family because his wife and children had been there. When he was in critical condition, his wife had made an all day, daily ritual of being by his bedside, in his room, even when he was asleep. She was also an important part of his therapy and assisted the therapists with him in every way possible.

Of all the coworkers, especially the ones that worked almost daily with Lee, he seemed to remember me mostly. On occasions when a coworker came into his presence, he had to think hard to recall their name and on occasions he had completely forgotten their name.

I found it interesting that he always remembered me and always referred to me as his very close friend.

One of his close friends and coworker was SA Harold Kent, also a pilot. They both had an Asian wife and had flown missions together.

Kent was an older pilot and had flown numerous dangerous missions in Vietnam for a U.S. agency. Like a number of other U.S. agency employees, after Vietnam, he found a less killing agency through which he could continue a federal career, the DEA. Kent was a strange character and a tad shy. When asked questions about his former U.S. employer, he merely smiled and always skirted them like a professional politician.

One day, I joined Kent in a DEA twin-engine airplane at Lindberg Airport for a flight to the U.S. Penitentiary (USP) at Marion, Illinois; a level 6 federal prison. Shortly after "wheels up" SA Kent offered, "Boss if you are thirsty, you can reach back there in that cooler and get one of those cold ones." After telling him that I was a non-drinker, he apologized for having the beer in the aircraft and related that he had only brought it along to make me comfortable. While en route, I assuredly answered his inquiry letting him know that he had not "stepped on his Johnson with both feet."

I met the warden at the entrance of the USP at Marion. During my federal career I had been inside of Terminal Island Prison (TIP) at San Pedro, California and the Federal Correctional Institution (FCI) at Lompoc, California (not to be confused with the USP at Lompoc, which is a high security facility). The Lompoc FCI facility is a minimum-security facility that resembles a country club. It houses political prisoners— politicians convicted of crimes. The last time I was at TIP was to interview a female inmate. At that time, TIP housed both women and men. When interviewing the female inmate, it was almost like watching a fashion show. They were all wearing civilian clothing and dressed as if en route to a party. The USP at Marion was awesome, rather petrifying.

As we entered the electronically controlled double entrance gates, I immediately became apprehensive and felt my blood pressure increase and my heart beating faster. I immediately became aware that I was somewhat claustrophobic and that prison life is a life I could not endure. I was taken through two electronic control stations on the inside. We had to be buzzed in electronically to each unit. At one area, an inmate was escorted by two guards from a 6' by 8' cell, in handcuffs and shackles on his ankles, to a metal cage the size of a large living room. He was placed into the cage and the handcuffs and shackles were removed. The inmate started jogging and exercising. We visited a work area inside of the prison where certain inmates made and assembled components of certain military helmets. According to the warden, the USP at Marion was a level 6 prison, one of the most secure prisons in the United States. It was opened almost the same time Alcatraz was closed; built to house the most dangerous inmates in a very controlled environment. The most dangerous of the population are kept in isolation, like the inmate that was taken to exercise. They are not allowed to congregate in the yard, cafeteria or at religious services and are left in their small cells an average of 22-23 hours per day. There are no close visitations, that is, visitors are separated by Plexiglas, preventing them from kissing or touching relatives.

According to Main Justice statistics, I learned that there are over one million prisoners in facilities in the United States. Over half of the prison population consists of Blacks. I further learned that there are more Blacks in prisons, in the United States, than there are in colleges and universities. A sadder revelation indicates that one out of every four Black males is projected to go to prison in his lifetime.

After completing the prison tour, I felt frightened and still apprehensive. If I were a teacher or school administrator, I would strongly recommend that parents of wayward children consider taking their child for a visit like the USP at Marion. I still remember the coldness of the building and believe visits to it, or other prisons, would be major crime deterrents.

I found it alarming that Whites committed 80% of the crimes, but

Blacks were more susceptible to going to prison. I am not naïve to think that there are no innocent people in prison. I am also cognizant that there are people, not in prison, who should really be in prison. I often think or rethink and old adage about letting 10 people go free, rather than to convict one innocent person. Of late, I have started to opine that there is, in certain circles, a tendency to convict 10 innocent Blacks than let one guilty one get away. Sadly, I have seen Blacks convicted on scanty to no evidence beyond being arrested and accused. There is something inherently wrong with associating Blackness with guilt and lawlessness. Often Blacks are found guilty outside of the courtrooms based on the color of their skin and demeanor.

Shortly after SA Lee was transferred, SA Kent was walking in front of the divisional office when a car making a left turn struck him. He was taken to Barnes hospital in an ambulance. I arrived at the hospital and found him on a gurney in a supine position in the emergency room. When I tried to determine his well being, he asked if I could please get him a mirror. After a nurse gave him a mirror, Kent immediately rearranged his wig and related that he was okay. Kent was an example of a man, whose physical appearance was more important to him than his physical well-being.

I found it interesting that often those who are highly exposed to danger, as SA Kent was with DEA and more so while flying combat missions in Vietnam, are often injured in the weirdest places and at very unusual times. I surmised that Kent's priorities in life mirrored those of SA Lee; flying was very important to him. Another lesson I learned is that those things that are of high priority to you, are often of little to no importance to others.

For a long period, the U.S. Department of Justice (Main Justice) and most all other U.S. departments had celebrated Black History Month and urged all components to fully support the program. Later, the celebration of Hispanic History, Asiatic and Pacific Rim and Women were included in these special interest programs. It was in 1993 when Main Justice strongly emphasized the recognition of women. I received a large package from Main Justice containing photographs, pictures, drawings, lithographs and brochures for use in the Women's Special Interest Program. In reviewing the material, I saw a huge photograph of Ethel Rosenberg. The only Ethel Rosenberg of historical note I could recall was the wife of Julius

Rosenberg; both had been executed for spying. I placed a telephone call to Main Justice and conferred with a Special Interest Specialist I had previously met. He thought I was putting one over on him about having the picture of Ethel Rosenberg to be used in the women's recognition program. Like the old adage, if things can go wrong they are likely to, in fact, go wrong. I learned you should pay more attention to details, not only in carrying out your duties, but in everything you do, whether large or small. I further learned from this incident, that because a person is in a position of authority such as a priest, doctor, dentist, lawyer or teacher, that they are not always correct in their assessments, beliefs, opinions or actions. I also learned not to prejudge every situation or judge every situation with suspicion or be hypercritical of the actions of others. I found it reasonable to believe that what I believe is wrong, could easily and often be seen, and in reality be correct to others.

XXII

WHEN 1994 CAME around I immediately concentrated my energy toward retiring. I attended a one-week retirement seminar, in Houston, Texas, to prepare for the transition. The U.S. Government was ahead of private industry in several areas. One was establishing an Employee Assistance Program to assist individual employees and immediate family members in handling stress and other related matters. Since mobility was a condition of employment, a relocation service was established to assist families moving from one location to the other at the benefit of the agency. Retirement seminars were conducted to assist employees in handling this important life transition.

The seminar stressed important factors that affect retirees. The financial part was very important, but was something the employee should have stressed earlier in their career. Often retirees, especially those under mandatory plans, found themselves with insufficient savings to make the transition. Paying employees for unused annual leave offered some relief. Over time, federal employees started saving annual leave as a kind of retirement bonus. The cap was set at about six weeks for certain employees and unlimited for employees in the Senior Executive Services.

One of the more interesting subjects involved time-management, how to manage all of the time newly available when retired. It warned against over volunteering and joining too many organizations and boards. Examples were given showing how a retiree could end up working more, on committees, boards, clubs etc., than when fully employed.

One of the important issues involved having vocations, varied interests, friends and things that you enjoy doing. Examples were given about retirees with nothing to do after retiring that left them sad all the way to the end of their life; they were the employees for whom the job was their life; they had gone a lifetime never finding anything more meaningful to them than their work, the job and their coworkers. They took retirement harder and many died shortly thereafter. There were others that frequently visited their old office "to see how things are going along." It epitomized the worker who never really had a life outside of the job. When the job ended, in essence their lives ended also. I learned that there is a major change in a person's personality that results from retiring. Initially there is angst that there will be nothing to do and thoughts about how one will survive on retirement pay. There is strong consideration required that a retiree, in most cases, adjust to having a monthly income instead of biweekly. I felt prepared, especially having varied interests in: golf, fishing, hunting, travel, writing, gardening and landscaping and a desire to become more involved in the developing years of my grandchildren. I was proud of my accomplishments, rising from a street agent to a senior executive level in a federal agency that had once been hesitant to employ too many of my kind. Emerging from a small town in Mississippi, where no U.S. president has ever visited and meeting two presidents, were feats I had never imagined. It was another accomplishment meeting the nation's first female U.S. attorney general. Having met, John Ashcroft, who later became the U.S. attorney general was interesting.

In 1994, President Clinton came to St. Louis. I requested that the Secret Service SAC arrange a photo opportunity with President Clinton, which he did. I accompanied several federal and local officials to the Adam's Mark Hotel, in downtown St. Louis, where President Clinton was speaking. When he was departing, for security purposes, we met him in the hallway leading to his limousine. SAC Snyder introduced me to President Clinton as the head of the DEA office in St. Louis. We shook hands and were photographed. President Clinton thanked me for the job we were doing and added that it was a pleasure to meet me. After the group of officials had taken photographs with President Clinton, we walked to the parking area to his limousine. There were eight Black men wearing partially dirty smocks and cook's caps from the food service of the hotel, standing and watching President Clinton walk to his limousine. When he started to get in, he paused and said, "Wait a minute." He started walking toward the eight Black males. Most of them turned and looked to their rear, as though, wondering where he was going. President Clinton walked up to the eight Black men, shook each of their hands and stated, "I want to thank all of you for making my visit nice while I was here." One of the most respectful things that I watched him do was, not immediately wiping the grease from his hands in their presence.

President Clinton, I strongly believe, is one of the kindest, caring, interesting, sincerest, honest presidents we have ever had. He has an angelic aura about him that reflects goodness and a desire to help others. Of all the White males I have encountered, even including Jack from early childhood, for some reason I believe President Clinton was the most sincere in his love for all people, including the ugly, deformed, dispossessed, fat, thin, robust, with different sexual preferences, rich and all people per se. He seemed to live and believe that there is only one race: the human race.

President Clinton, despite holding the most powerful position in the world as U. S, President, displayed a humbleness not seen in other heads of states worldwide. The position itself made him the Commander-in Chief (CIC). In reality, the CIC is also the ultimate authorizer and director of coup d'etat and coup de grace activities throughout the world. The CIC is responsible for a lot of killings that take place in various parts of the world. Although not the actual killer, the CIC is the person authorizing coup masters to contrive situations that result in others killing others. I believe that as president, Clinton exercised his authority in this area sparingly.

We, as Americans, are extremely naïve to the fact that when we elect a president, one of the most important prerequisites is the ability to order the killing of others for "our interests" whether in the form of a coup, clandestine assassination, or war. As Americans, we do not invade countries, instead we engage in incursions and pre-emptive strikes. We do not kill thousands of innocent people during these incursions or pre-emptive strikes; they die from collateral damage.

When we elected President Jimmy Carter, we elected a Christian lacking the conscious or power to kill. While in the eyes of some, he was viewed as a vacillator, in reality, although he attended the Naval Academy, in the Iran hostage situation, he could not muster the courage to kill; as his predecessors had readily done and what his successors readily do today without hesitating.

The persons most aware of President Carter's inability, to kill or order or approve the killing of many, were the Iranian hostage takers. It was no surprise to many that President Carter was later awarded a Nobel Peace Prize. He is to be highly lauded for his work with Habitat for Humanity, and the monitoring of peace and election processes in various parts of the world. I often wonder, in his peace monitoring efforts, if he is fully aware of the purveyors or the real force behind the violence in many of those countries.

Despite the foregoing, one of President Clinton's strongest assets is his public acknowledgement of his love for God. He seemed to possess a strong desire to help, to have a positive impact on everyone he encounters.

In electing President Ronald Reagan, we elected a president who had no qualms of killing when America's interests were involved. The Iranian hostage takers were very cognizant that Reagan was not nearly as tolerant or indecisive as his predecessor. As I recall, after he was sworn into office and asked if he would negotiate with the hostage takers, Reagan answered, "You cannot reason with barbarians." The American hostages were immediately released after being in captivity over 445 days.

I was surprised that President Reagan did not send a retaliatory bombing mission to Iran, as a gesture of his resolve that you cannot attack the United States or any of its properties without suffering dire consequences. I laud him for his decisiveness in Iran, Libya and Grenada.

I abhor President Reagan's peripheral involvement—although he denied it— in certain parts of the Iran-Contra incidents, especially for allowing certain members of his cabinet to actually get involved in cocaine trafficking as means to finance the Contras. I believe that this cocaine was intentionally shipped into Black communities, where it was sold as crack. Sadly even today, I strongly believe that this U.S. Government Cocaine Trafficker (USGCT) lied before the U.S. Congress. The public, somewhat unaware of the USGCT's criminal chicanery and skullduggery, elevated him to the status of some kind of a hero. The USGCT and his indicted, but pardoned, coconspirators should be in prison. I strongly believe that President Reagan was cognizant of these criminal acts and that he orchestrated and approved the sale of arms to Iran via Israel.

I still favored President Clinton over his four predecessors. Although, without being pressured, he was the only U.S. President to publicly apologize for slavery and admit that it was wrong. He was the only U.S. President that tried to have a Cabinet reflective of the make-up of America.

President Clinton did more for the American people than many of our prior presidents. Albeit, a special prosecutor, whose mandate was to determine any criminal activity on the part of the president and his wife prior to being elected, went beyond his mandate and ventured in a non-criminal area. In doing so, the special prosecutor contrived a situation for the president to not be candid.

As a result, the president was subjected to impeachment procedures based on a non-criminal act that most males find difficult not to succumb to; regardless, whether married or single. During the impeachment process, it was revealed that many of the pro-impeachment Representatives involved in the process, had worse skeletons in their closet than what they were using to "dirty up the president."

One proponent, leading the charge, was caught involved in egregious behavior, and decided abruptly to step down. The proponent's behavior was reprehensible, compared to that of the president's indiscretion. The proponent went a step further and recommended that the President also step down.

The American people could easily see the games the special prosecutor and his supporters were playing, and ironically gave President Clinton, during the impeachment process, a rating almost two times higher than the younger President Bush has during his last two years in office.

I was cognizant that when President Clinton was governor of Arkansas, he did what was politically correct, even at the cost of being partial toward Blacks and favoring Whites. Like many of his predecessors, whether governor or president, they went with the political flow by trying to placate the largest number of people, despite how detrimentally it affected others. Some were quick to reverse play the race card, by alleging that a minority was playing it. Somewhere along the way, many politicians and office heads quickly learned that it is advantageous to have more friends than enemies.

In 1994, a lot had changed in the greater St. Louis area. A significant number of cities and towns had Black mayors, Black police chiefs, and some even had Black fire chiefs. The city of St. Louis had its first Black mayor and Black chief of police. President Clinton appointed a Black U.S. Marshal for the Eastern District of Missouri and one for the Southern District of Illinois.

1994 came quickly, bringing my retirement date closer. I had no angst regarding retiring and knew that it was a type of life I could easily enjoy. I could do those things I had procrastinated doing for so long. It would be another adventure in life to enjoy, and not like it was for some: the end of life. I looked back on my life and decided that there is nothing that I would have done differently. I am proud of my humble beginnings and very proud of where I went and what I accomplished.

I retired on August 31, 1994 and was honored a few days prior with three retirement events; two parties and a golf tournament. I was honored that SA Roland J. Talton, one of my junior partners from Los Angeles attended the events and roasted me during one. During the first party, SAC Snyder gave me a photograph of my meeting with President Clinton and related that the president had personally signed it. Congressman William Clay's aide gave me a proclamation from the honorable congressman proclaiming August 31, 1994 "My Day". I received a similar proclamation from the honorable Mayor Freeman Bosley.

I was shocked when special agents, Gene Crosby and Johnny Fisher, called me to the podium and presented me with a trip for two for a one-week vacation in Freeport, Bahamas. During the presentation, they related that it was from many of my friends within DEA who related that I had helped or touched them somehow in a very positive way. It was a very exhilarating and wonderful feeling learning that I had had a positive impact on the life of someone and that there are many people positively affected by me.

It was during my retirement that I learned another definition of testimony. A testimony is living an upright and righteous life that causes or influences others to emulate you or desire to be like you.

There are insufficient words to adequately thank my mother and father for everything they did for me. Perhaps foremost, I would thank them for being married and together until death.

I often look back and highly praise my mother for her nurturing, guidance, testimony, love, faith, teachings, parables, metaphors, euphemisms, strength, perseverance, sage advice and her ability to communicate with many people in a kind and caring manner. I admire her immensely for having experienced such horror in her life, yet remained godly in her ways and never questioned God regarding any of his actions. I remember her ability to cook nutritious meals for family members with different likes, dislikes and appetites. I thank her with all my soul for being the mother she was to all of us, including my friend Norman. I admire her more for having the foresight to predict eminent racial turmoil and for allowing me to move, so far away from Mississippi, to California with my uncle.

On occasions while walking or driving, I think of some of the things I heard her say and break out in laughter from the humor and wit in them: girls jumping through fire; praying for children, and not to be blessed with more children, can never be forgotten. I am sure she is now residing with our heavenly father.

I thank Jack for being my friend in a place and during a time when Whites and Blacks were rarely friends. I further thank him for being a major influence to me, reflecting goodness and will always remember him as a man of high moral values and kindness. Although not mentioned earlier, when seeing him walk inside the prison compound, often our neighbors remarked, how he was highly respected by others and even the German prisoners of war.

If I could ask a favor, it would be one that should have been asked over 60 years ago of those German prisoners, in Greenwood, Mississippi, who escaped after the war and went through the Black neighborhoods for help. I would have asked them to be more tolerant in their treatment of Blacks; not to hate Blacks merely based on skin pigmentation; not based on how we're often portrayed in the media; but harbor no preconceived idea of a collective behavior pattern applicable to Blacks or any person. I would ask the same of all communities. I would hope and pray that not only the ex-prisoners, but that others would see what I see.

XXIII

SOME OF MY mother's old sage advice often resurfaces. One deals with the acceptance of things free, wherein, she harbored a strong aversion that in most cases there were some underlying reasons for "free gifts."

I recall one of those free gifts involving the medical treatment of illiterate and uneducated Blacks in a Tuskegee Institute program. In this free medical treatment for bad blood; Blacks, specifically Black men, were unwittingly used by the U.S. Public Health Service (USPHS) in experiments for syphilis studies for 40 years, from 1932-1972. It is ironic that the USPHS selected a learning institution established by one of our most noted Black inventor/scientist—George Washington Carver— for this heinous project. The Tuskegee Syphilis Study, which has been dubbed "the most infamous biomedical research study in U.S. history", also utilized a few Black employees in this process. It is possible that some Black employees were aware, while others were used unwittingly. Perhaps more alarming is that U.S. presidents Herbert Hoover, Franklin Roosevelt, Harry Truman, Dwight Eisenhower, John F. Kennedy, Lyndon Johnson and Richard Nixon were fully cognizant of this atrocity, but since it involved Black men they all remained politically correct and did absolutely nothing to correct it. Blacks and non-Blacks were utilized unwittingly in other atrocious experiments; one involved

245

the testing of Lysergic Acid (LSD). Since the human guinea pigs were in the U.S. Armed Services, there was no subsequent possible redress in any U.S. court system after this atrocity became known. These American atrocities, America and other countries' germ warfare arsenals, give credence to many that Herpes Simplex II, Human Immunodeficiency Syndrome Virus (HIV) and Acquired Immunodeficiency Syndrome (AIDS) are the results of man's testing and stockpiling them as weapons for germ warfare. This belief is further augmented by the emergence of these diseases after the end of the Vietnam War and the revelation of the utilization of Agent Orange during the war. Sadly the Department of Defense denied the adverse impact that Agent Orange had on soldiers that were exposed to it.

President Franklin D. Roosevelt threw the Black community a bone when he went against the politically correct and allowed Blacks to receive aviation training (become pilots) at Tuskegee Institute, ironically during the same period this atrocious medical experiment was in full operation.

America has long stepped wide of reasonably identifying the disparate treatment it has subjected its Black citizens to and continues to do little to rectify it. As previously stated, in the South, Blacks were often separated from their land on alleged back taxes, failure to pay taxes or failure to pay certain loans. Contemporaneously, the USDA has historically provided White farmers adequate assistance with loans, grants and even compensated them for certain programs not to cultivate certain acres. The USDA relegated the administration of these programs to the local agencies, which resulted in many Black farmers being denied access to the programs. They were not provided even a small amount of the assistance that was often provided to White farmers. This pattern was widespread throughout America, whether in the South, North, East or West and peaked during the 1980's and 1990's. As a result, many Blacks farmers lost their farms. The USDA made no effort to discern if the programs were being meted out fairly. This led to a Black Farmers' class action suit against the USDA. Sadly, the USDA had no choice, but to acknowledge that it had actually discriminated against Black farmers. Rather than correct the mistakes and remedy the wrongdoings; the remedy continues to be mired in an imbroglio. This leads one to believe that it is intended to send a strong message that you, Black farmers, have won the war; but the battle continues. Many of the Black farmers, while with a favorable ruling, have yet to realize any of the intended results of the ruling.

I recall a former head of the USDA drawing a little public heat by describing the ultimate wants and desires of a Black male as, "a tight p---y, soft shoe and a warm place to shit." Needless to say this USDA official did little, to nothing, to correct any disparate treatment involving Black farmers.

I am cognizant that Title VIII of the Civil Rights Act of 1968 and Presidential Executive Orders (Fair Housing Act) prohibit discrimination in sales, financing, rental or other financial related matters involving housing based on: race, color national origin, sex, religion or handicap. Historically, Blacks have and continue to be charged maximum allowable interest rates, mostly based on being Black. Banks and lending institutions often utilize a credit rating scale to justify this malpractice. Despite being found guilty of these practices in court, unscrupulous lenders continue this practice and utilize witting and unwitting Black employees in perpetrating it. Many lending institutions tend to have a consensus that Blacks are historically on the dole, non-debt or poor debt payers. Often, they use skewed statistical data, garnered from certain segments of the Black community, involving unskilled to lowly skilled Black workers who are often the last hired and first fired, to justify their acts. Some Blacks are fired when they reach the journeyman level in order to hire a younger less expensive employee or non-Black.

Some corporations/companies have taken this malpractice beyond the Black community. They have started terminating senior employees from all ethnic groups and hiring younger employees at a lower salary. They have taken this further by hiring a large cadre of part-time employees to obviate paying certain required benefits. Others have taken it further, skirting many loopholes, by hiring aliens at a minimal hourly rate; many contract overseas vendors who run sweatshops to save on labor. I would postulate that over 70% of our clothing is produced overseas, with the most being made in China. Not only does China manufacture most of our clothing and other items, but it is also a major source for the theft of American and foreign intellectual properties. It is likely that China also makes and sells more knock-off designer goods, in the United States, than the actual designers. Many companies further avoid numerous labor requirements and employee benefits by not allowing their employees to unionize. It is not alarming that some of our biggest employers are non-union corporations. Some of these same corporations utilize mostly temporary employees to avoid paying the attendant benefits, usually required for full time employees.

I am cognizant that most all U.S. federal agencies have discriminated against Black employees, which has been found true via many class actions decisions in U.S. courts.

I have a strong belief that most Americans, especially Blacks, desire to work and earn sufficient wages to care for self and family. As mentioned earlier, I was able to earn enough money during the summer school vacation to buy my first car, school clothing and have money left over at the age of 17. I pride myself for never receiving an unemployment check or benefits because there was always work available.

It has become very difficult for college graduates to earn sufficient wages to purchase a car or house. The cost of a college education has increased to unreachable levels for many American families. Professional athletes, some with less than two years of college are now earning five and ten times more wages than top surgeons, lawyers, engineers, and architects. In the past, parents who encouraged their children to become doctors, lawyers, engineers, architects and other once highly paid professions; are now encouraging them to become professional athletes. It is possible that in a few decades, there will be no Black male doctors or Black pre-med students. They will likely become millionaire professional athletes or millionaire rappers.

I see even the highly intelligent students pondering, whether to pursue a medical career to devote long training, hours, efforts and years to become a doctor and have the attendant high malpractice insurance, further reducing their earning capacity. A college education has now become very difficult for most Americans to afford. As a consequence, we are seeing an increase of foreign doctors and foreign medical students in our hospitals and clinics. Most of our medical doctors will soon either be: foreigners or former foreigners.

I see America using a trend analogous to placing a Band-Aid on a cancer, as it involves our students. Student loans are offered with low interest rates. In this little set up, the student graduates with a huge debt, in some cases more than $50,000 that has to be repaid. The government has, in some cases initiated garnishments, against some students. As this

248

applies to White students, the brunt of the garnishments is often levied against the Black students.

The cost of medical treatment has risen to cost-prohibitive levels, leaving over 25% of our population, mostly Blacks, without medical insurance. Older Americans, from all ethnic communities, now have to choose between eating or purchasing needed expensive prescriptions. We now have to smuggle in or purchase certain needed drugs from overseas in order to afford them. This is prevalent because many of our politicians are deeply beholding to the pharmaceutical and medical industries.

We have arrived at a stage in America where many jobs have been sent overseas; while others are being held by aliens. In our quest for academic excellence, we have completely overlooked the need for skilled laborers like plumbers, carpenters, electricians, brick masons, sheet rock installers, roofers, painters, construction workers and other professions. Meanwhile, jobs for Blacks continue to become scarce.

I described many incidents of police corruption, especially as it related to the Civil Rights Movement. I like to think that they were merely unknowledgeable and were following orders of their employer; nevertheless, these hired civil servants were major purveyors of evil acts against minorities, especially Blacks. I am not so naïve to think that, even today law enforcement no longer has such evil officers. Corruption as it existed years ago is also prevalent today, but to a much lesser extent. Today, many law enforcement managers have adequate training to forecast corruption and the abuse of power by their officers.

As little boys, seeing the police run roughshod through the Black neighborhoods violating Black peoples' rights and causing fear, even today, proves difficult for younger Blacks to grow up with any degree of respect for the police. In Black neighborhoods when a Black male states, "I ain't never been to jail" in essence he is saying I am not a criminal, nor have I been falsely arrested by the police. We saw firsthand those elected and public officials, who by virtue of their positions should have been a solution for many of our racial and other problems; actually being major catalysts propagating them.

Albeit, there is corruption in many areas of the government, it is not now as widespread as it was earlier in our history.

Despite all of my experiences, good and bad; I learned from negative and positive influencers that despite races being described as white, red, brown, yellow and black, that there is only one race of people on earth: the human race.

In reminiscing about the multitude of countries, cities, towns, islands, hamlets and villages where I have been, there is nothing close to the wonders of the United States of America. Albeit the Euro is currently providing a united currency, the U.S. Dollar remains the world currency, that is, it is spendable worldwide. Many of the things we take for granted in America are often things many foreigners dream of and wish for on a daily basis. For example, we throw away more uneaten food than many developing countries have access to on a yearly basis. Additionally, because of our wide cosmopolitan make up of numerous cultures, we have almost every type of food consumed in the world, available right here in America.

There is no other comparison to the beautiful ambiance of New York City, Chicago, Detroit, Philadelphia, Los Angeles, San Diego, San Francisco, Oakland, Santa Barbara, Sacramento, Houston, Dallas, Miami, Ft Lauderdale, Tallahassee, Destin, Jacksonville, Tampa, Savannah, Atlanta, Charlotte, Raleigh, Durham, Charleston, Myrtle Beach, Baltimore, Washington, D.C., Richmond, New Orleans, Baton Rouge, Cleveland, Indianapolis, Louisville, Minneapolis, Milwaukee, Memphis, Nashville, Jackson, Biloxi, Gulfport, Little Rock, Tulsa, Oklahoma City, Kansas City, St. Louis, Seattle, Portland, Palm Springs, San Juan, St. Thomas, St. Croix and a host of other American cities and towns; each with a magical aura of its own that foreigners can only dream about or imagine. The lights of Las Vegas and Reno, Nevada flickering 24-7, in a kind of kaleidoscopic, magical symmetry, are sights to behold with awe.

We have the Pacific and Atlantic oceans, the Caribbean Sea and Salton Sea, the world's only inland sea. At Salton Sea we have the Corvina Charlie fish. We have the Great Salt Lake, magnificent mighty rivers like the Missouri, Colorado, Mississippi, St. Lawrence, Arkansas, Tallahatchie, Ohio, Yazoo, Red River, Black River, White River, Sewanee and a host of other beautiful fish filled rivers, lakes and streams.

When singing, "America the Beautiful" we realize that God did share his grace on America, the land of the free, the land of plenty, the land where there is so much to see and so much to do. There exists a paradisiacal aura in America, unlike any other place in the world. We are the trendsetters, moviemakers, music-makers, car-makers, millionaire-makers, and makers of some of the best food in the world.

We are a free country in which we can express our individual opinions about the government and governmental officials, without fear, threat of arrest or revengeful adverse action.

We have the best educational institutions in the world, the best army, the best aircraft industries, the best publishers, the best medical facilities, best doctors, more importantly, when we even think of America, we think of having the best of the best.

Despite the foregoing, we have become complacent in many areas; having lost our desires to strive to work hard and excel in difficult areas of discipline. Nevertheless, I love America, the various beautiful trees including: the sequoias (giant redwoods), china berry, elms, cedar, pines hickory, ash, oleander, myrrh, cherry, Bradford pear, fig, apple, orange, grapefruit, guava, persimmons, peach, plum, lemon, lime, banana and the lovely magnolia grande flora with its huge white fragrant flowers. We have a huge array of other beautiful trees and a larger number of beautiful flowers, some the most beautiful in the world.

Despite all of our shortcomings, America is a fabulous place, a paradise on earth, a place where a young Black man can come out of prison and become a multimillionaire rapper. Although, I am not a great fan of certain rap music, I admire numerous young Blacks who have been cast out of mainstream America and handed almost total defeat by a non-caring and insensitive society; for having the artistic ability to survive legally on an inclined playing field. I further admire them for realizing that it is a dare to be Black; realizing that being Black is a constant uphill fight for equality.

It is not surprising in that we have taken God out of our way of life, out of our public schools and many institutions, including our court systems. Americans now frequently go overboard, at the expense of the majority, in efforts of pacifying a few. It is postulated that over 80% of all Americans believe in God, however, we are careful not to offend the other 20 % who are atheist, agnostics or believers in a different supreme being. We continue to tolerate elected officials in fiduciary positions that act unprofessionally, at times criminally. We make special dispensations for them; we send them to country club type prisons or give them pardons. We allow unscrupulous purported ministers to preach and pedophilic priests to conduct mass and other services in our churches. Under the guise of religion, we allow the forming of various sects and idly, watch them venture into isolated areas and engage in widespread sexual and mental abuse of young females as they enter into puberty.

We, along with seven other world powers, in concert and sometimes unilaterally, launch coup d'etats around the world for the sake of a favorable ruler that is a purported U. S. ally. When the once favorite leader goes south or grows tired of being manipulated and pursues a different path; we crank up another coup to unseat him, often resulting in a coup de grace. Even Third World or developing countries are now fully cognizant of the identities of the real trigger pullers.

We disclaim that Osama Bin Laden, Fidel Castro, Manuel Antonio Noriega, Saddam Hussein and a host of others were once close allies and good friends of the United States. Of all of the former friends, it has become difficult to discern, who actually "cut and ran."

We let our elected Representatives and Senators, take various gifts and things of value from lobbyists and corporations for favors that are completely against and contrary to the desires of their constituents. Because it is America, we do not say they are bought-off. Some of our representatives have actually aided the enemy, foreign enemies in their acceptance of gifts from certain lobbyists. It is understandable why it is difficult for our elected Congress to resist these "gifts in kind" and monetary temptations since there are approximately 50,000 lobbyists with almost unlimited funds in the Washington D.C. area to effectively influence our 535 Representatives (Senators/Representatives).

We have lost all consciousness of the adverse impact that corruption, on the part of elected and appointed officials in fiduciary & Christian leadership positions, has on our youth and the public. We are fully cognizant that today, the hate for America throughout the world is higher than it has ever been.

We have become addicted to debilitating drugs and extravagant oil consumption, both likely taking us into a major depression. The days of American extravagance are peaking, requiring a new life style of smaller cars, smaller homes and the need for major urban and interurban mass transportation systems and major car and van pooling efforts like in Washington, D.C.

Despite the foregoing, America is still a land of plenty, land of op-

252

portunity, a land of beautiful people from all ethnic corners of the world. There will always be racial ands ethnic divides all over the world. In America, there are no exceptions. Today, the racial divides are less intense and do exist in many facets of American life, but minimally detracts from the wonderment of being an American and enjoying a life on earth that is almost paradisiacal. When I hear "America the Beautiful" despite all other shortcomings, I smile in awe and pride for the privilege of being a citizen of this beautiful fourth Roman Empire. I pray that a fifth one never exists. America despite the foregoing, I love you unconditionally.

The Author with President George Bush circa 1993

Printed in the United States
By Bookmasters